# In One Word

Michael Behnke

# In One Word

## The Power of Razor-sharp Brand Positioning to Lower Costs and Improve Results

 Springer

Michael Behnke
The American University of Paris
Paris, France

ISBN 978-3-031-88201-2     ISBN 978-3-031-88202-9  (eBook)
https://doi.org/10.1007/978-3-031-88202-9

© The Editor(s) (if applicable) and The Author(s), under exclusive license to Springer Nature Switzerland AG 2025

This work is subject to copyright. All rights are solely and exclusively licensed by the Publisher, whether the whole or part of the material is concerned, specifically the rights of translation, reprinting, reuse of illustrations, recitation, broadcasting, reproduction on microfilms or in any other physical way, and transmission or information storage and retrieval, electronic adaptation, computer software, or by similar or dissimilar methodology now known or hereafter developed.
The use of general descriptive names, registered names, trademarks, service marks, etc. in this publication does not imply, even in the absence of a specific statement, that such names are exempt from the relevant protective laws and regulations and therefore free for general use.
The publisher, the authors and the editors are safe to assume that the advice and information in this book are believed to be true and accurate at the date of publication. Neither the publisher nor the authors or the editors give a warranty, expressed or implied, with respect to the material contained herein or for any errors or omissions that may have been made. The publisher remains neutral with regard to jurisdictional claims in published maps and institutional affiliations.

This Springer imprint is published by the registered company Springer Nature Switzerland AG
The registered company address is: Gewerbestrasse 11, 6330 Cham, Switzerland

If disposing of this product, please recycle the paper.

# Preface

When we think about branding, we usually imagine product, service or corporate brands, which comprise most of today's branded entities worldwide. Nevertheless, states, entire countries or regional destinations, people, political parties, programmes, NGOs or simply a movement may be turned into a brand using the exact same techniques that prevail in product and service branding. Once you fully understand the principles and dynamics of branding, almost anything can be turned into a successful brand.

*In One Word* will analyse and discuss the underlying dynamics, as well as the unique techniques and methodology of defining a brand's value proposition in just *one* word. This book offers deep insights for marketers, communication professionals, CEOs and senior managers or anyone interested in the world of branding to better understand what it takes to build successful brands. Many of today's power brands have succeeded in defining what they stand for with just a single word. A one-word brand positioning, if executed properly, has the potential to unleash powerful synergies in the brand-building and management process by pointing everyone involved in the exact same strategic direction.

This way, a company's resourcefulness, energy and creativity are bundled together and directed towards the same objective. In this unique approach to branding, a single word will ultimately drive the entire brand-related marketing and sales operation. "Glamour" drives the L'Oréal Paris brand, while Nivea stands for "Care". *In One Word* is a practical guide on how to build power brands, providing tangible advice and real-life illustrations to empower branding professionals in their quest for building unique brands that deliver rewarding results.

While this unique one-word branding technique may be applied, almost literally, to all different kinds of brands, this book focuses primarily on product, service and corporate branding. These represent the traditional branding areas, offering the best potential to explore and explain the principles of branding. At the same time, they provide vivid and tangible illustrations and benchmarks from the real world and a lifetime in branding to better understand the process of building them.

*In One Word* aims to provide a holistic view on branding, starting with a tangible discussion on how brands function and what has and will continue to turn them into indispensable components of consumers' lives. It will then look at the theory and practical implication of the one-word branding process before taking a closer look at its application in specific business domains and brand types.

With the arrival of artificial intelligence and in the overall context of the third industrial revolution, brands will also go through a major transformative process in the next 10–15 years. However, their primary role of guaranteeing consumers a consistent, reliable and highly emotional experience will not change. As a matter of fact, these very functions that all brands must deliver on will most likely further cement their role as an essential component in consumers' lives.

Paris, France  Michael Behnke
February 2025

# Acknowledgements

I'd like to dedicate this book to my dear friend Alan Lambert, a former student of mine and ex-CEO of Aciprosalud C.A. in Venezuela. This book never would have been written if it weren't for his relentless push for me to pass on my knowledge in branding to future generations. I would also like to thank my wife Yvonne, an incredibly talented artist painter, for helping me to find an editor. And a big thank you to all the people that read my book, particularly, my two sons Timo and Mitja and my longtime friend Axel Pfennigschmidt for commenting on the manuscript, providing critical and valuable input and logistical support in the process.

I would also wish to thank Susanne Wiesmann, one of the finest research professionals I have met throughout my professional life and who largely contributed to the chapter on morphological research, to Beate Steil, who realized many of the graphic illustrations in the book, to Chase Doolan, who helped me with the final editing, to Marion Ranoux, a colleague at AUP who kept me company in the office during a full year of writing, to Jorge Sosa from the AUP library, who helped document this book and to Robert Payne, chair of the CMC department at AUP who supported my project by providing me with an inspiring office space where I could work on the book.

I would also like to express my gratitude to my editor Springer Nature for accepting my project as a first-time author and for providing an incredibly professional and transparent process to finish it.

**Competing Interests** The author has no competing interests to declare that are relevant to the content of this manuscript.

# About this Book

**IN ONE WORD**

A practical guide to building powerful brands

Can you summarize what your brand stands for? Can you do it with *ONE WORD*?

Positioning a brand is a challenging task that most brands fail to master, consequently turning them into poor performers that waste valuable funds and energy. They rarely ever live up to their true potential.

Successful brand positioning must deliver on three fundamentals: clear **differentiation** from the competitive set, **relevance** for target audiences and **competence** that truly reflects and supports the positioning and potentially allows the brand to stretch into new market segments. For each of these aspects, the *one word* can make the difference between relative success and failure.

Most brands that fail struggle to define what they stand for. Complexity is your worst enemy in branding. Multiple brand dimensions, lack of message prioritization and unclear wordings all turn brands into complex, overcharged vehicles, too unfocused to communicate a single-minded, consistent and relevant message to consumers.

Boiling the brand positioning down to a *single word* or a *precise angle of attack* empowers brands way beyond their own market scope. It has the potential to provide focus for the entire parent organization and helps get everybody on the same track. It summons the creativity and energy inherent to successful businesses, pointing everybody in the same direction, providing the roadmap and the measurement tool to channel creativity and professional energy.

For instance, the BMW brand stands for *driving pleasure*. This focal point gives the brand and the entire organization a clearly defined, single-minded direction. Hence, the role of every single person at BMW is to deliver *driving pleasure*—through product innovation, marketing action all the way down to the sales pitch and the post-purchase user experience. Every little detail of the BMW brand, product and service offer will be measured and evaluated by this central, highly operative brand positioning concept. *Driving pleasure* works like a prism through which all brand activities will be seen, executed and measured.

This book leverages the experience and expertise of over 40 years in branding, working with hundreds of brands from different geographies and industries around the world, to define a brand *IN ONE WORD*. The unique methodology to do so may translate into a significant competitive advantage and has been proven to produce strong in market results.

Can you say what your brand stands for?

This book will enable you to say it in just *ONE WORD*.

# Contents

1 Introduction 1

2 The Central Role of Brand Positioning 21

3 How Do Brands Interact with Consumers and How Do Consumers Interact with Brands? 41

4 The Essentials of Power Brands: Why Competence, Differentiation, and Relevance Are the Key Dimensions to Focus on? 53

5 Perception Versus Reality: The Two Sides of the Brand Evaluation Process 73

6 How Self-Expressive Human Values Boost Brand Appeal? 83

7 The Essential Role of Consumer Insights and How to Unlock them via Morphological Research? 95

8 Simplicity on the Other Side of Complexity: Identifying the One Word that Defines your Brand 113

9 *One Word* Positioning and Brand Vision, Mission, and Purpose 137

| 10 | Brand Positioning and Brand Behavior: Successfully Translating Brand Positioning into Marketing Action | 143 |
|---|---|---|
| 11 | The Revival of Vintage Brands | 159 |
| 12 | Sharpening Established Brands (Product and Service Brands) | 173 |
| 13 | Brand Creation: Getting It Right from the Start | 185 |
| 14 | B2C Versus B2B Branding | 197 |
| 15 | Branding in the Corporate World (Crucial Implications for Corporate and Employer Brands) | 207 |
| 16 | Organizing the Brand Message Mix | 219 |
| 17 | The Current and Future Role of AI in Branding | 229 |
| 18 | The Transformative Responsibility of Brands in the Advanced Twenty-First Century | 241 |

# About the Author

**Michael Behnke** has spent over 40 years working in international branding and communication and has lived in Europe, the USA and Latin America. He is founder and president of the Belly Button Paris brand consultancy in Paris, France and has been teaching branding, marketing and communications at the American University of Paris for the past 10 years.

# 1

## Introduction

According to The Nielsen Company, a global research institute, 90% of CPG[1] brand launches fail within the first 2 years. The Harvard Business Report[2] states that 75% of FMCG[3] brand launches in the US market do not even reach first-year target sales of a modest $7.5 million, while less than 3% meet objectives of 50 million € or above in the first 12 months. L'EUIPO, the European trademark office, registers close to 135,000 brands every year—but only a few of them will ever reach a sustainable level of sales.

While these numbers are purely indicative and highly dependent on the fields of industry, there are usually multiple reasons for this rather disappointing performance: poor product performance, weak distribution, insufficient marketing funds, or the strength of the competitive response. Oftentimes, however, this is due to a brand's failure to develop a sharp and unidimensional value proposition, also referred to as *brand positioning* or *brand essence*, that helps set it apart from its competitors and makes it relevant to consumers.

It is important to note that there are nuances in the definition of failure. Some brand launches crash and burn resulting in brands falling off the map completely, while others struggle to gain market traction or fail to meet their desired goals. Successfully launching or repositioning a brand requires several distinct steps, including thorough competitive brand research, scouting for insights into consumer needs, attitudes, and motivations, a deep understanding of product or service features, and the brand's history, just to name a few.

---

[1] CPG: consumer package goods
[2] Why Most Product Launches Fail —Havard Business Report/April 2011 by Joan Schneider and Julie Hall.
[3] FMCG: fast moving consumer goods.

Like in an investigation, every detail counts. Doing your homework during this planning and analysis phase provides the intelligence for effective marketing strategies that will give your brand the push it needs to succeed.

The most decisive factor for brand success is a unique brand value proposition, whose role it is to define what your brand will stand for in a tangible and actionable way. The *brand value proposition* or the *brand essence* becomes the centerpiece of all future branded activities.

Entire marketing and sales strategies will thus be driven by the brand essence, ensuring that all touch points between the brand and its consumers provide the same consistent brand experience. Summarizing your brand *in just one word* provides the focus and discipline it takes to build true power brands with global potential and reach.

Today, too many brands either fail to define what they truly stand for or lack the focus in marketing and communication to undeniably claim their difference with enough clarity and consistency to stress their relevance. Defining the brand essence is a complex exercise, requiring a methodological approach and strong focus. Still, many brand positioning statements remain either too complex or too abstract to prescribe tangible marketing and communication action. Complexity and abstraction obstruct a fluid brand experience, where each target contact reproduces an experience that is coherent and consistent with the previous and the following one. It is for these consistent brand experiences that consumers engage with a given brand over time, eventually truly embracing it in the long run.

The consistency of the tangible and intangible performance parameters of a brand is the first and most important condition and the primary reason why consumers to shop for brands. Consumer expectations toward brands are subjective, yet rather clearly defined. Generally, they are nonnegotiable and as a basic function, any brand must reassure consumers on its consistent quality and performance. Today's brands mostly deliver on quality and other tangible performance indicators. However, there are also numerous exceptions. Quality slips in production, increased raw material prices that tempt brand owners to adjust recipes or product formulations (as with the recent inflationary context), or a simple packaging format or design evolution might lead to a change in the brand's overall performance perception. A radical change to the packaging design of a German cat litter brand during a brand repositioning exercise in 2018 increased consumer quality complaints on the customer service platform threefold, even though the product composition had not changed at all. However, what had changed was the consumer perception of the product performance, triggered simply by the change in the packaging design. Consequently, it is important to recognize that even minor disruptions of the brand mix might already lead today's marketing-weathered consumers to suspect that product performance and, as a result, the entire brand experience may have been altered.

As a matter of fact, brand perceptions may produce a tangible impact on the actual brand experience. Research conducted in 2021 by the University of Sussex[10] revealed that brand messaging may significantly influence consumer taste preferences in beer. This phenomenon will be discussed in more detail in Chap. 5. Our interactions with food and beverages, but also other products and services, start with the brand cues we perceive even prior to the actual product experience. These cues generate expectations with target consumers that in turn may produce a direct and immediate impact on their product or service usage perceptions.

What appears less obvious is that brand messaging and communication also require consistency, not necessarily in form but in content. A brand positioning that lacks focus and sharpness will almost always offer too much scope and latitude to deliver truly consistent brand messages, which are indispensable to continuously reinforce the attitudes and beliefs that consumers have already started to associate with a given brand.

This uncompromising quest for consistency might feel like a constraint for marketeers, in their ongoing effort to build strong brands or to keep a given brand desirable and up-to-date. At the same time, brands must constantly perform a balancing act between consistency and change. Consistency alone is not enough. Consumers also expect brands to renew themselves in order to keep up with changing times and emerging trends. The point here is that the change must apply only to the form and not the content—providing reassurance and freshness at the same time, a phenomenon often referred to as the *branding paradox*.

Norman Berry, the Worldwide Creative Director at Ogilvy and Mather in New York, was one of the finest and brightest people in the advertising industry in the mid-1980s and used to claim *the freedom of a tightly defined strategy*. As an experienced advertising creative, he understood that only the simplicity and edge of a tightly defined strategy would give him the freedom to focus on how to translate a claim into powerful brand messages or how to imagine a new form for the same consistent brand content. Norman understood that his creative role was to redefine the "*how* to say" it, since the "*what* to say" was sacrosanct and written in stone by a brand's sharply defined brand essence.

All creative processes require a clear and mono-dimensional direction to produce a hard-working creative idea. In the process of building a brand, those ideas may and should differ, while the actual meaning of the brand message to consumers requires absolute consistency over time. His creative vision clearly illustrates the importance assigned to the actual definition of the brand message. He demanded absolute clarity in what the brand must say. Only a clearly defined, single-minded, and differentiated brand message provides the creative freedom to find the best and most effective way to communicate the *what*. Consequently, the *what* is the foundation of any creative process, where all creative energy is dedicated to defining only the *how*, or, the form and not the content of a brand's unique selling proposition. What a brand stands for must be regarded as consistent over time, impactful, and relevant to the target audience. Defining "*what* to say" clearly is the sole responsibility of the brand owner and the brand strategist.

Inconsistency in brand messaging often springs from poorly defined or overly complex brand positioning platforms, leaving too much room for interpretation and a false sense of freedom that will most likely lead to brand communication messages, which may not provide the necessary focus and consistency. This is where many branding problems begin. It is sort of a chain reaction: message inconsistency leads to somewhat diffuse brand images that generally result in weaker salience or relevancy.

Before we enter the process of defining what a brand should stand for, let us take a minute to consider why brands are such powerful means to influence consumer preferences or even to create entirely new needs. For over a century, brands have successively become integral parts of our lives. They are omnipresent and accompany us day and night. We perceive them consciously or unconsciously. However, only a few of them make it to our relevant set, and even less are eventually consumed.

Initial forms of branding can be traced all the way back to antiquity, where craftsmen would emboss or engrave a symbol to sign their piece of work. However, the origin of brands as we know them today was actually a consequence of the Industrial Revolution, where mass production enabled through energy-powered machines led to fiercer competition and an increased need for differentiation. As mass production started to generate mass consumption (an indispensable precondition for mass production to last), relationships between manufacturers and consumers grew more distant. Unlike the artisanal production of goods by craftsmen and their families, manufacturing was mostly anonymous, where consumers came to rely less on the trust of a personal relationship with the producer and/or the distributor. Eventually, brands emerged to fill this gap, offering consistent product and service experiences and building trust with their target consumers.

Undeniably, branding has grown more and more sophisticated and complex over the years, and the arrival of social media has forever shifted the branding paradigm. Brands today are built and managed via multifaceted stakeholder communities in which the consumer has become a decisive player. Essentially, branding has become interactive, and the "one-way" model of the past has given way to new forms of branding, increasingly built on dialogue with the target audience. Enabled by social media, consumers more than ever before have turned into cocreators in the overall branding process. While in the past, it was the brand owners who claimed what their brands should stand for, now brands are also what consumers say about them. This has led to a significant paradigm shift in branding: from simply buying a brand to buying into a brand.

When we talk about brands, we often refer to a product, a service, a destination, or a person. Brands as such are generally seen to materialize via distinctive color codes, logos, brand signatures, or a designated product or packaging formats such as the Dove beauty bar, the Nespresso capsule, or the iconic Coca Cola bottle. The latter was designed, deposited, and introduced in 1915 to underscore the brand's uniqueness at a time when hundreds of copy-cats had proliferated across the United States. By 1916, courts across the country had banned 153 imposters of the Coca Cola legacy.

However, in reality, a brand is not any of the above, but rather the simple recollection of the feelings and emotions that logos, slogans, advertising messages, and regular use have evoked in our minds. As a matter of fact, brands are intangible and developed through the accumulation of our subjective perceptions over time. These perceptions are formed in multiple ways and by multiple contact points such as the communication buzz around a brand, may it be advertising messages, a logo on a store front, word-of-mouth recommendations, or the simple fact of seeing a given brand in your immediate everyday surroundings. Brands only really exist in our minds.

The overall level of brand awareness, the actual product or service experience during and after use, and brand equity perceptions acquired over time, all play a significant role. Simply seeing a packaging on a supermarket shelf, at a friend's place, or observing someone checking out a product at the cashier terminal consciously or unconsciously contribute to the brand awareness level, its perception, or even the overall brand experience. Every single touch point between a consumer and a brand contributes to building the brand, or its image in the form of recollections generated by the perceptions produced during these contacts. As part of the brand equity, each brand contact is associated with the experiences they collectively trigger inside our mind.

Over time, the total number of contact points[4] has dramatically increased in our daily lives. Research suggests that back in the 1970s, traditional media

---

[4] The sum of all brand messages combined and beyond advertising.

such as TV, radio, press, and billboards produced an average of 600–1600 branded messages or brand contacts a day—obviously significantly more for consumers who lived in dense urban rather than suburban or rural areas. In 2007, the American market research firm Yankelovich estimated the daily ad and brand impact on an average urban consumer at 5000 contacts. The latest data from 2021 now suggests that contact frequency might have evolved to between 6000 and 10,000 branded (see footnote 4) messages per day.

There are many reasons to explain this dramatic increase. Traditional media, social networks, direct marketing, outdoor, and POS (point of sale)are just a few examples of brands that cross our paths during our daily habits, routines, and work. Every day, thousands of such brand contacts are accumulated, which challenge our cognitive capacity to selectively retain any meaningful brand information. First, the media fragmentation and later the democratization of the Internet and social media have greatly impacted the numbers of our average daily exposure. At the same time, marketing techniques initially designed in the 1970s to increase the level of real or perceived product obsolescence (such as practiced by most fast fashion brands, for example) have shortened the repurchase cycles of many product and service categories, pushing consumers ever more frequently to reevaluate their brand choices. This also explains why, driven by media channel proliferation and consumers' search for information, brand contacts during any given day have multiplied exponentially.

Nobody knows the exact numbers, and unquestionably significant variations may apply depending on consumers' lifestyles, occupations, and place of residence or work. However, even if these numbers are mere approximations, they still show that reaching a consumer with a branded message is one thing but catching his or her attention is quite another.

Even with a conservative estimate of 5000 daily branded hits, our cognitive capacity becomes easily overwhelmed when it comes to absorbing and somewhat considering even a tiny portion of this daily brand message activity. A 2014 study on media usages conducted by Media Dynamics, Inc., a US research media firm (see Fig. 1.1), arrived at the conclusion that on average, 58% of advertising messages passed unnoticed. As a result, for brands to gain relevance with consumers amid these crowded communication environments, message clarity and consistency become paramount. This requires a single-minded, differentiated brand positioning, defining for everybody in the organization what your brand shall stand for—ideally with *one single word*.

The other important element to keep in mind is that brands strive to create emotional bonds. Strong brands establish deep emotional relationships with their target audiences. These emotional connections allow brands to establish

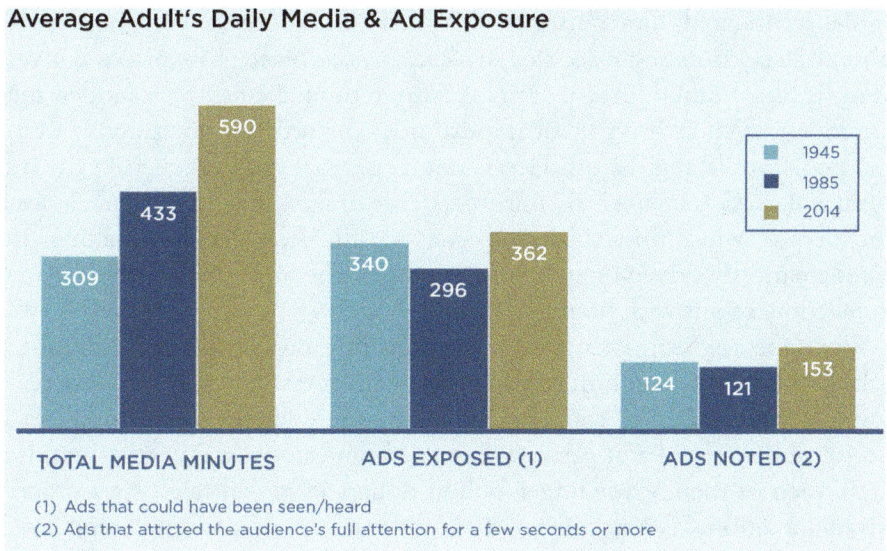

**Fig. 1.1** Average daily media and advertising exposure for adults. Source and permission: Media Dynamics, Inc.

trust and confidence, further enhanced through flawless consistency in the brand experience. Of course, brands have rational dimensions, too, mostly expressed by product or service attributes that suggest a certain desired performance, which, in turn, must be relevant to your brand's designated target audience. Rational attributes have the potential to designate a functional competence for which a brand will become known. While a functional competence may be instrumental in establishing brand differentiation, comparing alternative brand choices purely on functional attributes demands quite a cognitive effort, which often overwhelms the average consumer. As a consequence, consumers fall back onto more emotional brand dimensions during their decision-making process. Trust, confidence, value perceptions, and recollected past experiences finally outweigh the rational decision-making criteria, unconsciously pushing consumers toward an emotionally driven decision-making process.

The same principles hold true in B2B (business-to-business) decision-making processes, where rational performance criteria admittedly play a larger role. However, emotional triggers in B2B negotiations, such as trust and confidence, will also tip the balance in favor of those brands, which have established stronger emotional connections. The extent to which emotional decision-making represents a consumer truth has been demonstrated in numerous studies on behavioral finance. Nobel Prize-winning psychologist

Daniel Kahneman, a precursor in this field among others, concluded that a substantial portion of the decision-making process, even in finance and investment, is based on emotional logic. A simple bubble effect or a sudden mass movement, such as investment trends, often distort the conclusions rational data pools would suggest. And let us not forget that typical buyers in the B2B world are B2C (business-to-consumer) consumers outside of work as well. And despite what most consumers may claim, their decision-making processes are mostly driven by subconscious urges, the most powerful being emotional connections with brands.

While message consistency is paramount in building successful brands, it really unfolds its strength in combination with message repetition. Procter & Gamble (P&G), one of the world's leading manufacturers and marketer of successful household and personal hygiene brands, owned 22 mega-brands in 2020, each of them exceeding 1 billion dollars in global sales. As a process-driven operation, Proctor believes that "advertising works through repetition." This belief does not come out of nowhere. P&G figures among the most research-driven FMCG companies in the world. Repetition does indeed work, and not only in advertising. The principle of repetition applies to brand messaging in the same way. A simple, single-minded, and pertinent message, translating a product or service attribute into a differentiating benefit and reproducing it at every single consumer touchpoint, is what ultimately contributes the most to building leadership brands.

Hard-working and successful brand positionings are first and foremost about choosing the one discriminating attribute that lends itself to building relevance and differentiation. Successful brands translate these attributes into highly relevant consumer benefits, ideally leveraging exclusive consumer insights that have been previously revealed via intensive consumer research. *Morphological* research in particular, founded on the theory of Gestalt and Freudian psychology, is a powerful tool to unlock the unconscious sides of the consumer mind, digging for relevant need structures. Morphological research has become an integral part of the one-word branding approach for many years and will be discussed in more detail in Chap. 7.

Not only is it crucial to build a brand positioning around the product or service reality, but the equity a brand already owns with consumers or customers must also be considered. The only exceptions to this basic requirement are new brands, which must build their equity from scratch. Brand roots, graphic identity signatures, past positionings, iconic products and communication milestones, brand and corporate history, brand experiences lived, told or transmitted, the cultural space a brand might occupy, and so on are all important dimensions that need to become aligned within the future brand positioning platform.

A brand is a highly complex construct, and the objective in branding is to distill this massive complexity down, ideally to a single word or angle of attack. A complex brand positioning is almost always synonymous with a lack of focus, leading to confusion and, ultimately, to less consistent brand activities over time. That being so, successful brands stand for only one thing. The one dimension a brand may not only claim but also entirely occupy and ultimately own is always built on a tangible product or service reality. It is worthwhile noting that the product or service reality may not just refer to a product attribute but may sometimes be identified in the nature of the raw materials or ingredients, the formula or recipe, the production process or other elements of the larger brand universe. Every little detail has the potential to make a difference in the development of the final positioning platform. Accordingly, in branding any piece of information counts and should be gathered prior to the brand distillation process, which is indispensable to identifying the *one* magic word or angle of attack (see Chap. 8).

Pablo Picasso once claimed that *it took him 4 years to paint like Raphael and a lifetime to paint like a child*. What he was indirectly referring to is a thought by Oliver Wendell Holmes, a physician and Harvard professor of anatomy and physiology in the nineteenth century: *For the simplicity on this side of complexity, I wouldn't give you a fig. But for the simplicity on the other side of complexity, for that I would give you anything I have.*

True simplicity lies indeed on "the other side of complexity" and Picasso's artist vision does not apply better to any other domain than it does to branding. He was referring to the fact that as we learn and get better at what we do, first our reasoning, then our actions, become more sophisticated and complex. We acquire the indispensable skills to perfect our work. However, as we must consider more and more things on a daily basis, complexity makes us lose the intuitive lightness and agility of our youth. This is where most of us get stuck in the complexity of our know-how and expertise. True masters in their fields can shed that acquired complexity, refusing to focus on the details anymore. It is the result that attracts all their attention, skills, or mastery, leaving the complexity of the achievement process behind. This is when true masters achieve the second state of simplicity, the one on the other side of complexity. Masters focus on the one and only virtuous dimension that matters—all others are pushed to the backstage. While carefully weighing and balancing all elements of the brand equity in the process of defining or redefining the brand positioning, only the aspect of the product or service reality with the best potential for differentiation deserves particular attention. To design a one-word brand positioning, only that one feature counts—all others become deprioritized; however, none is lost.

This book is about how to define a brand positioning in *one word* or one angle of attack. It elaborates on the reasoning behind this unique methodology and the detailed process to achieve it. Using various brand illustrations, it demonstrates how to define a brand's value proposition in its ultimate state, boiled down to a single word or angle of attack. In this process, *simplicity, clarity, and focus* are the most important performance indicators for the brand positioning platform. A well-defined positioning is indispensable to providing clear and actionable direction for all marketing and sales activity, while also providing the groundwork for differentiated, relevant, and consistent brand messaging over time.

It is fair to say that identifying the single "word" or "angle" is a challenge, and only a minority of brands succeed in doing so. However, many of the brands that have managed to do so in the past have become leaders in their respective field or industry. Nike stands for *empowerment*, Oreo for *playfulness*, and Evian for *living youthfully*. Not only does each of these brands stand for one thing in consumers' minds, their precise and unidimensional value propositions also provide a clear and single-minded roadmap for all stakeholders who take part in managing and developing the respective brand. Virtuous in their own way, these positioning platforms were conceived to attain *simplicity on the other side of complexity*.

Be that as it may, the single-minded thought process that led to their creation has made them entirely operational for everyone in their parent organization. They are easy to understand and execute. They succeed in fusing human know-how, diverse competencies, energy, and creativity on an everyday basis. They become highly instrumental in pointing the combined talent of your organization in the same direction. A simple word such as *playfulness* serves as the ultimate guide in every aspect of a complex marketing, innovation, sales, and communication mix—to external and internal target audiences alike. In practice, this means that if a given idea or initiative is believed to produce *playfulness*, it is worthwhile pursuing; if not, then why bother. As Norman Berry would say, unidimensional brand positionings give all stakeholders the freedom that comes with *a tightly defined strategy*. Leaving no margin for interpretation, these brand value propositions channel every bit of energy and creativity in the same strategic direction. Nevertheless, the full understanding of what a brand truly stands for empowers people in the entire company, potentially leading to more productivity, innovation, higher levels of motivation, and profitability.

If things are that simple, why are not all brands built on one-word positioning platforms?

The origin of overly complex brand positionings can often be traced back to the branding process itself. *Not invented here* attitudes, extensive management hierarchies, and complex power structures, lack of senior management support, weak internal branding competencies, or insufficient external resources all too often produce negotiated brand positionings, which are built on the smallest common denominator, meant to get everybody in the company to agree. In these cases, the branding process turns into an internal political show, on a local, regional or global level.

The simple lack of focus produced by a somewhat negotiated brand value proposition, as described earlier, almost becomes a minor problem. Much worse is that *negotiated* positionings all too often merely reflect the brand-owner perspective rather than the one of the target audiences. Therefore, these brand value propositions generally fail to truly address consumer needs. They almost always ignore relevant consumer insights in the process of their formulation. In addition to being too abstract to point a team's energy and creativity in one and the same direction at the operational level, they are also most likely to fail to produce the necessary salience and urgency to get the brand onto the consumer's shopping list. In fact, branding projects that result in single-word brand positioning platforms demonstrate that the stronger salience or relevance generated in the process may be leveraged to add urgency to the brand proposition, ultimately impacting consumer choices.

To unleash the real power of any given brand, its positioning must be single-minded and therefore, expressed in a *single word*. This principle applies to all brand types, no matter whether they concern FMCG, corporate, destination, or people brands or whether they are directed toward B2C, B2B, B2B2C, or even political target audiences. *America First* and *Get Brexit Done* are striking examples in political branding. The underlying principles of this unique approach to branding always remain the same. Applied correctly, with discipline and a sole focus on the result, one-word brand positioning platforms do deliver a tangible pay-off for their stakeholders.

When BMW decided to differentiate its luxury car brand by claiming the high ground of *driving pleasure*, the company took a clear position for one single-minded angle of attack. As a highly relevant benefit in the car market, BMW decided to distinguish its brand via this single-minded positioning platform, across all models and at all price points. Furthermore, BMW has done so consistently, allowing the brand to eventually fully own *driving pleasure* in the car industry. By no means does this suggest that BMW cars do not offer engineering quality, safety, technological innovation, comfort, or reliability. The focus on *driving pleasure* simply provided a single-minded platform for differentiation to address the consumer, simultaneously empowering the entire BMW organization.

Single-minded brand positionings provide meaning for internal and external target audiences alike. In a certain way, they function like a prism through which all brand activities are envisioned, conceived, and evaluated. They work as guidance and measurement sticks at the same time and may extend all the way to the dimension of employer branding, which has become ever more important in today's context of the "war for talent."

While *driving pleasure* defines a tangible and highly relevant benefit to consumers, it points everyone inside the company in the same direction. BMW employed roughly 155,000 people in 2023.[5] Imagine the effect of every single one of them using his or her inherent energy, creativity, judgement, and imagination to find new ways to enhance, reinvent, and build on *driving pleasure* for BMW.

*Driving pleasure* is the "one angle" the BMW brand truly stands for and owns against the competition. As such, this brand positioning directs everything that the parent company and the car brand does and strives for—no matter the model. While a different dose of driving pleasure may apply to every single model line, *driving pleasure* as the brand value proposition is the predominant and perceivable attribute all BMWs share, including the BMW motorcycle brand. A brand with the intelligence and courage to stand for only *one* thing, truly stands for something.

It is fair to say that within the luxury car market, BMW is not the only one to offer its buyers *driving pleasure*. Mercedes, Audi, Porsche, Jaguar, Lexus, and so on all offer a pleasurable drive, as much as all of them, including BMW, offer an attractive design, engineering quality, advanced technologies, safety, and reliability. The point here is that BMW has decided to make *driving pleasure* a focal point of its brand equity. Single-mindedly and prioritized over all other relevant brand messages.

At the same time, the brand leverages *driving pleasure* to differentiate itself from the other salient car industry performance indicators. As such, BMW does not simply aim to offer safety. It may strive to imagine a safety feature that simultaneously preserves and enhances driving pleasure.

Producing the maximum amount of *driving pleasure* across all car models, all features, and all consumer touch points become BMW's brand mantra. This way, *driving pleasure* becomes and remains the key image cornerstone of the BMW brand in consumers' minds. In short, via each and every BMW brand experience, *driving pleasure* provides the fluidity and consistency

---

[5] BMW Group 2023 Annual Report.

necessary to constantly strengthen and reinvent the BMW brand experience for its target consumers. *Driving pleasure* is the one and only strategic message the brand communicates, while all other relevant benefits indispensable to match customer expectations in the luxury car industry have become tactically assigned to subordinate positions in the communication mix. Hence, one-word brand positionings do not only rely on a mono-dimensional angle of attack but also lead to a well-balanced and prioritized message hierarchy (see Chap. 16).

It is quite easy to imagine how the focus on a one-word brand value proposition also helps to turbo-charge the overall brand development process. A single-minded brand message repeated over and over at all consumer touch points clearly speeds up the awareness and brand equity-building process. It increases the productivity of the resources applied to execute it.

Like all well-defined power brands, BMW defined relevant spots for each of its tactical messages in its overall message mix. In this approach of message prioritization, each tactical message has its exclusive place in the message hierarchy. This way, it can best unfold its strength single-mindedly, and without the message clutter that usually comes with a poorly defined message mix, where too many messages compete at the same identical level.

Stakeholders often get the impression that when hierarchizing strategic, tactical, and *politically* relevant brand messages, some are lost in the process. However, standing for only *one* thing does not mean that other messages are lost. Successful branding is also a question of message ranking and prioritization. Not every message should have the same importance in the message mix, and to choose does not mean to eliminate. There is a place where every brand message may maximize its impact and relevance to help your target audience along in the brand image formation and the purchase decision-making process.

In most cases, prioritizing a message simply means assigning it a precise position within the message mix, a position that it may truly own. Indeed, BMW also communicates on design, engineering quality, safety, technological innovation, comfort, and reliability. However, none of these attributes are used for the brand's strategic differentiation. As a matter of fact, most of these *tactical* attributes are owned by competitive car brands, respectively, who use them on their behalf and for their own strategic brand differentiation. As much as BMW stands single-mindedly for *driving pleasure*, Volkswagen owns *reliability*, Mercedes *engineering excellence*, and Volvo *safety*. However, it is fair to say that this single-minded brand positioning focus may also trap a brand. As a brand, Volvo has become somewhat stuck in *safety*. What used to be a real point of differentiation has become somewhat banalized, as all car brands now feature similar or the same safety features. While *safety* remains highly relevant, it has lost its capacity for differentiation.

Especially in corporations with hybrid brand systems and in product-centric master brand organizations, a strategic brand positioning that relies on just *one word* offers great potential as a multidimensional driving force behind the brand's development in its category and beyond. From marketing to communications and from sales to product innovation and manufacturing all the way to dealerships and SAV. *One-word* brand positioning may also provide differentiation in the way you might deal with your partners and suppliers or how you define the corporate brand, guiding the definition of the corporate vision, the employer brand, and the CSR strategy or, to a certain extent, tomorrow's growth strategy.

The "one-word" brand positioning also defines a brand's core competence, the one thing a brand is best at, what it will become known for and desired by its customers and consumers. The definition of the core competence is the natural secondary outcome of any sharp brand positioning. Like the brand positioning platform itself, the *brand competence* provides strategic input and helps to translate the brand positioning into operational action steps in areas such as the innovation process and brand stretching exercises. For example, this allows a brand to enter new market segments or to develop product line extensions. Ensuring that new products or services stay on track is strategic and highly relevant to building strong and consistent brand equities over time and across different market segments. Thus, providing a clear understanding of the brand competence may stimulate and support the process of defining and tapping into new sources of business for the brand.

Few companies have given their brands the role they deserve, allowing them to drive entire organizations. Obviously, a product or service brand, being part of a larger brand portfolio may never drive a hybrid or diversified parent company organization. However, within these organizations and as part of the overall brand portfolio, these brands may well drive all brand-related operations, from marketing to sales, communications to talent management, and innovation to manufacturing and supply chain partnerships. In the transformation process, unleashed through one-word brand value propositions, the brand essence ideally commands and guides all management functions and all subsequent activities. It is also a great tool to enhance brand differentiation within the brand portfolio.

In today's consumerism-dominated world, most market segments are saturated. They no longer offer the comfort of organic growth. For most brands, the only way to grow is to gain market shares from competitors in the brand's core market and in line extended subsegments alike. At the same time, decades of frantic marketing activity have created a plethoric brand offer that simply overwhelms today's average consumer.

A typical supersize hypermarket, such as Walmart or Target in the United States, Sainsbury in the United Kingdom, Carrefour in France, Coop in Italy, or Kaufland in Germany, may carry up to 50,000 product references. At the same time, statistics suggest that a routine weekly family shopping trip comprises an average of 150 items. For many consumers, simply finding and choosing a given set of products among all those branded choices often turns into a challenging, time-consuming, and tedious task. Facing such choices, the time consumers will spend considering new brands or lesser-known brands has decreased at the same rate that the offer complexity is added to the shelf. In that kind of context, brands that fail to effectively communicate relevance through their single-minded point of difference reduce their chances to compete effectively.

Decades of massive marketing activity have also made consumers way more marketing savvy as mass consumption has contributed to shaping and conditioning purchase behavior in a way and speed never seen before. Today's consumers have developed more opportunistic approaches to marketing and promotion techniques in their role as shoppers. In this context, branding missions have become more complex, not least because some of the brand-building control has moved over to the target audience itself. At the same time, stakeholder communities have grown more multidimensional, with consumers themselves playing an increasingly active role in the ongoing brand development process—as mentioned earlier, a phenomenon referred to as the *multifaceted stakeholder communities*. This is a direct result of the arrival and democratization of the Internet in the late 1990s and its powerful search engines (Google launched a first Google Search in 1998), followed by social media with Facebook taking the lead in 2004.

While the traditional and rather static brand development model remains widespread, ever larger, often global consumer communities have started to impact branding processes in virtually all areas of branding by leveraging conversations about, experiences with, and suggestions for a given brand, using brand-owned and user-owned social media channels to share their thoughts and feelings. Facebook, then YouTube, Instagram, Twitter, LinkedIn, and more recently TikTok and WeChat or Sina Weibo for China, to cite just the main ones, have given consumers powerful platforms to make themselves heard.

The democratization of social media channels with local, regional, or global reach has no doubt contributed to shifting the paradigm. Brands have become less about what brand owners want them to be and more about what consumer communities say about them. Branding has simply become more complex and now must seriously consider consumer opinions and feelings in its process. In the context of this cocreation, brand owners have no doubt lost some control over their brands. In essence, today's consumers do not only have their own views about brands but also the means to make them heard.

Many books and essays have been written about *meaning* and *purpose* in relation to branding, and Millennials and Generation Z represent the first-ever generations to consume with a view on the future. These consumers want to buy *into* a brand before putting their money down. Consequently, these two generations undeniably place a higher importance on these more recent brand traits. To successfully target these generational clusters, *meaning* and *purpose* must become more central to any future brand equity. In the twenty-first century, successful branding is becoming less product and more humanity centric. The consequence of this is that functional branding, as it is still practiced by many companies, will have to cease and become more emotional in its approach. Also, the evolving dynamics in today's cocreated brand-building process suggest that future branding projects might have to increasingly incorporate branding dimensions such as "transparency" and "trust."

Progress in technology and the transition into a post-globalized economic world are transforming our societies at an ever-faster pace. *Acceleration* is perhaps the word that best describes the way our world has changed over the past 30 years and, in particular, since the democratization of mobile IT devices, the Internet, and social media channels. Be that as it may, climate change, with its massive environmental impact, geopolitical instability, and the aftermath of the pandemic, all have a lasting impact on consumer perceptions, consumption patterns, and ultimately on the role brands play in consumers' lives.

According to some historians, 1500 years were necessary to double the combined knowledge of humanity—a period stretching from Antiquity all the way to the Renaissance. Only 250 years later, by the time mankind entered the First Industrial Revolution, our combined knowledge had doubled again. During the twentieth century, knowledge is believed to have doubled every 50 years. In today's context, of the often decried Third Industrial Revolution with its ever more powerful IT technologies, some experts estimate that knowledge doubles every few years, maybe even faster. Obviously, this does not happen homogeneously across the world or across all regions and all areas of human life, but the speed of change is perceivable for everyone no matter one's age, social status, or level of education. With artificial intelligence (AI) and quantum technology applications on the verge of going more mainstream, not only the perception but also the reality of speed is most likely to enter a new round of acceleration.

In this global context of ever faster change, brands offer powerful opportunities to provide stability. The consistency of the holistic brand experience will play an even bigger role in the years to come, as we move through the rocky and destabilizing times of this Third Industrial Revolution. In an amorphic world where everything seems to change at a breathtaking speed, more than ever, brands will provide reference points, allowing consumers to touch ground and to find and define meaning for themselves. The brands, which have succeeded in making *meaning* intrinsic to their brand identity, will be the ones that will emerge stronger in the period ahead.

One way to achieve this is to define a self-expressive human value of brand personality, quite likely the most powerful tool enabling marketers to connect and bond with their designated target consumers today and in the long run. Self-expressive human values help to inject fresh dynamics into brands and may turn out to be instrumental in building strong and lasting competitive barriers. Again, this underlying principle applies to all kinds of brands in similar ways. The principles of self-expressive human values will be explained in more depth in Chap. 6.

Times of increased speed also produce environments of increased complexity in which brands must operate. Increased offer complexity, self-checkout cashiers, digital payment methods, and inflationary pressures, all produce perceptions of change, which introduce new and unknown dimensions into established shopping routines, especially in grocery distribution channels. At the same time, long-proven push marketing techniques are starting to lose some of their grip as consumers grow ever more marketing savvy and, most importantly, increasingly wary of overconsumption.

European FMCG distributors have experienced continued change in consumer purchase behaviors for several years. Shoppers have been abandoning the overwhelming product choices and temptations of large hypermarkets and are focusing grocery shopping on smaller formats. Mostly inner city or neighborhood formats such as Monop, Franprix, or Carrefour City in France are offering reduced choices, improved product visibility, and shopping hours better adapted to modern urban lifestyles. Hence, an increasing number of consumers are at least partially shifting their shopping trips toward these retail formats, which offer more manageable, less tempting choices on the shelf. Hard discounters and, more recently, bargain outlets such as the Dutch distributors "Normal" or "Action" are deliberately reducing the cognitive barriers for consumers, selling end of series consumables, and stock from insolvencies to offer attractive pricing that alludes to the perception of regained purchase power.

Monop, a franchised city format of the French Casino group, has been leading in this development. Situated in inner-city, high-pedestrian traffic locations, these stores generally offer some 6000 product references (compared to the up to 50,000 references in a traditional French hypermarket). They operate on a surface ranging from 150 to 500 m² and use extended opening hours to address the busy lifestyle of today's urban dwellers. These formats offer easier, more spontaneous access while giving consumers a sizeable portion of control over their shopping expenses.

Also, inflationary pressures are seen as having lastingly impacted shopping behavior in many markets across Europe. In France, for example, food prices increased by close to 13% over 2023. Data suggests that this has not only driven consumers to smaller grocery outlets but that it has also motivated them to take shorter, but more frequent weekly shopping trips where fewer items end up in the shopping bag. A study recently conducted by Kantar,[6] an international research institute, found that while grocery shopping trips in France increased by 4.9% in 2022, the number of items purchased decreased by 4.5% during the same period, translating into an average reduction of 5–6 items purchased per visit. At the same time, and to preserve their purchase power, consumers are shifting their purchase choices from leadership brands to private label brands or from the latter ones to "first price" value brands.

Inflation might be temporary and the impact on consumer behavior might be limited over time. However, the effects of 60 years of consumerism, the speed of change, and the general geopolitical and environment instability are undeniable vectors that will produce lasting effects on how shoppers shop and how their brand choices will ultimately map out. The environmental impact of the products we consume and the values that brands stand for will become increasingly central to consumers' decision-making processes—not just in high-involvement categories but also for their day-to-day consumables. Apps such as Yuka in France, which allow consumers to scan and evaluate food and cosmetic products based on their composition and impact on the environment, have gained remarkable traction with younger target audiences recently underlining this trend. More than ever, brands have to "walk the talk" or risk being downranked or even dropped from consumers' shopping lists.

In times of great change, brands, too, must change. They must become more apt at managing the *branding paradox*, providing continuity and change at the same time. Providing a consistent brand experience is the role of any successful brand in its quest to build a loyal consumer base. However, while a brand's strength lies in providing consistent quality, performance, and overall brand experiences, brands must continually evolve to stay contemporary and

---

[6] Quand l'inflation s'invite à la table des Français, Le Monde, March 30, 2023.

desirable. In practice, this should translate into a homogeneous and consistent brand experience, delivered in a constantly refreshed and new way.

This demand for refreshment does not necessarily imply a constant flow of product or service innovation. True innovation is hard to achieve, and to reactualize a brand, even minor actions such as a new packaging format or design, a refreshed visual identity, or even a promotional offer may contribute to project a dynamic and contemporary image dimension for your brand. In most cases, it is the perception that counts more than the reality.

The extend to which this is true has been demonstrated by multiple research studies. A study conducted in 2021 on Food Quality and Preferences[7] by the University of Sussex in the United Kingdom proved that both sensory descriptor information provided on the label and beer color generated sensory and hedonic expectations, which directly influenced how participants appreciated a beer sample in reference to its flavor, taste, or mouthfeel. Brand messaging, promotions, package design, and so on offer the potential to produce expectations, which may positively impact brand perceptions. We will come back to this important lever to influence brand preferences in Chap. 5.

The era ahead offers great opportunity, particularly for those brands that succeed in defining and enacting a clear and mono-dimensional positioning that answers the evolving needs and decision-making criteria of tomorrow's consumer. A differentiated, mono-dimensional brand positioning derived from deep motivational consumer insights, continuous brand innovation, and hierarchized communication messages that all capture the brand essence as defined by the one and only *magic* word will become even more so a decisive factor for success in tomorrow's operating environments.

This is not to suggest that brands that are not managed by these principles are likely to fail. My point here is to suggest that organizations that design their operational activities entirely around what their brand claims to stand for succeed over time in producing stronger results. I trust that most of the world's CEOs can say what their brands stand for—however, how many can say it *in just one word*?

Leveraging a unique methodology, tangible tools, and many real-life benchmarks and illustrations, this book will show you how to define any given brand in just one word. It is a hands-on operational guide designed to improve the performance of your brand.

---

[7] A taste of things to come: The effect of extrinsic and intrinsic cues on perceived properties of beer mediated by expectations. University of Sussex, 2021. Helena Blackmore, Claire Hidrio, and Martin R. Yeomans.

# 2

# The Central Role of Brand Positioning

The brand positioning defines what a brand stands for; in essence, a unique, differentiating, and highly relevant brand proposition that it will own against the competition. The brand positioning is the foundation on which the brand will ultimately be built. It impacts each and every aspect of the marketing and sales activities and often also casts a halo on the corporate, parent company brand. At the same time, the brand positioning provides the roadmap for all future brand activities. It not only defines the brand promise, the rational and emotional benefits, as well as the most pertinent reason to believe, but it also affirms the brand's personality and a set of values to act upon. Together, all these elements will determine the specific nature of the brand activities and help shape how the brand will be perceived by its target audiences.

The primary goal of the brand positioning is to clearly define what a brand stands for: single-mindedly, unambiguously sound, and actionable. I have seen many brand positioning definitions that remain strikingly abstract and since they do not naturally and intuitively translate into actionable marketing programs. They almost always end up forgotten in the company archives. From my experience, this happens most often in multilayered company structures such as global corporations. Entire marketing teams and branding agencies get so caught up in the information and data complexity of a historical brand, and with its internal approval processes and hierarchies, that the brand usually falls victim to the *not-invented-here syndrome* of internal politics. Branding work under these conditions has a fair chance of culminating in an agreement called a *positioning comprise*, i.e., accepting the smallest common denominator that somewhat satisfies all stakeholders. Positionings developed under these circumstances are almost always non-actionable and rarely produce tangible results. They are a waste of time and valuable resources.

To position or reposition a brand is not an easy task, since it always implies digging through a massive amount of information complexity: the product and advertising history, competitive brand positionings, and their image dimensions, which may compete for the same target consumer, evolving consumer expectations, new media channels, and communication venues. The past 20 years have particularly generated a tremendous amount of change in the world of branding, triggered by the global democratization of internet access and the arrival of social media networks in 2004. Both of these technological advances have profoundly impacted how brands are successfully built and managed over time. We will examine this subject in more detail later on.

Established brands usually come with a long history, accumulating many different facets and dimensions throughout their entire brand life. These facets and dimensions always provide first important clues for a successful positioning platform, inspired by the advertising, the product or brand history, and other elements of the brand's equity. Together, all these components have left a mark on consumers over time, contributing to shaping the image and equity perception they have of the brand. Nascent brands do not offer these reference points and need to be defined from scratch. However, they usually benefit from a reduced information complexity and the fact that their core proposition is derived from an innovative idea that, at that stage, remains fairly essential and pure. The challenge in any brand positioning or repositioning exercise is to overcome this complexity, distilling all the available and relevant information to define a brand positioning in an absolute state of simplicity. *The simplicity on the other side of complexity.*

In the brand positioning or repositioning process, every tiny detail of information counts and defining a powerful brand positioning always starts with a thorough analysis and investigation of all aspects of the brand's equity. This implies scrutinizing the product, its composition and the exact role and benefit of every component or ingredient, the provenance of the raw materials, the manufacturing process, the product performance as measured in lab situations and as perceived by consumers alike. Brand, product, and packaging histories count equally as much, as a brand's past communication and promotion messages.

Starting with the *product*[1] is paramount. Any brand positioning must be anchored in the product reality. There is a lot to study and discover in the

---

[1] In this definition, the term *product* also refers to a service, a place/destination, a person or any other entity which may be transformed into a brand

archives and to learn from people who have been in the company and with the brand for a long time. Often these people are the living memory of the brand equity, and may be able to explain the rationale behind a certain name, logo, or slogan and the exact role of the brand's attributes at a time when it was at its peak performance and desired by its target audience. Also, do not hesitate to talk directly to the people who are working in the innovation and manufacturing process, the developers, engineers, and line workers. You should also talk to the consumer and, most importantly, use the product yourself: not just once, but over a prolonged period of time. Product usage information usually provides deep insights into the performance attribute that allows you to differentiate and turning a *product* into a successful brand. It also lets you slip into the consumers' shoes, not solely through their feedback, but made tangible by your own personal experience. The exact same procedure should be applied to service, place, and people brands. The more you know and understand your *product*, the better your chances are of identifying that little element of difference, which will ultimately allow you to formulate a differentiating and relevant brand proposition.

We once worked on a popular fresh cheese brand in Germany. It had been around for decades and competitors both from the branded world and the distributor brands had somehow diminished its brand differentiation. At first sight, all brands in this market segment used the same recipe. They also all claimed the unique origin and quality of their milk, being sourced from small human-size farms located in well-known and protected natural geographies. These places in themselves were image-laden and came with many positive, but stereotyped image connotations held by the target consumer community. Also, the recipes used to make this cheese were pretty much the same across all competitive offers. We looked at all the details, analyzed ample consumer research available on the brand, and on product usage and attitudes. There simply was nothing that turned up to help us define a tangible point of difference.

Then one day, we happened to talk to one of the senior food engineers, who had the longest experience in the company and with this particular product. We went over the entire sourcing and production process again, step by step and when we finally approached the pasteurization process of the milk used to make this cheese a small detail inadvertently emerged from his explanations. We will develop in Chap. 4 how this tiny detail eventually provided the lead for the new brand repositioning.

To be successful, any brand positioning or repositioning must be actionable. This means it has to translate easily and almost intuitively for everybody into concrete and tangible actions, including marketing and communication as well as sales and product innovation. For this to happen, a pertinent brand positioning needs to fulfill three key preconditions: (1) it must be built on a *product* reality, (2) it must be differentiating against competition, and (3) it must have relevance and salience with target audiences.

## Understanding the Product Reality

The *product* reality is the starting point for any brand positioning, repositioning of an existing brand or positioning of a future brand. Consumers expect brands to perform in a consistent and reliable manner. They evaluate a brand's performance via their own personal experience, referred to as the *user experience (UX)*, while third-party opinions from friends or online communities might equally impact these performance perceptions. While the actual use of a product or service largely determines its subjective performance perception, there are also various other criteria and stimuli that might impact performance perceptions (to be discussed in Chap. 5).

Most packaged goods today, independent of the market segment where they compete, are likely to struggle to define a unique product reality based on a recipe or product formulation. Branded competitors and distributor-owned brands tend to copy any offer that has not previously been patented. This might considerably limit the amplitude or scope on which positioning claims can be made. The same holds true for service offers or destination brands. Consequently, defining a differentiating positioning platform requires deeper research into the history and the product reality of a given brand. Here, the goal is to identify that tiny piece of *product reality* that allows you to make a differentiating claim, giving your brand the indispensable level of *differentiation and relevance*. Unfortunately, the holy grail of differentiation does not always come in ready-to-use formulas. In most cases, only a creative transcription of the basic positioning platform into powerful wording will turn it into a valid brand proposition. This book is about how to eventually get there by settling on *one single word*. It was not only Picasso who had a passion for simplicity, but Antoine de Saint Exupéry, a world-famous French aviator and book author, also shared this same vision: *In anything at all, perfection is finally attained not when there is no longer anything to add, but when there is no longer anything to take away, when a body has been stripped down to its nakedness.*

Take the case of Evian mineral water. At the beginning of the twenty-first century, Evian had lost most of its competitive edge not only to its closest alpine water competitors, but also to numerous spring water brands that had recently entered the market. The simple promise of authenticity was no longer differentiating enough against all these new competitors who were also leveraging their origin in reference to the Alps. Evian went back to discover its brand roots: minerals and trace elements absorbed during a 50,000-year filtration process through the rocks of the French Alps. In fact, doctors in 1935 had recommended giving Evian to babies due to its mineral composition. But again, minerals and trace elements are what is considered one of the dominant attributes of the bottled water market—they are no longer sufficient to differentiate a water brand in today's crowded marketplace. However, it was the unique role that Evian assigned to its ingredient story that did the trick. Minerals and trace elements are vital for certain body functions, such as cell renewal. Evian decided to leverage this biological evidence to propose a functional brand claim, lightly linked to a health promise. Since the mid-2000s, these claims have become increasingly regulated in Europe and any direct link between the consumption of a product and a health claim must be proven using scientific evidence.

Evian got around this with a clever move, linking cell renewal to *youth*. However, instead of claiming a *fountain of youth* positioning that the brand could impossibly prove, Evian lifted the *youth* proposition to a visionary level, as well expressed in its new slogan at the time: "Live Young." As a brand, Evian elevated the claim of *youth* to a form of attitude, elevating its benefits from the biological to the cognitive level. This is clever and highly relevant to its affluent, health-conscious target audiences. The claim also uses a call to action (CTA) technique, somewhat adding a sense of urgency and reinforcing the attitudinal spirit of Evian's brand essence turned brand vision.

During the late 1980s, consumer research revealed a significant paradigm shift in terms of how people relate to their individual lives. Advances in medicine, more efficient treatments, nutritional science, and the growing popularity of physical activity had changed the way people looked at their life. For centuries, mankind had aspired to *add more years to one's life*. All of a sudden, *adding more life to one's years* had become the new mantra. The definition of growing old had been revised by an entire baby boomer generation and life aspirations had transformed from a definition of *years* to one of *enjoyment and fun*. *Live Young*, Evian's brand signature that summed up this new positioning into a catchy advertising claim, clearly struck a nerve with its target audience and continues to do so to this very day.

Apart from this being a brilliant and creative brand repositioning move, it was also a positioning that was highly actionable and operational. For everyone working with and around the Evian brand, *youthful living* can easily be translated into marketing and sales messages or activities. It also provides a clear direction for product innovation. Proof of this were Evian's brand image communications in the form of the award-winning *roller-baby* TV ad from 2009, which really gave the brand's repositioning work worldwide visibility, generating over 130 million views as the most viral advertising message of all times. The campaign is still up and running after 15 years (see Fig. 2.1).

The Evian example shows how clever thinking and creativity may compensate for a lack of real product differentiation at the attribute level. Admittedly, Evian uses more than one word to define its brand essence; however, *live young* still represents a very sharp and single-minded angle, which leaves little room for interpretation when approaching the operational applications of the marketing and sales effort.

Evian, like most brands, used intrinsic product attributes to differentiate: minerals and trace elements. Although the composition of these elements in Evian water is unique, the fact that mineral waters have a unique mineral and trace element composition is not. As a matter of fact, for a water brand to receive this denomination, the mineral composition must be stable over time—except for spring or source waters where mineral and trace element density may vary. The uniqueness in the Evian case comes from the fact that these intrinsic attributes were simply used as a reason to believe a clever new brand vision. A good illustration of what makes the difference in successful brand positioning is creativity, an open mind, and the capacity to think outside the box.

Nonetheless, extrinsic attributes are also suitable for the brand differentiation exercise. Take the example of Absolut Vodka. This Swedish Vodka brand could neither rely on the traditional origin credentials common for vodka (Russian or Polish), nor did it have any specific product attribute that made it

**Fig. 2.1** Current Evian advertising, the United States. Permission Danone Waters

unique. The brand simply claimed the high ground with its name and supported it with a unique round transparent bottle and label. This bottle is a remarkable extrinsic product attribute and functions somewhat like a showroom window to the product's purity—a main quality feature of vodka for consumers. The bottle also disrupted the conventions of the market by naturally standing out and generating impact on the shelf. First established in 1879 in Ahus, in the south of Sweden, Absolut Vodka was initially sold just outside the Stockholm city limits as a value product with the intention of undercutting the city's monopolistic pricing that, at the time, was referred to as "Rent Bränvin" (literally "royal burn-wine"). Nationalized in 1971, the brand was relabeled *Absolut Rent Bränvin* and continued to be produced from locally sourced wheat and spring water. The brand does not claim a competitive edge via its distillation process. The only truly ownable point of difference for Absolut Vodka is its unique bottle, an extrinsic product attribute, which the brand started to iconize when it went global in 1981, launching what was to become the longest running campaign in advertising history (Fig. 2.2).

Ever since, the brand name alone allowed Absolut to claim the high ground of quality vodkas. Together, its name and the uniquely shaped and highly

**Fig. 2.2** First global Absolut Vodka print ad from 1981—"Absolut Perfection." Permission Pernod-Ricard

recognizable bottle have become the main product attributes on which this brand continues to claim its differentiation. Both of them are extrinsic. It is only fair to say that lucky incidents also helped Absolut to become number one. In 1986, Andy Warhol, who (abstained from alcohol consumption and is believed to have used Absolut Vodka from time to time to perfume himself) was so inspired by the bottle that he turned it into one of his most well-known works. The other element in the Absolut brand mix that is worth noting is the conceptional use of the name in combination with the bottle. Indeed, the word *absolut* automatically turns everything it refers to into a sort of reference. *Absolut* simply suggests *best among all others*. This simple but highly effective fact allowed Absolut to conceptionally leverage salience at a global level, independent of local cultural differences. Proof of this is the Absolut communication campaign that promoted hundreds of **local ads using** the exact same creative principle as shown in Figs. 2.3, 2.4, 2.5, and 2.6. *Absolut simplicity* is just *on the other side of complexity*: a name and a bottle to build a highly desirable brand by leveraging the potential of two extrinsic attributes.

At times, a product attribute that looks like a weakness or threat at first sight may serve as a powerful differentiator. This was the case for the French

**Fig. 2.3** Absolut Manhattan print ad. Permission Pernod Ricard

**Fig. 2.4** Absolut L.A. print ad. Permission Pernod Ricard

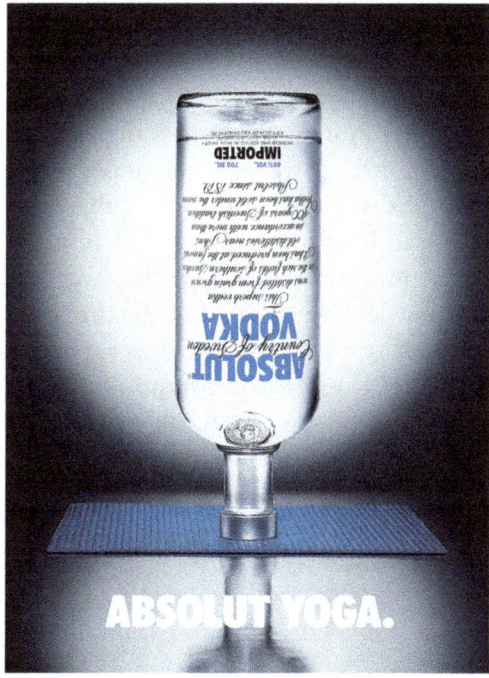

**Fig. 2.5** Absolut Yoga print ad. Permission Pernod Ricard

**Fig. 2.6** Absolut Bastille print ad. Permission Pernod Ricard

soft drink brand Orangina. Orangina's product difference is its pulp-based formula, giving the drink a more consistent orange taste and a texture closer to freshly pressed orange juice. However, Orangina had a problem. After a few days, the pulp usually settled on the bottom of the semitransparent bottle, suggesting anything but an irresistible appeal. The solution is to simply shake the bottle prior to consumption. Similar to the Absolut brand, which succeeded in iconizing its bottle, Orangina also used the shaking gesture to iconize its product usage; thus, turning a potential weakness into a strength. Over time, the shaking of the bottle prior to consumption became a ritual that gave the brand its differentiation in the soft drink market. The ritual of *shake it before you taste it* has been institutionalized for over 30 years, playing a central role in Orangina's communication messages all the way to the moment of consumption in French bistros.

## Differentiation

Brand differentiation is the process by which the selected product attribute is transformed into a unique positioning claim, usually referred to as the brand essence. As the term suggests, the brand essence is the essential message that a brand stands for. The claim that makes it stand out in the market and from the competition. The word *essence* further suggests that the designated brand meaning has been purified down to that very element, which will allow the brand to claim a unique benefit to its target audiences. The tighter the brand essence is defined, the more creative freedom it will provide in the process of expressing it at different levels of the marketing mix.

Differentiation may be achieved at different levels. Most brands are differentiating at product or service level. However, differentiation may also be achieved at market level, like Apple did when it decided to attack the entire PC industry with the introduction of the Apple Macintosh personal computer in 1984. Contrary to the average brand seeking differentiation, Apple did not decide to build its differentiation on any particular product attribute but offered its new Macintosh as a visionary and almost *ideological* alternative to all Microsoft-powered PCs—no matter the respective brands. The newsbreaking introduction at the time was achieved with a single 60-second TV spot directed by Ridley Scott and aired only once during the 1984 Superbowl in which Apple claimed that *with the introduction of the new Macintosh, 1984 won't be like 1984*. Taking on an entire industry and proposing an alternative to an established product standard can be a highly effective way to build brand differentiation under one condition: your product must offer a relevant benefit that is radically different from those the market is currently competing on. In Apple's case this was and continues to be the *user experience*. Lipton used a similar approach to propose its teas as an alternative to coffee. Nestlé leveraged the high-tech innovation behind the Nespresso system to attack and break into the roast and ground coffee market as a true game changer.

To achieve a solid differentiation, your brand does not always require a radically different product reality to build on. Any product attribute that allows your brand to claim a distinctive point of difference that other brands have not yet claimed can be turned into an ownable and defendable brand positioning claim. If this point of differentiation turns out to also have high relevance or saliency with your consumer target, you might have a winner. Most brands do not actually differentiate on a radically different product attribute; they simply decide a point of difference that allows their brand to develop a recognized and ownable competence over time. In other words, they transform a claim for differentiation into the focal point of their innovation activities.

Take the example of the car industry. All car manufactures own the necessary hardware skills to claim a safe driving experience for their customers. Also, almost all of them offer the same or similar product attributes like ABS breaking systems, front and lateral airbags, car stability systems (EPS), and so on. At a given level of their brand messaging, they all claim safety as a benefit. The difference is that none of them, except Volvo, has made safety central to its brand positioning. As perceived by consumers, it is Volvo who owns *safety* as a brand and who has the highest legitimacy to claim safety as its core competence. Volvo consistently developed its *safety* positioning platform as its main point of differentiation over the years. The same holds true for BMW, which owns *driving pleasure*—a set of features and a benefit that most cars may claim legitimately on their own. Or Mercedes, which differentiates its brand on *engineering excellence*, a claim for high quality finishings that most luxury car brand successfully deliver on, too. For each of these brands, the difference lies in the fact that their respective claims have been made brand-centric, allowing these brands to truly own them and therefore define what each of them stands for.

Together, the above examples demonstrate that differentiation can be achieved via almost any intrinsic or extrinsic product attribute that translates into a relevant benefit for the target audience, if it is not already owned by a competitive brand in the market you operate or plan to operate in the future. You might come across certain brands from different industry sectors that may claim the same identical word for their own differentiation. As long as these brands do not compete in the same market segment and for the same consumer, there is nothing wrong with it. Coca Cola has finally settled to stand for *happiness*. That is also the differentiated brand proposition for Hamlet, a cigar brand, while Cadbury chocolate differentiates on *joy*, which is very closely related to *happiness*, too. Or Oreo cookies and Trader Joe's retail chain, both of which share *playfulness* as a brand positioning platform. Neither one competes directly with the other.

## Brand Relevance and Brand Salience

Successfully differentiating a brand on a tangible or intangible product or service attribute will not do the job. The brand positioning must also be perceived to have relevance with its designated target audience. Relevance refers to the extent to which a certain brand is perceived as addressing a given consumer need. These needs may be physical or cognitive. In an abstract way, one can imagine needs and brands like *problems and solutions*. When a need arises, a consumer will seek to satisfy the need in the most convenient, accessible, and qualitative way. The role of a brand is to simplify the selection process, allowing consumers to identify and decide on the *solution*. Throughout this subjective process, brands play an important role as shortcuts to tangible product or service *solutions*, while brand image dimensions simultaneously contribute to increasing the value perception of these solutions.

Obviously, this is not as simple and mono-dimensional as it sounds and the brand's perceived capacity to address a given need is just one element within the purchase decision-making process. Other criteria, such as previous brand experiences, the perception of the brand's price value perception, its equity and brand statue, its accessibility, and so on, also play a role. Needs may be conscious like craving a refreshment or a sweet treat or more subliminal and unconscious like the need for social recognition or belonging. However, unsatisfied needs over time will lead to a certain sense of urgency that motivates consumers to act.

Relevance has several dimensions within the branding context. For a brand to be seen as relevant by a consumer, it must first claim a benefit for which a consumer has a basic need. In other words, if you do not own a dog, you most likely will not develop a need for dogfood.

The next level of relevance concerns the actual product category in which a brand competes. Here, consumers have already preselected respective brands for their relevant set, meaning that a given brand under consideration will be compared against alternative, competitive brand choices. This is where brand relevance plays a key role. The question here is no longer whether a brand caters to a relevant need, but the extent to which it is seen as doing so. Often a brand's relevance is reduced to its price-value perception. In other words, the equation between a perceived value of a brand for the consumer and its actual cost. While price has never been as important in consumers' decision-making processes as it is today, the price level also has never been more relative than at any given time. If the value perception of a brand is capable to project high enough, it might enable to successfully compete against a competitive brand even if this one offers a significantly lower price.

However, even in a context where brands have an intrinsic relevance within their specific market segment and with their designated target audiences, the level of relevance they can count on may vary over time, often in relation to changing lifestyle needs. Take a couple who is about to found a family. The relevance of their actual brand choices will certainly evolve as they move into parenthood with all it entails, from food and transportation choices to preferences for leisure activities, travel destinations, even furniture and home choices.

Another factor that might impact relevance is the risk perception consumers associate with a given product or service selection and purchase. The risk perception may be monetary or image-related, such as the purchase of a high-ticket item or simply the acquisition of a product or service, which is felt to make an important image statement about yourself. In both cases, consumers will get deeper involved in the brand selection and purchase decision-making process. A consumer's perception of relevance is strongly influenced by these high- and low-involvement processes or high- and low-risk assessments. As a brand owner, it will be important to address these in the decision-making process models that consumer-centric brands develop with the intention of producing a smooth and rewarding purchase experience (see Chap. 4).

Contrary to relevance, saliency refers to a brand's presence and strength within the decision-making process. Salience is a marketing term that essentially combines relevance and other brand-related factors such as brand awareness, brand image, and possibly past brand experiences as a total measurement consumers use during their purchase decision-making. Salience relates to the positive information a brand has left in a consumer's mind that is spontaneously available. It differs from brand equity, which is usually broader and comprises all the information a consumer holds about a given brand, may it be spontaneously available or simply remembered when triggered by an external stimulus. Some exceptional brands have even succeeded to establish their brand name as a descriptor of certain consumer activities. Many of us refer to internet searches as to *google for information*, while Kleenex or the German Tempo brand have become synonymous for paper handkerchiefs. Usually, brands with strong top-of-mind awareness ratings also have high salience, such as Coca Cola in soft drinks or FEDEX in delivery services, at least as far as the US market is concerned.

Saliency may have a big impact on a brand's value perception and, consequently, its pricing strategy. Take the example of the German Volkswagen Group. Volkswagen owns numerous car and truck brands in Europe. To demonstrate the effect of brand saliency, let us look at Skoda, VW, and Audi. To maximize its conception and production efficiencies, VW uses the same engineering platform for three distinct cars in its branded offer: the Skoda Octavia, the VW Passat, and the Audi A4. While there are certainly some differences in the engine design, the materials used for the interior, and the car design itself, the fully loaded versions of these three models all offer very similar levels of engineering quality, finishing, and comfort. The price positioning, however, tells a different story. At the time of this comparison and according to the Argus 2021 data in France, a Skoda Octavia retailed at 43,260 €, the VW Passat at 54,000 €, and the Audi A4 at 63,015 €: a price difference of roughly 83% between the Skoda and the Audi models. Clearly, not all of this price gap can be explained according to the saliency factor, but a large portion can. The salience aspect is also demonstrated by the price comparison for regular take-out coffee versus the same coffee from Starbuck's as shown in Fig. 2.7.

A few years ago, an analysis by Millward Brown, a global research firm, revealed that among the S&P 500 companies, an average 30% of their market valuation was represented merely by the brand. All of these are examples of how saliency is the ultimate marketing measure that drives the brand value perception and will transform relevance into consumer desire to purchase a brand.

As laid out above, the definition of the brand positioning is a crucial exercise, indispensable to define what a brand stands for and how it will differentiate with high relevance from its competition. It must be anchored in the product reality, while simultaneously taking into account the brand's history (product and communication) and relevant target data, with a specific focus on consumer insights. For maximum impact and efficiency, the brand positioning must be defined by a single word or angle of attack. We will discuss at a later stage how to define a one-word positioning, using powerful and proven tools of the branding industry. As the brand positioning will seal the brand's performance for years to come, it should be given all the available resources within an organization.

**Fig. 2.7** Price comparison regular take-out coffee versus Starbuck's. Author's own image

## The Brand Positioning Within the Branding Exercise

To leverage its full potential within the marketing and sales process, the brand positioning assumes the role of a prism through which all brand, marketing, and sales activities are seen. The brand positioning is strategic and will form the groundwork for all brand development steps to follow. This implies that from now on, every little detail of the brand universe must be imagined and decided in tune with the brand positioning platform. As a first step, this will usually concern the development or renewal of the brand identity. Here, the best way to start is by defining the brand's values and in a second step the brand personality. Both definitions are subjective and will allow you to translate the brand positioning into first actionable steps that will provide the direction and guidance for the development of the *graphic* brand identity.

Values define what a brand believes in and what it will live up to, in all its activities. This means that once you have defined your brand's values, you and your brand must walk the talk. A good way to decide on the brand values is to first define the vision and mission statement of your brand. Take Nike as an example. Since its creation by Phil Knight and Bill Bowermann in 1972, Nike believed that *anyone with a body is an athlete.* This brand vision is still alive and enacted everyday by the Nike brand and its employees. It was and still is the starting point for Nike's brand mission, which it defines as *bringing inspiration and innovation to every athlete in the world* (again an athlete being defined as any person with a body). Nike has defined a strong and ambitious vision for its brand and, in particular, the vision and mission statements somewhat prescribe the values Nike will live by: diversity, inclusiveness, encouragement, and positive change. (Nike does not communicate its brand values directly, the selection represents what the author believes Nike's values to be.) Brand values are an important element of the brand positioning, and they are a crucial part of what your brand will be seen to stand for by its target audiences. Chosen carefully, each brand value must be easily translatable into action and lived day-by-day, actively providing tangible proof that your brand not only says what it does but also does what it says.

Following the definition of the brand values, you can decide your brand's personality. While this exercise is subjective, the definition of the brand personality should correlate and correspond to the values that you have just defined. Like with humans, brands can be given distinctive personalities. The brand personality sort of humanizes a brand and sets the tone and manner by which consumers will relate or identify with it. Also, consumers might simply feel more drawn toward a brand when the brand personality corresponds to a scheme that allows them to relate to it on an emotional, somewhat humanized level. This form of identification may occur at two different levels: in relation to a consumer's *real* (actual) self-perception or in a more aspirational form, referring to a consumer's *ideal* self-perception. The principles of *real* or *ideal* self-perception will be discussed further on and in the context of self-expressive values of brand personality (see Chap. 6). However, in both cases, it is the brand's personality traits that facilitate consumer identification and bonding with the brand.

To illustrate this, let us have a look at the work of Jennifer L. Aaker, Assistant Professor at the Anderson School of Management, University of California, who researched the topic of brand personality in 1997.[2] In her publication, she identifies the following five dominant dimensions of brand personality:

1. **Sincerity** with subdimensions of "down-to-earth, honest, wholesome, cheerful," a personality that might fit the Warby Parker or Toms brands
2. **Excitement** with subdimensions of "daring, spirited, imaginative, up-to-date," a personality that might fit the Tesla brand in its early days
3. **Competence** with subdimensions of "reliable, intelligent, successful," a personality that might fit the Volkswagen car brand
4. **Sophistication** with subdimensions of "upper class, charming," a personality that might fit many of today's luxury fashion brands such as Yves Saint Laurent, Dior, or Nespresso
5. **Ruggedness** with subdimensions of "outdoorsy and rough," a personality that might fit The North Face but also the Harley Davidson brand

Nevertheless, these are just a few examples that help to illustrate the concept of brand personality. They are not meant to be comprehensive and by the end of the day, it is you who will have to decide on the brand personality that you want to assign to your brand. However, while this definition remains subjective, the brand personality must be closely related to your brand values and should allow your target audience to easily project itself and identify with your brand.

Once brand values and brand personality have been decided, you may now also define the *brand identity* (ID). Again, this should be done in coherence with the brand positioning and in line with the values and the brand personality. Both of them will set the tone and manner that will guide your ID choices: primary and secondary color codes and fonts, iconography and other illustrative elements, logo and brand block, brand signature, and so on. The brand ID represents a direct and tangible expression of what your brand stands for.

---

[2] "Big Five"—Journal of Marketing Research, Vol. 34, No. 3 (Aug., 1997), pp. 347–356

It translates brand values and brand personality into relatable image clues, allowing your target consumer to form concrete image dimensions for your brand. Brand ID also enables brand recall and brand recognition, as for instance during a purchase decision-making process.

In this context, the role of the brand signature or brand slogan is to translate your brand positioning into a punchy and meaningful phrase. If done right, it will stay with your brand for years to come, thus favoring a better assimilation of your brand signature by your target audience. Only very few brand slogans will ultimately be recalled and remembered by consumers and if you try the exercise yourself, you will quicky see that your personal recollection will probably not exceed ten slogans at best. This does not at all diminish the importance of the brand signature. Its core role is to become the spring board for your brand story, allowing you to develop your brand narrative and storytelling further down the line. In that sense, the brand signature may be used not only in marketing communications but all the way through a consumer's purchase experience, including the sales pitch. Nike's *Just Do It* perfectly sums up the brand's positioning as a visionary brand that believes in *everyone having a body to be an athlete*. At the same time, Nike instrumentalized its slogan right from the start as a call to action in the brand's sales pitch all the way down to consumers shopping in a retail environment. As of today, Nike sales staff still employs the Nike slogan to close a deal with a shopper hesitating between two models of running shoes ... *just do it*!

Once the principal components of the brand identity have been decided and finalized, you will need to decide how to use them. In organizations with multiple brand stakeholders, such as independent local marketing, promotion, or sales teams, the establishment of a certain set of rules on how to use the key elements of the brand identity will ensure that the brand will present itself in the same coherent and consistent manner everywhere it is introduced. This is usually done through the development of a brand book. The brand book essentially defines all the elements that are designated to define the brand. It provides guidance and rules for how to use these brand signals in the context of any given marketing, promotion, or sales activity. The brand book provides detailed directions for the brand logo, shape, and color, as well as how to use them. The required white space that must be observed around it to improve logo visibility, suggestions for print layouts or video formats, or the design and ergonomics of local brand websites, to quote just a few. There are numerous examples of brand books that may be found on the internet.

The brand book defines all visual brand ID elements, and it summarizes core brand messages that are all directly derived from the brand positioning. The brand book is the strategic guideline that must be observed by everybody who manages and impacts branded activities. It assures the proper translation of the brand positioning into executional elements of the brand identity and their respective communication formats. Its role is to provide maximum visual and message consistency across all brand activities and geographies.

Brands that observe a strict consistency in their identity codes and messaging build salience in the short-term and brand equity in the mid- to long-term more efficiently. Both identity codes and messaging must be derived from the brand essence as the single central brand message. All other brand messages will be organized and hierarchized in relation to the brand essence and as part of the brand message mix (see Chap. 16). This implies that the brand is thought of in terms of the brand essence itself. The moment the brand essence is turned into the roadmap for all brand-related decision-making processes, starting with the selection of values, the brand personality, identity codes, advertising and promotion messages, the sales pitch, and even the innovation process, your brand will strive through total message consistency at all consumer touch points. This principle works best by developing one-word brand positioning platforms, which, as we will see, have the capacity to unite entire teams providing focus and mobilizing their respective energy and creativity to push the brand in one single-minded direction, as defined by the brand essence.

# 3

# How Do Brands Interact with Consumers and How Do Consumers Interact with Brands?

Consumers may form lasting relationships with brands. These relationships are primarily driven by emotions. I have come to believe that brands that are able to establish an emotional relationship with its target audiences will be able to bond more persistently with consumers, developing lasting relations of personal engagement. This holds true, in particular, for B2C brands (business-to-consumer), but as we will see it also applies to a certain degree to B2B (business-to-business) and corporate brands. At the same time, this does not mean that *emotional* brands will operate solely on an emotional level. To succeed, any brand will need both a functional and an emotional benefit, which relate to each other in total coherence and consistency.

Functional benefits define what a brand will do for us as consumers. Emotional benefits define how a given brand will make us feel. This basic difference already highlights the potential of emotional branding, seeing as most of what we do is strongly influenced by a fundamental human desire or need to feel good. The principle applies to all types of brands, no matter whether they concern products, services, destinations, a political party, or even a person.

Comparing brands on a functional level may quickly turn out to be a difficult and tedious exercise for consumers (less though in B2B where professionals generally process the technical qualification as well as the respective performance indicators to compare competitive brand offers on factual grounds). Consumers often simply lack the knowledge to compare brands on their functional dimensions. Take the example of shower gels sold in different formats, with different ingredients and at significantly different price levels. Even if some of us take the time to read the label, without a solid knowledge in chemistry or willingness to research individual ingredients online, it will be quite hard to identify the differences between the individual brand offers on the shelf in front of us. You do not see many shoppers either using their smartphone to calculate the price advantage of one brand versus another based on the respective product volume format. Most of the time, consumers will simply resort to the lowest price. In a shopping environment, shoppers quickly get overwhelmed with choices that are cognitively complex and revert to emotional decision-making. Here, the brand plays a preponderant role.

This principle applies even more to high-risk or high-involvement purchase situations. The more functional aspects there are to consider, the more likely the average consumer will feel overwhelmed, eventually resorting to an emotionally driven decision-making process. In this context, rational or functional brand information is used to rationally reason the emotional decision-making. The decision to choose a given brand or not might involve consumers' own convictions and feelings but also those of others. Brand reviews or simply word-of-mouth recommendations may play a decisive role in the decision-making process. Like for the consumer decision-making, most of these external factors are emotionally motivated, through that person's own brand experience or hear-say. *Social shopping*, for instance, provides vivid testimony to this behavioral pattern, allowing consumers to reach out for peer approval prior to making a purchase decision.

Nevertheless, functional brand claims are still important. Their role is to provide important reassurance that helps to justify an otherwise emotionally motivated purchase decision. Functional benefits provide *rational underpinning* especially in purchase situations with high perceived risks, where consumers need to rationally justify their emotional decision-making through functional criteria or attributes. This helps to introduce some objectivity into the process, thus reenforcing confidence. Even in the simple selection process of a shower gel and without a deeper understanding of chemistry, some functional criteria might still play a role for most of us, such as the presence of a fairly well-known active ingredient (such as argan oil or aloe vera extracts) or simply the absence of others such as parabens or other preservatives.

In the perpetual repetition of purchase decision-making processes, each shopping experience contributes to building the expertise consumers gain as shoppers. The more consumers shop in life, the more past shopping experiences feed into the way we make brand and product choices. No matter whether we shop at a grocery retailer or in a high-end boutique. Over time, they all contribute to establish a set of individual skills by which a consumer searches for information, selects, and purchases a given brand. The concept of shopper marketing, which researches how consumers behave as shoppers, has provided valuable insights to this effect that may be translated into effective marketing and promotion techniques.

Functional benefits also play an important role in another shopping-related context referred to as *post-purchase dissonance (PPD)*. Post-purchase dissonance describes a form of post-purchase evaluation by consumers that relates to the pros and cons of their purchase act. PPD generally sets in after a purchase decision has been reached and acted upon. At one point or another, we have all experienced the feeling of doubt or regret after having fallen for a certain product or brand. *Post-purchase dissonance* most often occurs in buying situations that are associated with a higher perceived risk or a higher involvement. This psychological phenomenon has been vastly researched and is understood to increase in frequency and intensity in relation to a consumer's level of self-confidence, while the level of discretionary income may also influence PPD. As it happens, low self-confidence and/or lower income levels are likely to increase the propensity and frequency of *post-purchase dissonance*, while more affluent consumers or those with a more affirmative self-perception seem less concerned by this state of mind. However, this is not a black-and-white scenario, and consumers experience *post-purchase dissonance* on different occasions and levels of intensity. *Post-purchase dissonance* can also occur for other reasons, such as identifying a seemingly more attractive brand offer after purchase, experiencing a negative side-aspect, simply by reading about a negative evaluation of the product or service or an unmatched expectation triggered by the product usage itself.

*Post-purchase dissonance* has been found to be closely related to impulse buying—purchase decisions that are chiefly motivated by spontaneous emotional behavior. Referred to as "wardrobe rage," fashion purchases for example are frequently less reflected and planned. A recent UK study found that roughly half of fashion shoppers claim to experience some kind of *wardrobe rage*, with the average participant owning 57 unworn items. However, there are other more serious side-effects as well. On average, e-commerce brands must deal with an up to 30% return rate on consumers' online purchases, especially in textiles.

Needless to say, *post-purchase dissonance* that generally produces a feeling of doubt or even regret may also negatively impact brand loyalty and ultimately your business results. As brands constantly lose loyal customers due to competitive offers or brand usage experiences, the recruitment of new customers becomes a perpetual *must do* exercise. This is costly and it will, in one way or another, always affect the bottom line. Joey Coleman,[1] author of the book

---

[1] Joey Coleman, *Never Lose a Customer Again*, Portfolio, April 2018.

*Never Lose a Customer Again*, comes to the conclusion that in many industries, a 5% improvement in customer retention rates will yield a 25–100% increase in profits, depending on the product categories. Especially in purchase decisions that involve a high level of consumer involvement, a recent purchase (even researched) does not necessarily stop consumers from seeking alternative brand or product choices in regard to the one they just made. Engaging in window shopping activities, for example, after an important purchase is one way how *post-purchase dissonance* manifests itself in consumer behavior. Also, the intensity of *post-purchase dissonance* may increase with the number of alternative choices available in any given market environment. As a result, brand owners are advised to develop designated programs targeted to reduce *post-purchase dissonance*. Doing so persistently will significantly improve customer retention.

In fact, many brands are still predominantly built on functional benefits, in particular in those market segments where performance matters. Personal hygiene brands like Dove have been pushing functional benefits since its launch in 1957. *Cream while you wash* is a 2-in-1 product formula that allows the brand to successfully claim a functional performance as its core element of differentiation. Or the Mars, Inc. brand M&M's introduced itself with the functional benefit of *the chocolate that melts in your mouth and not in your hand*. Today M&M has strongly emotionalized its brand with the introduction of the M&M characters. First developed in the mid-1950s, these *candy personalities* were created by the graphic artist Will Vinton. Relying on the vibrant M&M colors, he imagined the unique brand characters, each with a distinct personality.

Strategically, this allowed the brand to create and leverage a multitude of differentiated brand ambassadors to promote its brand and product range on an emotional level. Each character represents a different product formula and has its own distinctive personality somewhat inspired by a stereotyped human counterpart. The yellow character (peanut) is kind and endearing, however, a bit naïve and not the sharpest pencil in the box. Blue M&M's (almond) comes across as cool and laidback, while the red clan member (milk chocolate) behaves like the classic alpha male. The diversity of theses personalities is well chosen and gives the brand the means to connect with consumers on different emotional levels and according to personal preferences. While M&M's still *melt in your mouth, not your hand*, the brand has taken a big leap toward connecting emotionally with its target audiences.

Emotional benefits come in different formats. They allow brands to interact and engage with consumers on multiple levels and different dimensions. These dimensions include brand values, brand vision and beliefs, or brand personalities, just to name a few. Although brands are not literally perceived as people, their messaging and behavior may resemble the fundamental traits, also found in interhuman relationships. Brands often function like role models for their target audiences and as such can provide direction, reference points, and orientation to consumers, just like humans do. In this sense, consumers' worshipping of brands may have some limits. Take the example of Nike. The Nike brand positions itself somewhat as a coach that helps you find your *own personal greatness*. In this role—almost anthropomorphically—Nike inspires people to gain self-confidence through achievement in sports. Achievement equals a form of success and the confidence to succeed in sports easily relates to succeeding in life. This concept of success was widely popular in the *power-focused* 1980s and 1990s, represented not only by Nike but also other brands like Tag Heuer or Rolex. This is the period when consumers started wearing clothes with oversized brand labels (referred to at the time as *label on the outside*), something that is still in fashion to this day.

One way Nike's emotional strength becomes visible is the ostentatious way its brand followers are ready to make a statement by the size or the prominence of the Nike logo featured on their apparel or the number of people who proudly carry a Nike swoosh tattoo. There are fewer and fewer limits when it comes to customer engagement with and commitment to brands. I once briefly met a young woman at a gas station in northern Namibia during a self-drive safari road trip. Namibia has two million inhabitants living on a territory one and a half times the size of France. You can easily drive 200 miles without finding any significant settlement and even further before you locate a gas station. Therefore, you do not think twice before pulling over when you see one to fill up your tank. Her name was Berta and she worked as an attendant at the local gas station in a town called Kamanjab. About 10,000 people live in this community, making it a sizeable hub for the distribution of groceries, building materials, and, of course, gasoline. Now, you might ask yourself, what does this have to do with branding? Well, for Berta, Nike was the brand of all brands. So much so, that she wore with natural pride the Nike swoosh as a gold inlay in one of her front teeth. Each time she smiled at a customer, it shined like a flashlight from her bright white teeth. When I asked her why she would risk destroying a tooth with an inlay of a brand logo, she responded joyfully: *I love this brand so much and want everyone to see that I do*. Without question, Nike had achieved a very solid level of consumer engagement with this young Namibian woman, despite being far from concept stores and shopping malls.

This little anecdote is an example for the grip brands may have on its customers, if they provide the tangible meaning for emotional connections. Of course, not every brand will achieve the same level of influence as Nike, not least because consumers can only focus on a limited number of brands to engage with on such a deep level. Nevertheless, there still is ample potential to build a brand on emotional rather than functional dimensions. Emotionalizing brands requires focusing on their values, beliefs, and defining a clear understanding for what they stand for.

Brands that decide to engage with consumers on an emotional level have various approaches for doing so. The process for building brand engagement starts with the target audience a given brand aims to address. The target definition is important from a sociodemographic perspective; however, even more so from a generational and psychographic perspective. Generational targeting looks at consumers from a sociological point of view. We all grow up in different worlds, not only geographically but also historically. Technological advances, political and economic conditions, cultural trends in music, movies, or art all have a formative effect on how we evolve as people.

The context we grow up in has a significant impact on how we see the world, what we believe in, and also how be behave as consumers. Millennials and Gen Z, for example, are the first generations to have no recollection of a world without internet and for most of them, without social media, too. While these are of course simple media and communication channels like the traditional offline channels through which brands still heavily communicate, they have had a significant impact on how these generations interact, see the world, or what they aspire to and what drives and motivates them as citizens and consumers.

Consequently, the attractiveness of what a given brand stands for is not necessarily defined by the same parameters for Baby Boomers as for Millennials. Since the late twentieth century, emotional brands have evolved first from a proposition built on statutory elements to the use of values and finally the elaboration of a brand vision. Twenty-first-century brands are increasingly defined by *brand purpose*. The reason for this is that Millennials and Gen Z are more driven by a search for "*meaning*." The most obvious indication for this is visible in the area of employer brands where *meaning* has gained at least as much importance as *money*, if not more. However, both visionary and purpose brands will not be effective unless they produce tangible evidence and proof that the talk is also walked.

Other game-changers are the worldwide democratization of the internet and social media networks that have increased the reach and scope of *multiple stakeholder communities*. Since consumers have evolved from the passive receivers of branded messages to now actively engaging with brands through various touchpoints, still through word-of-mouth, however, via a much larger scope and with significant more reach through social media channels and rating platforms like online shops or Trustpilot, Glassdoor, Yelp, or Trip Advisor for example. That being so, consumers' personal opinions have become a decisive vector in how the brand image is being shaped. Brands today must include their target communities, addressing not only their needs but also catering to their beliefs. Branding has evolved and is no longer just about what you want your brand to stand for, but increasingly also about what consumers say about it.

The discrepancy is obvious. While in the past brand owners controlled their brand positioning almost entirely, they now must reckon with the target audience as the ultimate judge on whether a brand is perceived as sincere about what it claims or not. *Truth* has become a new, important currency in branding. Admittedly, it has always been, but mostly limited to the physical brand performance. Today the concept of *trust* has evolved. According to a 2019 study conducted by the global branding agency Edelmann, roughly two-thirds of consumers are *belief-driven buyers* who connect with brands on emotional values while functional benefits have become reduced to the simple *price of entry* in many product categories. The study also demonstrates that a brand's ethical behavior now ranks almost as high as the actual user experience (82% versus 87%, respectively) in consumers' decision-making processes.

However, the Edelmann study also points to another insight. Branding is in the process of moving from a *human*-centered approach to a *humanity*-centered approach. Or as Tim O'Reilly,[2] author of *What's the Future and Why it is up to us?*, points out, successful brands now must evolve *making better things to making things better*. In summary, the humanity-centered brand approach refers to using brand competence to deliver not just products and services but also positive societal impact.

O'Reilly's philosophical approach is already evidenced by an increasing number of brands that claim a *purpose* to define what they stand for. Purpose branding can be considered the next generation of *emotional* branding.

Multinational corporations have been among the first to adopt the concept of *purpose branding*, claiming various benefits their activities will produce in the larger context of society. However, purpose branding does not only apply to corporate brands that have been dealing with multiple stakeholder communities for a long time and that generally work with elaborate CSR policies. Most companies have increasingly started to realize the impact of their activities and actions beyond just financial returns. Environmental impact, diversity, societal integration of operations, and staff have all added further

---

[2] Tim O'Reilly, *What's the Future and Why is it up to us?*, Harper Business, October 2017.

dimensions to the corporate branding concept. All of the above also apply to FMCG (fast moving consumer goods) brands, with the only difference being the type of stakeholders, their needs, beliefs, and motivations.

While some of the purpose brand initiatives may be considered serious and impactful (Unilever—*making sustainable living commonplace*), others raise questions about their true motivation (Nestlé—*unlock the power of food to enhance quality of life for everyone*). I do not want to elaborate further on the differences between these two *purpose-driven* package good giants, but you might want to take a closer look and judge for yourself.

The most striking example of positive change, however, is *Patagonia*. Longtime committed to protecting resources and the environment, *Patagonia* has a long history of a sustainable approach within the (extremely polluting) textile industry. Founded in 1973 by Yvon Chouinard as a company initially specializing in mountain gear (the original products were hand-forged steel pitons), the company then evolved to produce and sell an extended range of mountain gear until introducing its first textile line (rugby shirts imported from Scotland, which were made from sturdy fabric, with a protective collar, preventing the hardware slings from cutting into the neck). As a company, Patagonia had an extraordinary environmental consciousness right from the start and throughout its developmental years. And as a brand, Patagonia developed a vision for functional excellence and for protecting resources and the environment, using recycled polyester fiber from plastic bottles and recycled paper for brand communication material as far back as 1980. Despite being a *for-profit organization* at the time, Patagonia increasingly focused on the impact its business model would have on resources and the environment. The brand started to communicate not only about what it did well, but also shared publicly what it did not do well. Transparency, unlike many other brands, has always been and still is part of Patagonia's DNA. Today, most brands claim some sort of environmental and societal responsibility; however, Patagonia was already doing so way before most businesses around the world had even heard about the larger concept of sustainability.

As of 1986, Patagonia decided to donate 10% of its profits to environmental protection initiatives (1% of its sales as of 2002). It became a B-company in 2012. In 2018, Yvon Chouinard redefined the purpose statement of the Patagonia brand: *we're in business to save our home planet.* And Patagonia lived up to it and walked the talk! In 2022, Yvon Chouinard transformed Patagonia, worth roughly $3 billion into a charity and a nonprofit organization, with only one single shareholder: the plant. Today, any profit that is not reinvested into the Patagonia business goes to the charity that exclusively supports environmental projects around the world with roughly $100 million every year, in line with the overall business results, of cause. As a matter of fact, Patagonia is not alone, and many successful entrepreneurs have turned to charity formats to claim that their brands help *to make things better*: the Bill & Melinda Gates Foundation, the Musk Foundation, to cite just a few of them. However, several media investigations shed doubt on the true motivations behind the real objectives of these "purpose-driven" branding initiatives. As we have seen before, "trust" is increasingly important, and I am personally convinced that the only way to build trust for tomorrow's brands will be through "transparency"—a concept that Patagonia, unlike others, has fully embraced.

However, as a purpose-driven brand Patagonia is about much more than high-performance products and the protection of the environment. It is also a clever way to emotionally engage with its core target audiences by protecting and restoring natural reserves, which at a given time attract loyal brand consumers in Patagonia wear. With its current format, Patagonia has also demonstrated that there is scope for an alternative way to marry business success and sustainability, potentially leading the way toward a next-generation business model that creates value that is truly mutually shared in a sustainable way. This might also prove effective in reducing the potential for personal greed, so emblematic in our hyper-globalized world run by the principles of neoliberal capitalism. After all, and with a view on younger consumer generations, doing good might indeed become the best way to grow. In conclusion, emotional branding has many different forms, formats, and nuances and the right approach to take will depend on the *product or service* reality of your brand.

So far, we have discussed how brands can engage with consumers. Let us now change the perspective and look at how consumers engage with brands. On a first-degree level, consumers relate to brands through trust. Trust in consistent quality and in the overall user experience of a given brand. Trust in brands is also delivered through consistency and from a consumer's point of view. Consistency may be evaluated by various subjective parameters, such as the actual brand performance that is constantly matched with consumers' expectations. The established packaging design identity as well as formats and functions such as the shape, size, and ergonomics of a given product format provide consistency and strengthen consumer reassurance as a side effect. Here, down-sized formats (unfortunately increasingly practiced these days via *shrinkflation* techniques), packaging changes that might affect the product handling, or a disruptively new design identity, all carry the risk of negatively impacting the perception of consistency. Most frequently, a too radical change in the packaging design may severely disrupt the perception of consistency and consumers frequently assume that the product itself has also changed. When we introduced a brand-new packaging for one of our FMCG clients in

Germany a few years ago, consumer quality complaints jumped to all time heights despite the fact that the actual product formulation and hence the product performance had remained unchanged. The best way to avoid these forms of disruptions is to properly communicate and explain the change to consumers, using the packaging itself as a primary media channel for the brand.

Jean-Noël Kapferer—a professor at the renowned HEC school near Paris—defined the function of brands as *simplifying consumer choices*, while simple products (commodities) make these more complex. Consumers indeed also relate to brands, because they allow them to reduce the cognitive stress involved in shopping. Brands function as shortcuts between consumer needs and expected experiences. Consumers engage with brands out of trust and the expectation of a consistent brand experience is a desired fundamental outcome of the consumer decision-making process. Performed convincingly, it may even help to get your target audience to accept a higher price point.

Beyond *trust*, brands may leverage a more psychological approach to create potential for consumer buy-in. This is based on the theory of *real* versus *ideal self-perceptions* all consumers develop to some degree throughout their lives. Fundamentally, this concept is about perceptions versus aspirations. The *real self* refers to perceptions consumers have about themselves such as traits or characteristics that are subjectively perceived as strengths or weaknesses. On a first level, brands with a deep understanding of their consumers' *real self-*perceptions may succeed in building longer and more authentic connections. Here, again trust is the main driver, and consumers may engage with brands on this level as they see their own identity addressed in a more genuine and authentic way.

However, the theory also suggests that consumer decision-making is also guided by their aspirations in life, or in other words, by their quest for their *ideal self-perception*. This second and superior level of how consumers engage with brands offers great potential for bonding and active engagement as it allows brands to tap into consumer aspirations, hence catering toward the *ideal self*. Self-expressive human values allow your brand to align with the aspirations consumers set for themselves. One way to leverage this approach is by defining a *self-expressive human value of brand personality* for your brand. This refers to the one self-expressive value your brand will stand for and act upon. Here, the self-expressive human value takes the place of the *brand essence*. It is the brand essence translated into a value. This value, expressed in just *one word* or single-minded angle will point toward a consumer's aspirational journey from the *real self* to the *ideal self*. Under the condition that your brand's self-expressive human value is universally recognized and shared by a given target audience, it has the capacity to provide multiple functions in the context of consumers' search for their *real self-identity*.

Nike embodies this theory in its branding approach. The self-expressive human value that Nike claims is *empowerment*. *Empowered* is Nike's brand essence, expressed in form of a value. The value makes Nike's brand essence more relatable for consumers and prescribes tangible brand actions (walk the talk). Addressing its target's ideal self-perception, the Nike brand provides meaning and aspirational value well beyond the simple product performance. Berta from the Kamanjab gas station in Namibia being living proof of it. Understanding how consumers engage with brands allows you to define a brand positioning that not only differentiates your brand from competition. It also makes your brand more engaging. The whole delivered in just *one word*. The full potential of self-expressive human values and the methodology to define them will be discussed in Chap. 6.

Yet another way consumers can engage with brands is through their *legacy* or *nostalgia*. This has always been the case as consumers are usually introduced to certain brands indirectly and during their infancy simply by the fact that their parents bought and used certain brands at home. Also hearsay or the fact that certain brands have a long history and a wide user base gives them status, which may translate into legacy and nostalgia. Nostalgia and legacy both imply a sensation of trust, and trust is what drives consumer motivations and purchase decision-making processes.

However, you may ask yourself why legacy and nostalgia are still relevant in a world driven by technological innovation and its inherent acceleration? One could argue that both these dimensions are simply opposing the notion of progress and the overwhelming speed of change that come with it. First, the arrival of the worldwide net, then connectivity, and now artificial intelligence offer consumers of all ages less and less tangible reference points to hold onto in their daily lives. Rarely has the world on our doorstep been so amorphous. In a world where everything is constantly on the move, brands are inspiring a certain sense of consistency, providing trusted reference points and a sense for orientation. In this context, brands function somewhat like a cognitive antidote, taking away some of the pressure of the continuous, accelerated change. Is it a coincidence that vinyl records outsold CDs in 2021, that fashion, retro-design in furniture and household appliances, and music from the 1960s to the 1980s are so popular? Or are these design references so desirable because they provide cognitive comfort in those places where we all retreat from the complex outside world. This is only hypothetical but underlying motivational patterns might well be that *legacy* and *nostalgia* from a time when the world was still easy to understand and where life appeared to be somewhat under our personal control, which help to ground us before having to surf the next wave. Brands through their legacy and the nostalgia that they trigger provide meaning in times where meaning has become a scarce currency.

# 4

# The Essentials of Power Brands: Why Competence, Differentiation, and Relevance Are the Key Dimensions to Focus on?

## Perception Versus Reality: The Two Sides of the Brand Evaluation Process

Why do some brands succeed, when others fail? Why do certain brands grow faster than others? Why can certain brands claim a premium, when others must fight in the price war trenches? Why do certain brands become global brands, while others remain local niche players? The reason clearly is not that the few who succeed are the lucky ones hitting the jack pot while the others are less fortunate.

Brands become power brands because their DNA was carefully designed for it. Either right from the start or following a thorough repositioning process. There clearly is no secret to successful branding, but rather a process of discipline and rigor that culminates in defining what a brand stands for in just *one word* or one narrow angle of attack. The definition of what a brand stands for in just *one word* ensures absolute focus not only in managing the brand but also in terms of maximizing its market potential.

Successful brands are founded on three main and equally important pillars: competence, differentiation, and relevance. These pillars are interconnected and codependent. As a group, they are indispensable and neither one can fully define the brand on its own. Competence, differentiation, and relevance all have a defining and a prescriptive function. They provide the input for what your brand will eventually stand for and guide your brand over time in its quest for innovation and change. Essentially, brands live in a paradox: they must simultaneously provide continuity and change. Well-defined brands provide that bespoken continuity when markets and its products are busy navigating through an environment of perpetual change. Change affects consumers' needs and brands must demonstrate great sensitivity and agility to recognize and address these evolving needs.

In branding, competence refers to a brand's unique expertise: the one thing a brand is best at. Milka's competence is to produce the most *tender chocolate taste*. BMW claims to master *driving pleasure* better than its immediate competitors. Disney is the king of *magic*. Competence defines a brand's unique know-how and expertise and supports its differentiation at the same time. Differentiation is always derived directly from a brand's core competence. One does not work without the other and defining a brand's competence based on an exclusive attribute, feature, or process will directly impact its differentiating proposition. It is the brand competence that provides the input on which the differentiation will be established. The initial and raw concept of a brand's differentiation is then distilled in a single word or specific angle, which successful brands leverage to define themselves.

However, being competent and owning differentiation does not quite do the trick. Brands must also offer a benefit that is relevant to its target audiences. The stronger this relevance is felt by a target consumer, the higher the likelihood for a brand purchase. *Driving pleasure* is no doubt a strong relevance motivator in the car industry and *magic* has a similar attractive quality in the field of entertainment. Of course, in both the car and the entertainment industry, *driving pleasure* and *magic* are not the only drivers and BMW and Disney are not the only brands to claim these highly relevant benefits. However, they are the ones that have insisted on these *differentiation drivers* over time and with more consistency to fully own them. Both have also used their differentiation to develop products that deliver these respective experiences in a more tangible way, whether objectively or only perceived does not really matter. Disney has its own signature style of producing magic not only in cartoon productions but also in feature films. And experiencing driving pleasure in a BMW for many consumers will feel very different from a driving experience in a Mercedes. Most likely, any little detail in a BMW has been imagined enhancing the perception of driving pleasure: the engine sound, the sound of the closing doors, the resistance of the steering wheel, or the pushback of the gas pedal, for example. Every single one of these details feeds into and magnifies the perception of driving pleasure.

Mercedes Benz, on the other hand, stands for engineering excellence. Consequently, both brands are known for a distinctive competence that allows them to differentiate while proposing strong relevance to their target customers. At the same time, you rarely see a loyal Mercedes owner switch to buy a BMW and vice versa. This reveals yet another aspect. Through their competence definition and differentiation platforms, both brands also gain distinctive image dimensions. While both are somewhat associated with success in life, each has its own interpretation of *success* that simultaneously offers distinct types of relevance. Conceptually, Mercedes defines success as the ability to master the rules, while BMW defines success as an attitude that challenges them. The Mercedes brand behaves like a clever conformist, the BMW brand like a rebel who questions society's conventions. This might seem like a small detail; however, in consumers' perceptions these nuances make a decisive difference. It is these nuances that ultimately drive brand and product preferences over time developing brand loyalty.

Let us take a closer look at each of the three success pillars. The first place to look for your brand's competence is in its *root strength*. As the term suggests, the root strength—part of the *brand key* model that will be discussed in Chap. 8—refers to the original attribute or concept idea that your brand will leverages as a competence, allowing it to claim a unique product or service offer at the time of its launch. Nestlé, the world's largest food company, who owns and manages hundreds of brands around the world, started out in 1866 with the idea from a German pharmacist, who had formulated a new and better formula for powdered baby milk. Heinrich Nestle and his wife had immigrated to Switzerland a few years earlier and to better blend into the French-speaking culture in the western parts of Switzerland, he slightly changed his name to Henri Nestlé, hence the Nestlé brand name. The formula combined milk, grain, and sugar and was presented as a powder. Infant mortality was high in those days and next to hygiene issues, malnutrition was a major cause. Fresh milk was often difficult to come by in urban locations and breastfeeding had somewhat fallen out of favor with Swiss middle- and upper-class women. Nestlé baby milk, initially marketed as Nestlé Milk Flour, is still a core product in the company's brand portfolio. Powdered baby milk provided the original Nestlé core competence as a food brand. This core competence in processed milk allowed it to enter the chocolate market later on, using its know-how and competence to produce superior product quality also in chocolate.

In both product categories, Nestlé's know-how in milk processing allowed the brand to develop a unique product offer, while providing the brand competence to differentiate and to grow the business (organically in its core markets and over time through a brand stretching strategy). All this happened in a competitive context where other brands had launched similar offers onto the market, such as Liebig condensed milk in the United Staes. However, Nestlé's formula made it easier and more convenient to use and women quickly adopted Nestlé's Milk Flour, first in Europe and soon after in the United States.

Today, Oreo is recognized as the authentic American cream sandwich cookie. Launched in 1912 by the Nabisco company, the brand had sold over 500 billion cookies on the eve of its 100th birthday. Yet, another brand called Hydro Cookie had launched a very similar cookie 4 years earlier than Nabisco, in 1908. This proves that the ingenuity of an idea is not the only factor that assures success. To own a competence, it is not enough to develop it, but to claim and defend it in the market for years to come.

This is particularly relevant for start-up companies. Over the years I have seen many of them come and go and only a handful turn into the unicorn that investors and venture capital firms long for. Obviously, there never is only one factor at play, but from those that I saw go, finance and branding were generally their weak spots. Textbook marketing certainly is a good starting point, but from there to a well-defined, differentiated, and relevant brand value proposition is a long way to go. It is not just the root idea that provides the ground for brand differentiation but the angle you give it, making it truly ownable for your brand and irresistibly relevant for your target audiences. As we will see later, there are many facets of the brand positioning that may play a role but there will be only one for which your brand will eventually become known.

Identifying an explorable competence is not always the most obvious thing. Sometimes you have to look really hard, be persistent, and dive deep into a product or brand to identify a competence that is unique enough to be leveraged in the differentiation process.

This phase of the branding project very much resembles journalistic investigation. It implies looking beyond the obvious, scrutinizing and evaluating all the components, no matter how tiny they are. Instead of analyzing the details of a formula or recipe by yourself, have the technical people from R&D explain it to you in all details. Try to fully understand the role each ingredient plays in the product, where and how it is sourced, how it works in combination with all the others, why it is there, and what results it produces in the final product formulation.

Often R&D and marketing do not speak the same language and as a branding expert you may have to translate what one or the other says to offer a mutually understandable meaning. Way back when I worked on the repositioning of Danone's Actimel brand, marketing had a hard time understanding the beneficial effects of Actimel's unique yogurt cultures on the human gut and the role it plays in boosting natural immunity. They simply looked at the obvious and did not make the effort to probe and truly understand. Approximately 70% of our immune system is located in our intestine. Here billions of live bacteria settle and grow on the gastrointestinal wall. As long as the good bacteria prevail, the system is in a positive state of balance, thus constituting a dominant asset for our body's primary immune defenses.

Certain live yogurt cultures have the capacity to pass through the natural acidity barrier in the stomach to reach the gut, where they settle and reproduce. There is no place to settle, no reproduction. Bad bacteria simply cannot survive and are transited out. By providing millions of *good* bacteria in every single Actimel bottle, this little drink contributed to maintaining a positive intestinal balance. Admittedly, it is a bit more complex than that but essentially this is what it comes down to. Understanding these principles took quite some persistence in probing the R&D director at the time. But once the principle of the hypothesis behind the unique activity or the Actimel yogurt culture became visible, it instantaneously defined the brand's core competence, later translating into a highly differentiating positioning as one of the first functional food brands. Strengthening natural defenses became Actimel's single-minded angle of attack. Defining this tangible and relevant competence of the Actimel brand immediately provided a unidirectional sense and direction for the entire marketing and sales team, who quickly picked up the ball and played it across several scientific studies, which ultimately allowed the establishment of a scientific monograph to sustain Actimel's claims within the reglementary context. All this work subsequently provided the input to formulate Actimel's brand claim. The brand quickly became known for strengthening the body's natural defenses: a tightly defined, single-minded brand positioning and fully operational.

This single-minded angle clearly answered a universal consumer need (*protection*), allowing Actimel to swiftly expand into additional markets. Today, this global mega-brand is selling 2.5 billion Actimel bottles every year. Actimel's single-minded positioning angle also provided clear and tangible direction for its global and local marketing teams. The brand's marketing and sales efforts became harmonized in one general advertising and promotion concept, which was easy to adapt locally and provided consistency while remaining open to plenty of guided inspiration for fresh ideas. Here, Danone's "*glocal*" approach to business also helped, defining global brand strategies while providing the freedom for creative adaptations locally. This allowed local markets to address a different cultural context with subtle nuances.

A few years later we worked on a German processed cheese brand that had the ambition to expand internationally (I briefly discussed this brand already in Chap. 2). The particularity here was that this brand had many direct competitors as brands and private label versions and what was worse, no real differentiation in its product formula. Like its competitors, Milkana also ambitioned to differentiate on the protected and picturesque region where the milk to make its cheese was sourced. Although competitors claimed different regions for sourcing their milk, the stereotypical ads all pretty much looked alike. In their own and certainly ownable way, each of these regional references relied on positive cliché images consumers hold of them. This produced an illusion of differentiation while the brands were not really differentiated.

As it happens, the basic recipe for this spreadable cream cheese was developed back in 1911 by a Swiss-American cheese manufacturer named Walter Gerber, who patented his method of processing this particular cheese. Although there is no tangible evidence, the original recipe probably served as an inspiration for the brands who developed their own recipe later on. The production method typically involved heating cheese produced traditionally, in this case cheddar, with an emulsifying agent such as sodium citrate, turning it into a smooth and spreadable product formula, producing a cheese that was tasty, easy to spread, and rather affordable. In Germany, Milkana turned somewhat into an iconic brand after the war, becoming a symbol for the new abundance of food after years of rationing.

Here, again the starting point in the repositioning of the Milkana brand became the search for its core competence: something which no other brand could claim. However, our search did not find anything exploitable in the recipe. The *regional claim* was already somewhat banalized. The packaging format and the product variants offered no potential for differentiation either. We turned everything upside down. We talked to all the people involved in the making of Milkana, especially those with the longest memory in the company. Unfortunately, these staff members are sometimes sidelined and undervalued in corporate company structures. However, they are the ones with the longest memory, and they have the highest potential to turn up the invaluable detail you might be looking for. Finally, 1 day, when all options were pretty much depleted, we talked to one of the Milkana food engineers again. This time, the questions we asked were more detailed and more persisting than the first time around. We went over every little detail of the recipe, the production process, and almost accidentally a small difference in Milkana's cheese-making competence surfaced.

There finally was a difference in the temperature applied at this very moment of the process. Not in absolute terms—the process first described and patented by Louis Pasteur in 1865, which uses temperatures of around 85 °C to stop milk from fermenting—but the actual path to reach that temperature. This path was different from competition and allowed us to claim a superior quality, texture, and taste. It was this little detail, for many in the company without any significance, which allowed us to find a fresh angle on which to reposition the brand: a manufacturing process designed to preserve the natural goodness of the milk that went into making the cheese, allowing the brand to claim the differentiating and relevant benefit of a *simple, wholesome pleasure*. We had found what we were looking for and this small and seemingly irrelevant detail allowed us to claim the larger concept of *authenticity*.

The concept of *simple, wholesome pleasure* offered several dimensions and among them we identified one that had the potential to differentiate the brand claiming that the simple things in life are often the source of the biggest pleasure (see Fig. 4.1). This gave the brand a universally attractive benefit to serve its international ambitions. It also offered the brand a differentiated value proposition against its main global competitor, the French *Laughing Cow* brand from the Bel company. Campbell's Soup recently rediscovered this same positioning angle for its *real food that matters for life's moments* campaign in the United States. Yet another example of the intrinsic power of branding concepts that leverage the notions of nostalgia and legacy as an antidote to the accelerating change and complexity of our times.

Let us now take a closer look at the dimension of brand *differentiation*. Over time, established brands may lose sight of their root strength altogether, getting overwhelmed by the complexity of their own brand messaging,

**Fig. 4.1** Illustration of Milkana's *simple, wholesome pleasure*. Author's own image

accumulated over the years without real prioritization. Having lost focus, these brands inevitably start to decline. This is the moment to seriously consider a brand repositioning project, returning to the brand's root strength, which initially provided the fuel for its successful launch and development. When you do so, you will see there are many things to consider. First, potential product attributes must be identified and weighed against each other. Not in limbo, but within the context of the competitive set and always in connection with consumer needs. This is a complex task, and many potential claims will not make it to the finish line. Ultimately, only one will serve as the base for your brand's differentiation. However, not a single brand message will be lost. Brand positioning or repositioning work is all about establishing message hierarchies and claim prioritization by defining any message's ideal position in the overall message mix.

Then potential claims based on the chosen attribute must be formulated and matched against identified consumer insights and needs. Chapters 9 and 10 will explore this concept and others involved in the branding or rebranding process in more detail.

Brand differentiation may play multiple roles in the brand positioning exercise. It may be achieved via functional drivers such as quality, price, an attribute, a process, recipe, or a service. It may also be defined by emotional levers such as values, attitudes, or brand vision. To be effective and ownable over time, your brand differentiation must always be anchored in the product or service reality; something tangible that may be leveraged as evidence for your differentiation claim. No brand differentiation can be achieved without this tangible substance, as absence of substance almost certainly leads to consumer deception in a real-life usage situation.

Also, at first, differentiation is defined conceptually. The content counts more than the format. This ensures that your differentiation has substance and that you gain absolute clarity about what your brand shall stand for. The temptation may be strong to define your brand via a catchy slogan or communication claim, but this always bears the risk of falling in love with a phrase while missing the true point of your brand's differentiation.

Brand differentiation drives brand relevance. It allows the brand to make a substantiated claim that consumers are sensitive and responsive to. This will also help with memorization of your brand, generate interest over time, and may ultimately lead to a purchase decision. In the same way that *competence* and *differentiation* are inseparable, it is evident that differentiation and relevance are, too. All three must work in unison in order to influence consumer behavior in the direction of your objectives.

Defining a hard-hitting, differentiated brand positioning platform requires an intimate understanding or your target consumer's needs. The better and deeper you understand those needs or *consumer insights*, the more striking your brand differentiation will be. Simultaneously, this intimate understanding of your target's needs will guide your brand in its effort to produce higher relevance. Generally, consumers may have more than one need related to a given product or service category. The understanding and ponderation of the needs or *insights* will become very instrumental in the analytical process and during the evaluation of your product or service reality (see Chaps. 7 and 8). All features and attributes that do not correspond to an identified consumer need will be temporarily eliminated at this stage as they are not suited for your brand's differentiating positioning.

There are several generic forms of consumer needs that many brands often lean toward define their differentiation. The most common one is price. Consumers look for price value equations before making a purchase decision insofar as price corresponds to a consumer need. Since the 2010s and the fallout from the subprime crisis, price has become even more important in purchase decision-making processes. At the same time, price has never been more relative, meaning that the absolute price a consumer is ready to pay for a certain brand is less defined by his or her budget and more by the perceived value of the brand in question. Take the example of Apple's iPhone 15. According to Investipedia owned by the US-based Dotdash Meredith publisher, the entry level version of this phone is sold at $999. To manufacture, it costs Apple $599. This gives the brand a profit margin of roughly 66%, close to twice the standard margin of the electronic industry. The numbers are even more impressive for the high-end version of the iPhone 15. Here, the value perceptions of the Apple or iPhone brand clearly demonstrate how relative price has become. The brand value perception may simply discourage consumers from looking for the cheapest price. Apple products are sold worldwide at the same exact price, a level of pricing control that most brands struggle to achieve. Differentiation always commands price.

Nevertheless, pricing is a tricky field to tread when it comes to brand differentiation. Most importantly, a differentiation via price is often short-lived and any competitor may undercut your price advantage, unless your brand and your entire organization have been strategically conceived to become a *leader in price*. This requires the entire organization and its product offer to be designed to that effect. Differentiation on price might be difficult to sustain over time as low price almost always rimes with low margins and at the end of the day, you will lack the funds to properly support and build your brand.

Building brand differentiation on quality is a better option. Quality offers a higher degree of protection from competitive attack. This is particularly true for markets with high industrial barriers. Nespresso provides testimony to this. At first a market failure, the Nespresso system had unsuccessfully targeted the B2B office sector. Then in 1986, Nestlé relaunched the brand with a new B2C positioning, targeting consumers. Nestlé had acquired the technology from the Battelle Institute in Geneva in 1974: a closed-circuit system where coffee capsules and machines were mutually exclusive. The Nespresso system produced single dose expresso coffee in an electronic three-stage process: pre-wetting, aeration, and extraction all controlled by an incorporated chip technology, which gave Nestlé a 25-year patented protection. The differentiation Nespresso claimed and proved was in the quality of the expresso produced at the push of the button. Conveniently, it offered an ever-increasing variety and, as a side benefit to consumers, the feeling of cultivation and sophistication. The different capsule colors corresponding to the Nespresso coffee varieties and the constant "bistro-like" coffee texture and taste quality enabled consumer to feel like "baristas" with a unique skill to recreate different tastes of expresso coffee at home. However, the final brand differentiation came from the high taste experience produced by the coffee capsules, which was truly comparable with the quality offered by professional bistro venues. With the concept of *quality*, the brand had identified a unique product attribute to differentiate on. Nespresso's brand claim "What else?" clearly illustrated this. The taste superiority of the Nespresso brand offer was never matched until the day the patent protection ran out in 2017.

However, this remarkable success story also hints at the vulnerability of a brand differentiation platform established on a technology or the concept of quality. Even Nespresso's protected and high entry-barrier technology did not protect it indefinitely. Today the brand is under attack from multiple sides and from brands that often differentiate on price while reproducing (at least in consumers' perception) Nespresso's legendary coffee quality. While *price* feels quite real to consumers, *quality* is much more subjective. Generally, most consumers cannot really tell the difference, and few will go all the way to perform a side-by-side quality (taste) test, which is never free from subjectivity either. This is true not only for food brands but also for technical brands of all kinds. Here, consumers often lack the expertise and qualification to truly compare the effects of product or service features that makes them revert to emotional decision-making.

Using a product or service feature is yet another way to differentiate on a functional dimension. For this to produce tangible results, the selected feature must lend itself to formulating a unique brand claim. This refers to brand competence, which was discussed earlier.

You may identify either a feature or attribute that gives your brand a single-minded uniqueness, such as the Alpine milk used to make Milka chocolate or the ¼ or moisturizing cream that discriminates the Dove beauty bar (launched in the United States in 1957) and has by now become the differentiating attribute of Dove's entire product range. M&M's also owned a differentiating attribute in its sugar coating that allowed it to claim: *the chocolate that melts in your mouth and not in your hand.*

Unfortunately, few FMCG brands are lucky enough to have a unique and ownable attribute to differentiate on. In this case, you will have to work with what you have. This does not necessarily suggest a major problem for the brand positioning process. As always, any challenge also bears an opportunity, and you just need to be more creative to define your brand differentiation using a feature that might not be exclusive to your product formula or service offer. The point is that brand differentiation must produce relevance for your target audience and cleverly designed consumer research may help you see available attributes in a different light. Consumer insights provide a deep look at consumer needs and motivational patterns responsible for brand preferences. If you can manage to unlock these consumer insights, the evaluation of your product features might take a surprisingly fresh turn. You are likely to see a previously rejected attribute from a totally new angle that might reveal an unseen potential for your brand differentiation.

Take the example of the ONGO family-owned office furniture brand in Germany. ONGO had forged its differentiation and reputation in the German office furniture market through a unique stool concept. The stool had a slightly curved bottom that made it move in circular swings when you sat and worked on it. This was deliberate and the stool was designed to counter backpain inevitably produced by sitting endless hours in traditional office chairs, all ergonomically designed to provide ultimate comfort. Worldwide, backpain is the number one health issue for office workers who spend 8 hours per day or more without working their back muscles. The ONGO stool was designed to do just that. A person sitting and working on the stool would never reach a stable seated position. In a working position, people were forced to constantly counterbalance. As a result, the stool naturally solicitated people's back muscles, rebuilding them slowly and effortlessly: a concept that had given the ONGO brand true differentiation in the market based on a simple but clever product attribute—the curved stool bottom. However, soon competition caught up with them. Much larger furniture manufacturer quickly introduced their own versions of the moving stool. Owning decisively stronger brand equities, these brands successively pushed the ONGO brand aside. Built on just a simple product feature, ONGO had lost its differentiation in the German office furniture market. The brand urgently needed a repositioning to give it fresh, relevant, and ownable brand differentiation.

However, the curved bottom was not the only product attribute of the ONGO stool. Its base could be extended to provide seating support for a stand-up working position, at a height-adjustable desk for example. But competition quickly introduced this feature in their own models as well. Finally, it was the unsuspected and banalized product attribute that became the new target for differentiating the ONGO brand. The stool was light and therefore easy to carry to a different desk, a meeting room or simply a more inspiring location to work from. In an office world where open spaces are quickly evolving toward more nomadic working environments, ONGO recognized the opportunity and jumped on a trend, way ahead of anybody else. In fact, shared desks, flexible workstations, and environments had reached the office market way before the Covid pandemic made working from home a permanent option in today's offices.

So far so good, but how does this provide brand differentiation? We leveraged a dual insight from consumers (office workers) and customers (companies that manage office spaces). The lightness and ergonomic ease with which people could simply move the ONGO stool responded to a new emerging need in the office market: the need for *agility*. The ONGO differentiation started out with a simple aspect and built it into a vision for a new office world. The brand's differentiation simply shifted from *movement* to *agility*. To illustrate this shift, the actual brand claim of *keep moving* became *agility at work*, with agility having a physical, mental, and cognitive dimension, all highly relevant to the office work environment. This new brand positioning provided relevant differentiation for the ONGO brand and provided a perfect platform for a new and unique brand narrative.

However, there was a downside to this new positioning. The stool alone did not make the brand's differentiation big and powerful. The actual product range at the time was too small and largely dominated by the stool concept. There was no alternative it had to evolve, providing more substance to the new claim by proposing a full range of *agile* furniture. Here, ONGO proved agility on its own and developed a new range of office furniture, including desks, boards, and walls (see Fig. 4.2). All on wheels, easy to pull to any office location, allowing users to instantly build a meeting room or workplace in a bright spot where inspiration would flow more freely.

Not the feature itself, but the concept built around it and from it became ONGO's new powerful angle of differentiation. A differentiation that went

**Fig. 4.2** ONGO Spark and ONGO Free in an open space office location. Permission Köhl GmbH, Germany

far beyond a simple product range and was turned into a true brand vision that generated strong news value in the market and put ONGO back on the shopping list. However, this illustration also proves that small brands may have big ideas and that funding is not always the name of the game. If you cannot outspend your competition, you may outsmart it. The point here is that if you do so, make sure to quickly occupy your new positioning in all communication channels you access and use. Even faster than a product feature, a positioning, too, may be copied or taken away by the competition, which happened later in the ONGO case.

Now that we have covered competence and differentiation, let us take a look at *relevance* and its role in the branding process. Relevance is probably the most central and decisive element in a brand's path to success. For any brand to produce relevance within its defined consumer target, it must be perceived as answering a specific consumer need. These needs may be defined by preferences, beliefs, and even aspirations. Relevance is not exclusively limited to physical but also to emotional needs and habits that consumers may have established over time. Brand relevance assigns pertinence to a given brand in the purchase decision-making process. As we will see in Chap. 6, this process may be partly driven by perceptions rather than concrete functional realities. Combined needs, preferences, and aspirations produce feelings and attitudes that motivate consumer behavior toward a given brand.

One way to think about relevance is to use research in defining a formal consumer journey map for your brand. Journey maps differ by product category and market segments. However, they all follow the same basic principles that are then divided into phases. It all starts with the awareness of a need followed by the awareness of brands that are seen credible as providing answers to these needs. Consumers and customers alike establish relevant sets, a sort of short list of considered brands. This phase is followed by an evaluation phase, where features and benefits are compared and scrutinized until a purchase decision is being reached. Product or service usage follows, then leading to yet another evaluation phase entitled enjoyment. If this is conclusive, consumers will start to develop initial forms of loyalty that might evolve to a state of advocacy where brand users actively recommend the brand to others. Brand loyal consumers have a high tendency to buy the brand again, without going through the individual steps of the journey.

A phenomenon described by McKinsey's model of the *loyalty loop*[1] that applies to all industries and market segments (see Fig. 4.3).

The model is based on research conducted on almost 20,000 people and their purchase decision-making behavior, providing evidence that shows that the actual decision-making process resembles a loop instead of the traditional *funnel*. The *funnel* model assumed that consumers would start with a broad set of potential brand candidates that would be eliminated one by one in a linear manner until the last brand remaining is purchased. The model further assumed that all steps including brand awareness, consideration, evaluation, and purchase were equally relevant. However, evidence from McKinsey's research suggests otherwise. Given the large numbers of brand choices in many industries, consumers resort to a short list of brands they may ultimately consider and evaluate. Here, brand awareness remains important as it is a precondition for projecting brands into the relevant set of those that are actively considered and then evaluated during the prepurchase phase. Research reveals that brands that make it into the initial consideration set are three times more likely to be purchased. While consumers consider alternative brand choices, those not preselected might still make it onto the shortlist, while others already listed may drop out in the evaluation process. This is where relevance plays a decisive role keeping your brand in the loop and defending it as the best choice until the purchase decision has been reached.

---

[1] McKinsey Quarterly, June 2009.

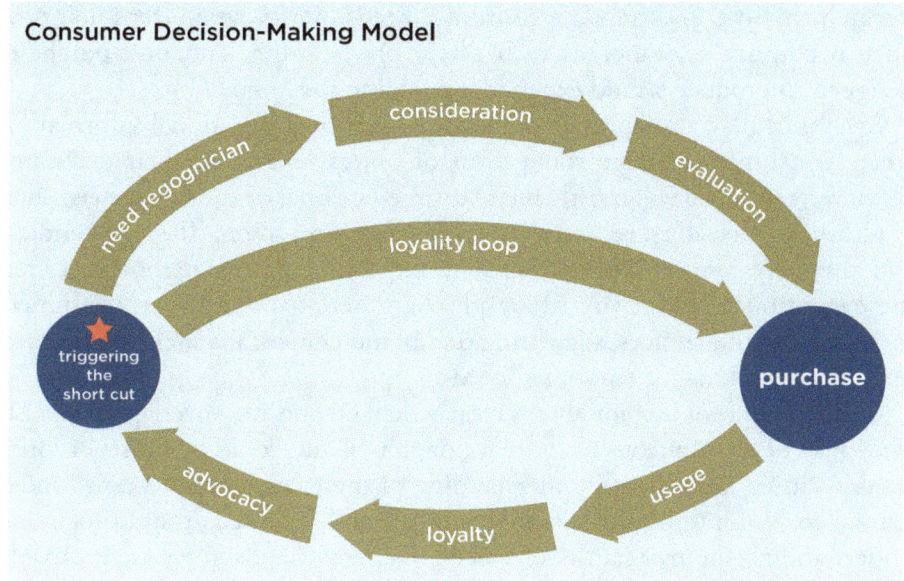

**Fig. 4.3** The consumer decision-making loop, McKinsey Quarterly, June 2009. Author's own image

This suggests that the traditional *push* marketing strategies used over the past 60 years might have lost some of their effectiveness. The McKinsey study demonstrates that consumer behavior has evolved and instead of simply absorbing brand messages, consumers increasingly resort to actively searching for brand-related information online in various media or simply among their peers. Brand websites, performance reviews, buyer evaluations, as well as past experiences with a brand now equal the importance of branded information during the purchase decision-making process.

Finally, the *loyalty loop* model also stresses the importance of the post-purchase period that many brands do not pay enough attention to. Contrary to common belief, the post-purchase experience is not only exclusively defined by product consumption or usage alone, but also through extrinsic perception triggers such as strategic post-purchase brand communication programs. To reduce the impact of post-purchase dissonance, these programs are designed to comfort consumers and customers with communication content that provides reassurance on the purchased product or service and offers easy access to after sales service platforms and dialogue. Apple has developed its customer journey into a swift, continuous process where nothing is left to chance and every little detail has been studied and designed to contribute to a positive and memorable consumer journey experience. Great efforts have been made to research, analyze, and translate consumer needs into program steps that produce maximum relevance at each phase pre-, during, and post-purchase, designed to produce a fluid experience enabling the *loyalty loop*.

Relevance may also apply to a need for functional or rational information where consumers leverage some form of objective data in their decisions. However, relevance will mostly relate to an emotional or subjective need such as pleasure, fun, safety, recognition, confidence, and so on. The list is endless and this why researching your specific target's needs is paramount. Often these emotional needs swing alongside the functional ones when consumers make their brand choices, suggesting that brand choices are rarely made based on either functional or emotional needs.

Consumer needs are not always clearly defined and may overlap or coexist. They may be spontaneous or more fundamental and could be short- or long-lived. Gaining an in-depth understanding of these consumer needs is fundamental to building brand relevance and researching needs should focus on understanding the *true* nature of a need. Generally, consumers are incapable of expressing their needs in traditional research settings. They simply do not really understand them or have difficulties describing them in a meaningful way. Similar to usages patterns and attitudes, consumers are mostly unaware of what they actually do and why they do it. They simply form opinions about their usage procedures and their attitudes toward certain product categories or brands. The problem is that these *opinions* are not neutral and usually also integrate societal standards, cliches, and beliefs. In a similar fashion, this also applies to needs.

When you research the underlying needs that relate to antibacterial household or personal hygiene products, consumers usually claim that they need to get rid of bacteria. On the surface this makes sense, and the entire category leverages this insight to position their respective brands. However, in morphological, psychoanalytical research (see Chap. 7), you will see that what really matters goes well beyond the elimination of bacteria. Here, too, consumers first express the same *hygiene* need. However, reaching into the unconscious reveals that the real motivation is directed toward eliminating what is *foreign*. The concept of and the tolerance for *hygienic cleanliness* clearly evolves from the deeper understanding of how consumers define the risk of *contamination* when the source lies outside the boundaries of the tightly defined *family tribe*.

When defining and leveraging relevance in any product or service category in B2C and B2B alike, consumer and/or customer understanding is paramount. The more you research motivations, aspirations, and preferences, the deeper you will delve into your target's soul.

Findings from this research will provide the necessary understanding on what to look for in your product or service offer to best formulate a claim that develops strong relevance and provides brand differentiation and competence simultaneously—all derived from and cautioned by the same product attribute or feature.

There are many different research methods to gain understanding of consumer needs, helping you to define your brand relevance in a more pertinent manner. Although not all offer the same potential, a first step may be to simply observe a target consumer, such as Procter & Gamble does in their LiveLab research facility (see Chap. 7). Observations may also provide first clues on a much smaller scale. In a retail shopping environment, among friends and family at home, etc. This will not necessarily provide highly reliable insights, but it will certainly deliver first hints for what to look for when you dive deeper, using more sophisticated research models at a later stage.

Screening product category-related forums and social media sites might also allow you to spot insights into consumer needs. The same is true for certain trends that also may point toward needs and motivations that consumers share for a certain product or service category. All these observational tools are low budget in nature and help to gain an initial understanding of consumer needs, allowing your brand to define relevance.

On the next level, qualitative research using focus groups and/or individual interviews in studio settings, *personas* in home settings, or online sessions may all provide a deeper understanding of consumer needs and motivations related to the category of your product or service. Qualitative research methodologies are widely used around the globe and help to collect intelligence on target consumers. However, these insights are rarely exclusive, and your competitors may own them, too. Do not forget that in branding, what is often more important than *what* you find out is *how* you will use it to define the relevance of your brand. Branding is a creative business and the way you play your insight could make all the difference. Therefore, the performance of your brand's relevance will highly depend on the creativity you will apply to transform your findings into a stronger and more attractive approach to relevance than your competitors do.

Another common research model used to gain insights into consumer needs, motivations, and aspirations are usage and attitude studies—either qualitative or quantitative formats. If performed in traditional qualitative focus groups, these research formats and methodologies do not dive very deep and bear the risk of providing understanding that barely scratches the surface. The advantage of quantitative U&A studies lies in their scale; they are capable of validating initial findings in need and motivation research through their larger consumer base. This validation process is often part of the processes designed to manage brands in larger corporations.

Nevertheless, in my view, nothing equals the power of morphological behavior research when it comes to understanding consumers' needs with the objective of defining brand relevance. For insight and U&A research purposes alike. Like no other research methodology, morphology allows you to gain deep insights into consumer motivations, attitudes, and believes. Less widely known, morphological research uses the principles or Freudian psychoanalysis and the theory of "Gestalt" to unlock the unconscious dimensions in consumer motivations related to a given product or service category. This qualitative research tool provides depth into insights for consumer behavior, motivations, and aspirations most of the conventional research models simply cannot match. Indeed, this research tool provides a deep look into the consumers' soul (it will be discussed in detail in Chap. 7).

Like competence and differentiation, relevance, too, must be directly linked to a product or service reality. It must be a direct and perceivable outcome of an attribute or a feature from your product or service offer. Missing that link or overstretching your claim will cause your brand to fail and lead to customer deception. In this sense, relevance, competence, and differentiation all share the same identical origin.

There are also several more tactical formats to improve the relevance perception in the short run, such as promotion activities, packaging or design updates, or genuine innovation. News value almost always produces some lift in brand relevance; however, it might be short lived as competition generally catches up quickly.

Other brand dimensions may also help to boost the perception of relevance, such as a brand vision, brand values, or genuine authenticity in words and actions. A brand that is seen as being authentic may enhance the feelings of credibility and trust, establishing emotional connections that favor the perception of relevance. I am convinced that *authenticity*, in particular, will become a key brand intangible over time. Too many brands have pushed their communication efforts too far onto beaten paths of increasingly meaningless semantics, often paired with deceptive deeds. Tomorrow, more than ever, brands will be obliged to walk the talk.

Emotional branding is yet another means to increase the relevance dimension of any given brand. Emotional ties usually go well beyond functional features and benefits, which, as mentioned before, may simply overwhelm consumers and their competence to evaluate them. Emotional branding aims to provide a tangible platform for consumer identification with the brand. Through incarnation (a celebrity, for example) or leveraging a value that may be relate to the self-perception of a distinctive target audience. Self-expressive human values of brand personality are further discussed in detail in Chap. 6. Expressed on behalf of a brand, they help consumers to transition from their perceived *real self* to their desired *ideal self*. They hint at how as a consumer the brand will help to transform myself. Therefore, they may become a powerful ally in your effort to boost your brand's relevance.

Finally, cultural dimensions, which by themselves are multifaceted, may boost brand relevance. Brands that adapt to cultural particularities may simply be perceived as more relevant by local target audiences. Even so, brands may leverage their cultural background and roots to generate relevance in markets abroad, such as McDonald's did when it first entered European markets with its brand. It became the first restaurant to propose an accessible, stereotyped *American way of life*.

At the end of the day, you must take your pick and see what works best. Competence, differentiation, and relevance defined and performed with consistency are what will build strong brand equities, while helping to optimize the time and the resources that you need to do so.

# 5

# Perception Versus Reality: The Two Sides of the Brand Evaluation Process

Evidence suggests that 80% of the value consumers perceive in any given brand is generated through product or service quality perceptions.[1] There is little doubt that a significant part of these perceptions is generated by the effects of tangible or perceived product or service attributes or features that consumers experience during usage. Taste, texture, sound, look, smell, along with a solid performance that can be perceived or measured, form the basis for the quality perception we associate with certain products and services. But what about the brand itself? Do brands by themselves also play an active role in this formative perception and evaluation process? Are consumers' quality perceptions purely derived from the *subjective* or *objective* (somewhat measurable) brand performance features or does the brand and its associated imagery or equity also play an active role? And if yes, how and to what extent?

The evaluation of any given brand and its performance is rarely objective and perceptions people articulate or resent when consuming or using a brand may be formed and influenced not only by intrinsic brand factors such as product attributes or features but also by extrinsic ones such as color codes, images or symbols, and messaging. Consumers rarely possess enough knowledge or pertinent information to evaluate a product or service objectively. Also, objective product or service evaluations may require a significant cognitive effort. If this effort becomes too demanding, consumers revert to brand image recollections, which are more comfortable to use during the decision-making process. Through the image recollections, consumers associate with certain brands, facilitating and speeding up the decision-making process. For instance, in a typical grocery shopping situation where we must make many

---

[1] David Aaker, Building strong brands, Simon & Schuster, UK, 1996.

successive purchase decisions in a relative compressed timeframe, brand choices are mostly based on previously accumulated perceptions rather than the functional product or service reality. In these processes, objectivity is replaced by subjectivity and emotional decision-making prevails over the rational. However, in more complex product or service choices, emotional decision-making also clearly prevails. While rational or functional decision parameters remain important during purchase decision-making process, they mostly play a secondary role of reassurance, thus somewhat underpinning the primarily emotional decision-making pattern. The Nobel Prize winning psychologist Daniel Kahneman, known for his work on heuristics, suggested that even in financial decision-making, largely considered to be exclusively based on hard facts and figures, 90% is emotionally driven and only 10% accounts for rational logic.

Consumers transfer brand impressions accumulated over time into brand equity that refers to the holistic image perceptions consumers have about brands in their mind. These image perceptions not only generate brand preferences, but may, as numerous research projects suggest, also impact the functional product or service performance evaluation itself. Positively or negatively alike. Thus, quality perceptions may be higher for brands with stronger equity, even where the tangible product performance is measurably lower. On the other hand, weaker brands may also generate lower quality perceptions even when the objective product performance is higher. Obviously, this evaluation is not black and white and the extent to which product performance is evaluated by perceived or real factors also depends on the product category and the risk perceptions associated with a potential purchase. In that sense, decision-making in low-involvement or low-risk product categories differs from those in high-involvement and high-risk categories. Brand equity may play a larger role when deciding on a bag of potato chips, while functional comparisons based on the list of promoted product attributes will prevail during the process of buying a TV set.

Brand awareness, brand identity codes, brand messaging, consumer-generated brand communications such as provided via forums, social media channels, or word-of mouth, as well as price, all play a significant role in how a consumer evaluates the actual performance of a brand.

Numerous studies have demonstrated the effect of brand awareness on the subjective evaluation of the product performance. First consumers buy brands they know and are familiar with. They also use brands to reduce their perceived risk when purchasing products of all sorts. The more consumers are aware of a brand, the more the brand will provide caution for the quality of a given product or service. Multiple research studies suggest that strong brand awareness induces a higher level of trust, which then also translates into higher quality expectations. Subjectively, these higher expectations may then lead to a more favorable product performance evaluation or service. A lesser or unknown brand will be evaluated more critically by consumers that consequently may induce a more skeptical performance evaluation.

However, brand awareness also plays an important role in the establishment of brand salience. Brand salience refers to the degree to which a brand is present in consumers' minds during a brand evaluation or purchase situation. Salience reflects the ability to recognize a brand and to recall its image impressions, beliefs, and attitudes during the purchase decision-making process. Brands with high salience are often the ones that are top-of-mind, coming first on the cognitive list of competitive brand choices. Usually, brand awareness and brand salience go in pair with market share and a high share may by itself produce a favorable effect on consumers' brand quality evaluations. Obviously, consumers do not reason by market shares, but brands that own a high share generally have higher visibility in the market, translating into image clout. Brand awareness is a crucial factor in any branding process and developing, strengthening, or maintaining strong levels of brand awareness should be a core objective of any marketing strategy.

This is particularly true for private labels, retail, or store brands—which all refer to brands owned by distribution entities such as any retail or wholesale entities on- or offline. These brands have gained significant ground in retail settings in most of the developed economies as retailers have over the past years successively replaced weaker industry brands with their own brand portfolio. In those markets, the fastest selling industry brand references or SKUs (stock keeping unit) have now been matched by comparable product offers from the respective store brand. In many European markets, retail brands now often own a combined market share of 70% in any product category. Store brands exist in several formats: as category brands with a distinctive product offer such as a line of foods, cosmetics, or drinks (Carrefour—*Reflet de France* or Target's *Good & Gather* in the United States) or as transversal store brands that cover almost all FMCG product categories offered in a given grocery chain (DM—*Dein Bestes* in Germany or simply *Tesco* like the name of the retailor itself in the United Kingdom). Thy are sold at mostly a 30–40% discount compared with the industry brands. These brands mainly succeed on a price/value proposition. While retail brands might have awareness with consumers who shop regularly at these outlets, they have significant less awareness with those who do not. Here, too, awareness induces trust and trust impacts the evaluation of the perceived product quality. In times where discretionary income is dwindling, consumers revert increasingly to purchasing private label brands. However, a recent research study shows that those same consumers also regularly return to the category-leading industry brands to remind themselves of the branded quality experience. It seems that only when the *real* brand experience is lived from time to time, that a private label brand can be tolerated.

Also, brand identity codes may have a direct and measurable impact on the quality evaluations of certain products. Remember that these evaluation processes are primarily subjective and that the quality experienced only reflects what consumers perceive. Before we experience a certain product or service for the first time, we have already been exposed to numerous brand clues and messages from the respective brand. We might have seen or heard about the brand in various occasions, we might have read reviews or seen advertising or promotional offers. All this might happen before we personally experience the brand in question for the first time. Accumulated over time, these clues raise expectations, and that may influence for example the sensory perception of a given food product in both ways, by either boosting or diminishing the quality evaluation.

Beer is one of the most consumed beverages around the world and many research projects have been conducted to study the impact of brand image perceptions on the consumer quality evaluation of respective beer brands. Unanimously, and similar to studies conducted on cigarette brands, consumers are generally incapable of distinguishing their favorite beer brand in blind taste tests. In one study conducted by the Carling Brewing Company[2] in the United States, six leading national and local beer brands where first blind-tasted by 326 regular beer drinkers in a home-use setting. Each six-pack deposited at participant homes, included one bottle of the brand claimed to be consumed the most. All of the bottles were unlabeled. Ratings for taste, flavor, foam, texture, aftertaste, strength, and so on were levied via a designated rating scheme. Results from the blind taste test showed no significant differences among the ratings for any of the nine attributes and across all beer brands, confirming the hypothesis that beer drinkers cannot distinguish their favorite brand in blind taste tests. The results were significantly different in the second phase of the study, where the same participants were given the same beer brands not in nude bottles but properly labeled. Not only did ratings for all nine attributes improve significantly (on average 18%), but also the preferred beer brand usually performed best in comparison to the five others. The findings strongly suggest that the physical product characteristics

---

[2] Influence of beer brand identification on taste perception, Ralph I. Allisson and Kenneth P. Uhl, Journal of Marketing Research, August 1964.

such as taste, mouthfeel, texture, and bitterness not only had little impact on the subjective quality evaluation of these beer brands, but also that product preferences were rather influenced by brand cues than by the actual product attributes.

Another small study conducted in the United States analyzed taste preferences in wine. Participants—nonexpert random wine drinkers—were asked to taste two different red wines, one designated on the label as being from California and the other one from North Dakota. The Californian red won hands down, despite the fact that both bottles contained the exact same wine. Although this study only leveraged product origin as a differentiator, it clearly demonstrates how brand cues may directly impede on product performance evaluation.

A rather radical experiment to demonstrate how product expectations may impact product quality evaluation was proposed by John Wheatly[3] in 1973. Participants were invited into a specially lit room to consume a meal consisting of steak, peas, and French fries. Halfway through the eating experience, which was utterly enjoyed by everyone, the lighting changed revealing the true colors of the food being served: the steak was blue, the peas red, and the French fries green. The simple variable of the coloration turned the food evaluation upside down. Many participants associated these colors with spoiled food and refused to eat anymore, a few even felt sick. Everyone had formulated expectations for the food served, which were clearly matched from an organoleptic point of view in the beginning of the experiment. Brand cues and messaging, too, generate consumer expectations, which inject more subjectivity into the quality performance evaluation process—although admittedly, not as radically as in the above example.

As consumers have grown more health-conscious, alcohol-free beers have become more popular. However, consumers often associate 0%-beers with inferior flavor, taste, and mouthfeel. To counter these perceptions, extrinsic brand identity cues have proven effective in research to influence product quality expectations. Brand cues such as certain words, packaging, product color, and even brand names together with previous experiences from the consumption of a product may generate expectations, which in turn will influence not only how we evaluate the product but also how we experience its taste, mouthfeel, texture, or aftertaste. As a result, expectations have the potential to change the sensory perception consumers experience in a

---

[3] A taste of things to come: The effect of extrinsic and intrinsic cues on perceived properties of beer mediated by expectations, Helena Blackmore, Claire Hidrio, Martin R. Yeomans, School of Psychology, University of Sussex, Brighton BN1 9QH, United Kingdom. Published by Elsevier July, 2021.

consumption moment. A study conducted in Denmark confirmed these assumptions in a project for alcohol-free beer.[4] The study was divided into two distinct phases: a blind tasting session where the product color strongly associated with taste was obscured using a red light in the test cubicles designated for the experiment and a situational session under normal light conditions. Both sessions were conducted successively. Participants were then asked to note their likings for four beer quality parameters: refreshment, body, bitterness, and overall liking of each beer sample. Both the beer color and the label descriptor "bitterness" significantly altered the product evaluation for "refreshment" between the blind tasting and the normal consumption phase for the exact same beer variant. The evaluation of the beer "body" dimension for the darker color was perceived as significantly "fuller" compared with the same beer during the blind test. This research provides some evidence for the fact that consumers evaluation of sensorial brand or product cues can well start before the actual consumption, impacting the perceived consumption experience in one way or another.

Another study focused on the impact of semantics on product quality evaluations. It is generally accepted that consumers in low-involvement/low-risk product categories use extrinsic brand cues more than intrinsic ones to form opinions about the products they consume. For example, a "phantom ingredient" test method was applied to analyze the impact on taste perceptions of the presence of soy as a key ingredient and *health* as a key brand message. Like alcohol-free beer, soy is increasingly considered by consumers as a healthy source of protein. However, soy, as a food or food ingredient has not managed to gain mass appeal and is perceived by many consumers as organoleptically less appealing. In consumer research, soy is often described as less tasty, with a somewhat grainy texture and an unpleasant aftertaste.

The test involved a normal consumption taste test with 155 participants, clustered based on self-declared recruitment quotas for 50% taste-conscious consumers and 50% health-conscious consumers. Participants were then asked to taste and rate a branded nutrition bar that did not include any soy ingredient. This zero-measure was performed on the product without revealing any brand clues via the labeling. Participants were then asked to evaluate taste expectations based on the packaging and later in a separate step also from tastings of the four alternative bars with different labeling options including messages on "soy content (10 gr)" and *health–no health* claims. Health claims were generally well received and did not alter the product taste and mouthfeel evaluations in any significant way for either the health-conscious or the

---

[4] University of Illinois at Urbana-Champaign, Champaign, IL 61820, USA.

taste-conscious participants. However, the revelation of soy as an ingredient via pack messaging significantly altered the taste expectations and perceptions of the taste-conscious consumer group in the test cell.

This measure also had a negative impact on the expected purchase frequency.

Now, you might rightly ask whether these finding also apply to non-food product categories, to high-involvement product items, and to service offers. While there is little or no available research on these product segments, it can be assumed that the same principles apply. Conditioning consumers through brand messaging and providing relevant information that triggers consumer beliefs, attitudes, or needs will most likely alter the perceived performance of those products in non-food and high-involvement categories as well. The reason for this is, as stated earlier, that the vast majority of our decision-making as consumers is emotionally motivated. And this also applies to high-involvement product or service categories, even if intrinsic brand cues clearly play a much bigger role here.

Another variable proven to impact product or service quality evaluations is price. Price almost always raises quality expectations with consumers and as we have seen through the research projects discussed above, expectation affects quality perceptions. However, this is not as simple as it looks and just increasing the price of a product or service might not lead inevitably to an improved performance evaluation by your target consumer. The concept here is that a premium positioning of your brand, which can be experienced through intrinsic and extrinsic brand cues, may positively impact the evaluation of your brand's performance from a consumer point of view. A higher-than-average price might then further boost these performance perceptions under one crucial condition: your product or service must deliver on it and perceived performance must be at least equivalent to that of your competitors. The reason for this is that consumers automatically assume higher-priced products are of higher quality compared to the cheaper alternatives. If you buy a household appliance from a premium brand like a German made Miele dishwasher, you expect a higher quality compared to the same item from Whirlpool, which is sold at a significantly lower price, despite having similar functionalities and features.

In addition, the brand name by itself and the brand equity associated with it may influence the way consumers perceive the performance of certain products. When we refer to the brand name as a stimulating factor in the evaluation of the perceived product performance, we obviously refer to not only the name but also the image or brand equity that is associated with it. The image value of a brand does not necessarily require years of brand building measures. Sometimes, the brand name by itself carries enough value to evoke a certain imagery, which might play a role in the performance evaluation process. Take for example the UK smoothie brand *Innocent*, which today belongs to the Coca Cola Company. Launched in 1999, the founding partners of the *Innocent* brand, Richard Reed, Adam Balon, and Jon Wright, performed a clever viability test on their concept, which not only gave them feedback on their product but also carried substantial buzz value for its launch. Being in comfortable job positions at the time, the four partners used a festival event to sell *Innocent* for the first time and to ask people if they thought this product would be worthwhile developing, which would then lead them to quitting their jobs. The feedback was positive, and *Innocent* was launched first in the United Kingdom and quickly thereafter in Europe. *Innocent* is a brand where the name is its positioning. Easy to understand and to remember, even for non-Anglo-Saxon audiences, the name spelled out what differentiated *Innocent* from its competitors: 100% natural ingredients, combined with a strong commitment to ethical sourcing and sustainability. This is exactly what health- and planet-conscious Millennials were looking for. However, from a product formula perspective, *Innocent* is less extraordinary; according to the brand's label, its largest volume ingredient is apple juice. Innocent has a Nutri-Score[5] rating of "E," designating it as unhealthy according to the scale developed by the French National Health Service in 2017 and applied to all food labels since. Even so, consuming exclusively healthy products might get boring after a while.

The performance evaluation of a given product may also be influenced by extrinsic brand cues, such as the name itself, color codes, symbols, or other elements. This is particularly true for product categories with few intrinsic brand cues that can be leveraged in the subjective evaluation process.

In that sense, a study conducted in 2010 by the University of Valencia in Spain[6] analyzed the impact of brand names on perceived quality evaluations in three product categories: tortilla chips, crayons, and facial tissues. For each category, the leading brand, a secondary, and a private label retail brand were selected. The product categories were chosen to correspond to three of the five senses: taste, eyesight, and touch. For the actual performance evaluation phase, all products were presented in four different conditions: (1) in their original brand packaging (Tostitos, Crayola, and Kleenex), (2) in the packaging of the secondary brand competitor, (3) in the packaging of the private

---

[5] Nutri-Score is an official French food label including five levels in different colors, indicating the nutritional and health value of a product.
[6] Hilgenkamp, Heather; Shanteau, James, Functional Measurement Analysis of Brand Equity: Does Brand Name affect Perceptions of Quality? Psicológica, vol. 31, núm. 3, 2010, pp. 561–575, Universitat de València Valencia, España.

label competitor, and (4) in a bowl without label. The packaging of all products was also presented by itself. During the test round that included 45 test points evaluated on a Likert scale, participants were asked to try and spontaneously evaluate the products. The packaging was rated on the likelihood of purchase based on past knowledge of the brands.

Not surprisingly, in each of the tested product categories the highest performance evaluation scores were obtained for the products directly associated with the respective category-leader brand (Tostitos, Crayola and Kleenex), followed by the secondary category brand and the respective private label brand. Product evaluations of the product by itself without brand revelation was ranked slightly above the secondary brand. The results clearly suggest that the exact same product is given different ratings in relation to the brand with which it was associated during the test. This once more confirms that the brand name and its associated equity may have a significant impact on the subjective performance evaluations of the product itself.

# 6

# How Self-Expressive Human Values Boost Brand Appeal?

Consumers connect with brands primarily on an emotional level. While product attributes or service features are important to rationalize the purchase decision-making process, the process itself is mostly driven by emotional motivations. The role of attributes and features is mainly to provide rational underpinning.

As already discussed, brands have numerous ways of forming emotional connections with their target audiences by deeply and intimately understanding consumer needs. Utilizing consumer insights (refer to Chap. 7), brands can not only position and differentiate themselves within a competitive market but also create a high degree of relevance. This perceived relevance, in turn, reassures consumers in their brand choices and fosters strong feelings such as *this brand is for me*. Brand identity elements, such as primary and secondary color choices, fonts, iconography, as well as brand narratives and storytelling, advertising and communication in general, to cite a few, all contribute to emotionalize the relationship between a brand and its designated target consumers.

Another source of emotional connections in branding are values. Brands that claim and defend a well-chosen, balanced set of values have a higher propensity of connecting with their consumer targets. To develop their full potential, these values must fulfill two central conditions: they must be the logical fall-out from the brand positioning and they must be actionable, or put differently, brands must be perceived as living these values in everything they do.

Carefully selected and enacted values might favor stronger engagement with brands and foster memorability of the brand itself and its messages. Dr. Carmen Simon, an expert in neuroscience and Chief Science Officer at the

Corporate Visions Consultancy in Reno, Nevada, suggests that 80% of consumers or customers usually forget brand content after 3 days. According to her research, there are three main factors why people forget brand messaging: message irrelevancy (55%), an excessively complex content to retain (30%), and a general lack of motivation (36%). Surprisingly, and contrary to what would be expected in today's highly fragmented media market, distractions during brand messaging accounted for only 18%.

Brands may use values at different levels. Corporate brands often define a set of core values. These values reflect what the company stands for and believes in not only with respect to its commercial target audiences, but also as an employer brand. For values to become effective within the branding process, they must be lived. There is no point in defining your brand's core values if the organization or the commercial brand itself does not walk the talk. Millennials and GenZ consumers, in particular, showcase highly critical attitudes toward value fakes and may adapt their brand choices accordingly. *Sharing, caring, authenticity, integrity, transparency*, for example, are typical and frequently used values in corporate brands.

While corporate brands generally play a subordinate role in the decision-making processes compared to consumer brands, they may provide reassurance to first-time brand buyers who are somewhat familiar with the corporate brand due to other brand choices they have made in the past. If, as a consumer, you have had good experiences with Tide detergent, you might also give Crest toothpaste a try, since both are made by the Procter & Gamble company (and brand). Thus, building direct and visible connections between a corporate parent company brand and its portfolio of consumer brands has become an integral part of the overall branding strategy. This may explain why parent companies of big, global FMCG brands have started to showcase their *umbrella* brands more prominently on the packaging of their mass market *sub* brands. (The Coca Cola Company started to sign all its consumer beverage brands as of 2011, P&G followed suit in 2012.)

Corporate values become indeed increasingly important in today's consumer decision-making processes where *parent company* or *umbrella brands* are more closely watched and scrutinized, in particular by younger generations who will swiftly grow into tomorrow's core target consumer. Over the years to come, the core values that these corporate brands claim will be increasingly matched against their deeds, and it might take way less than a major scandal for consumers to join the boycott of a specific brand. The Miller Brewing Company recently paid a heavy toll, trying to defend values of diversity and inclusion. Major controversy emerged after Miller Light used a transgender influencer to promote its brands in the scope of a new marketing campaign causing sales to drop 17%.

While the values of diversity and inclusion are entirely honorable, they did not match the expectations or beliefs of a large portion of its target audience. The controversy also highlighted the tensions that consumer and corporate brands may face when deciding to leverage cultural or societal issues in their brand management efforts and in the context of today's increasingly polarized world.

Values do not only apply to corporate brands, but also to consumer (B2C) or customer (B2B) brands. Like a person, brands use values to express their personality and to guide their activities and the way in which they engage with their consumer targets. Being a fundamental dimension of any brand, brand values must be carefully defined. They are a direct consequence of the brand positioning, the one word your brand will ultimately stand for. Therefore, prior to defining the set of values that will become associated with your brand, you need to first decide what your brand will stand for—a complex process that will be discussed and illustrated in detail in Chap. 8.

The selection and definition of a brand's values is strategic. Like the brand positioning itself, values are defined in relation to the brand essence, which defines the one single-minded stand a brand will take in its market and against all competitors. Your brand will be evaluated communicating these values, and it will be increasingly scrutinized truly living them. Just claiming a set of values is not enough and your brand must be perceived as living its values in everything it says and does. This requires that your chosen values also relate to your brand's product or service reality. Besides the will to live its values, brands must also have the competence to do so.

Your brand's values are strategic also in another sense. They provide a certain standard for which your brand will become known over time. This standard guides and prescribes how your brand and its entire product or service offer will evolve. Innovation processes such as product renewal, introductions of additional portfolio variants or services, the development of line extensions or co-branding efforts must all be aligned with your brand values. Values contribute to building a coherent and consistent brand equity that motivates consumers to engage with your brand, culminating in loyalty and advocacy over time.

Values assume multiple roles in branding. As discussed above, they commit brands to act and interact with their target audiences with consistency. Values contribute to providing authenticity across brand messaging, thus depicting the brand as more *genuine*. A brand that claims what it does and does what it claims will inevitably build trust with consumers, ultimately leading to more brand loyalty or even advocacy. Brands often underestimate the importance of their values. Once defined, they are given too little room for expression in messaging and tangible action. Unfortunately, the intensive and relentless marketing efforts over the past decades have not always demonstrated the openness and transparency, which is increasingly expected by today's consumers. Here values could make an important difference as they prescribe the talk and the walk.

Brand values offer potential well beyond building *authenticity* and trust. At the center of what a brand believes, values are instrumental to projecting and to enacting a genuine vision, which may lead over time to a concept of *purpose branding*. Patagonia, the US outdoor textile brand, founded by Yvon Chouinard in 1973, provides a good case for this. Right at its inception, Patagonia was built on a strong set of values: quality, integrity, responsibility (environmental), innovation, and simplicity. Quite likely these values were what its founder, an experienced mountain climber, at the time felt strongly about. This brand fully embraced its values and lived by them. They no doubt played a central role in the Patagonia brand and contributed to making Patagonia an example of authenticity and genuineness. Here is how Patagonia defines its brand *integrity*:

> Examine our practices openly and honestly, learn from our mistakes and meet our commitments. We value integrity in both senses: that our actions match our words (we walk the talk), and that all of our work contributes to a functional whole (our sum is greater than our parts).
> Source: Patagonia website

These values, which apart from minor adjustments remain relevant today and have also provided fertile ground to motivate and support Patagonia's brand vision. After imposing a 1% earth tax on itself in 1985 and extending this commitment toward a worldwide crowdfunding effort only a few years later, Patagonia was one of the first global brands to transform its entire business model into a charity, with only one shareholder: the planet. In 2022, Yvon Chouinard and his family decided to transfer all company assets into two nonprofit entities: the Holdfast Collective, owning all nonvoting stock and defending Patagonia's values, purpose and vision, and the Patagonia Purpose Trust owning 100% of the company's voting stock. Every cent of profit not invested back into the Patagonia business is now spent on fighting climate change and on protecting virgin land around the world. Patagonia is no doubt one of the greatest examples of how values can help define and guide brands by leveraging the power of emotional connections. Its current business model may even suggest an evolutionary path toward a less greedy and more redistributive vision of capitalism in the twenty-first century.

An important reason why brand values should be selected and defined leveraging deep target consumer insights is that they allow brands to build deeper emotional connections with consumers. Reversibly, understanding your target audience's needs, beliefs, and motivations will allow you to make a more informed decision about exactly which values to choose for your brand. As mentioned before, this selection will always be made within the scope of your brand's product or service reality. The more your target consumers recognize themselves in the values that define your brand's personality, the more likely they are to engage with your brand. This principle is best leveraged by the definition and use of a *self-expressive value of brand personality*, which consumers may use to define and position themselves in a social context. Consumers relate to brand values and see brands as a way of expressing their own values, aspirations, and beliefs. Expressed and lived explicitly, a brand's values allow consumers to signal their own identity by assuming these brands as deliberate choices in their everyday life.

This may be most evident with fashion or sports brands that prominently use oversized logos on the clothing or fashion accessories or more discreet color codes such as Prada's red stripe or Gucci's green–red–green banner. As established signs of brand identity, these visual codes embody the values and beliefs of brands and enable consumers to consciously engage with them on an emotional level while simultaneously revindicating their engagement to the world around them.

Nike is defined by a strong and coherent set of values: inspiration, inclusivity, innovation, authenticity, and distinctiveness. The brand has successfully leveraged these core brand values through its communication messages, in product design, and brand identity codes. All in absolute coherence and consistency and *walking the talk*. As the world's biggest sports apparel brand, Nike inspires its target audiences as a coach, suggesting the way to succeed is to *just do it*. Nike lives inclusivity by its brand vision: *if you have a body, you are an athlete*. This vision allows the brand to cleverly maneuver around the gender question. Its deliberate and outspoken inclusiveness also provides the brand with a powerful credo of authenticity. The innovation is lived via constant product and design renewal, while the sum of all values and their expression give the Nike brand its distinctiveness. Together these values cohabit with a self-expressive value of brand personality that defines the essence of the Nike brand: *empowerment*, which the brand leverages in its mission statement of *helping everyone to find personal greatness*.

Nike's values are central to its brand and brand activities. They are formative of the brand's vision and mission, and they relate directly to the Nike brand essence, which itself is defined by the value of *empowered*. Every single aspect of the Nike brand adds up to make it coherent and convergent, just like a little musical theme without a false note. This way all strategic messages and actions become aligned and produce a flawless notion of coherence and consistency. To its target audiences, Nike appears sincere about sports and competition as a way of life, regardless of an athlete's physical or mental capacity. This has allowed the brand to live its *commercial* life like no other in the field. As a sum of its parts, the brand has gained great distinctiveness with consumers all over the world.

To understand *self-expressive human values of brand personality* in the world of branding, we distinguish between two distinctive states of consumer self-perception, the *real* and the *ideal* self-perception. A consumer's *real* self refers to how consumers actually see themselves, i.e., the physical appearance, abilities, strengths, and weaknesses, including beliefs and attitudes. The *real* self is grounded in the actual, but predominantly subjectively perceived, consumer reality (see Fig. 6.1).

Whereas the *ideal self* is how we desire to be perceived or how we want to be seen by others. The *ideal self* is formed and defined by our aspirations, our ambitions, and by social prescriptions. In short, all those things we strive for physically and mentally. By definition, the *ideal self* is projective and future oriented. Both the *real* and the *ideal self* are perpetually evolving self-definitions—they are highly subjective and formed by our self-perceptions and the constant social stimuli and feedback we receive in our daily life. The *real* and the *ideal* self are in a constant state of tension, and consumers aspire to their respective *ideal self* by various means such as resolutions,

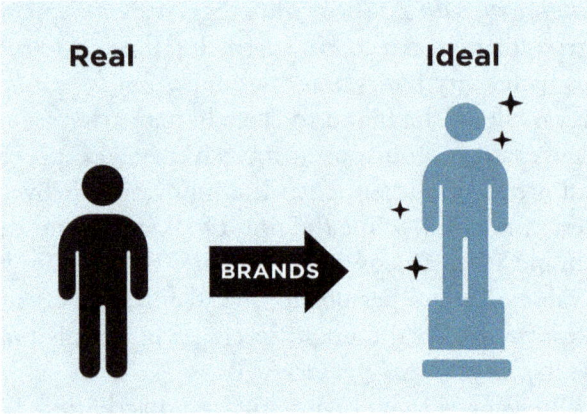

**Fig. 6.1** Simplified model of consumer self-perceptions. Author's own image

commitments, or interests that they believe will narrow the gap. Starting a new physical activity simply to lose weight or training to run a marathon or learning a skill, a language, or visiting a much talked about exhibition may all equally be driven by the need to approach the *ideal self*, projecting a desired image that is not part of the current self-perception.

In this perpetual state of mental strain, brands and their value set have a pivotal role to play. *Self-expressive human values* are ideal tools to fill the gap between the *real* and the *ideal* self. In the branding process, they define the brand identity (who am I?), the brand affiliation (to whom do I belong?), the brand competency (what am I best at?), and the brand vision (what do I strive for?). Brands that respond to these questions by a *self-expressive human value* offer consumers the opportunity to redefine themselves by emotionally connecting and embracing the brand and by demonstratively *wearing* it for the outside world to see.

*Self-expressive human values* also offer brands a unique way to define their brand personality. At the same time, they give consumers the opportunity to improve the sense of their personal *self*. Connecting with a brand via a *self-expressive human value* allows consumers to redefine themselves in the same way in which these values also help to define the brand: who am I?, to whom do I belong?, what am I best at?, and what do I strive for? These self-expressive human values enable consumers to express themselves using the same value dimensions claimed by their favorite brands. Boldness, responsibility, creativity, stylishness, confidence, modernity, authenticity, sophistication, empowerment, and endless others offer great potential to emotionalize a brand while offering a sense of perceived self-enhancement to the target audience.

Let us take another look at Nike to put this into a more tangible perspective.

Wearing Nike apparel defines you as someone with an affinity toward sports: a leisure sports enthusiast, a serious athlete, or just someone who is keen to project a sporty look. However, the brand also signals to your social environment that you belong to the community of determined sports practitioners, and it suggests that you have reached a certain level of competence in your chosen sports discipline. This then also legitimizes the fact that you strive for *greatness* in your sport domain: obviously, at your level of competence, ability, and ambition and not necessarily as a professional. Even for those people who just wear Nike as a fashion statement, they might, too, somewhat aspire to project the above personality dimensions within their social environment. The latter and the true enthusiasts all somehow belong to the same like-minded group of people, distinctively different from people who wear

Adidas, Puma, or Lululemon, for example. This also gives the Nike brand its distinctiveness.

Another example of *self-expressive human values* used in branding is Schweppes. Most of us associate Schweppes with a mixer brand in cocktail recipes. However, this predominant usage positioning somewhat cut the brand off from the soft drink market, which offers way more potential for volume and better prospects for growth than cocktails, which are generally consumed more randomly. It also made Schweppes vulnerable to shifting trends, as cocktail consumption became less fashionable during the 1980s and 1990s, before bouncing back more recently. When Schweppes decided to reposition its brand in the late 1990s, it leveraged a self-expressive human value to do so, giving the brand a distinct and highly relevant brand positioning that continues to differentiate it in the soft drink market today.

Schweppes looks back on a long heritage dating back to the late eighteenth century, where the brand first started to sell industrially produced carbonated mineral water. By a certain measure, Schweppes can be considered as one of the first soft drink brands. Awarded the British Royal Warrant in 1836, the Schweppes product range then evolved over the course of the twentieth century to become a reference as a cocktail mixer. Throughout its history, the brand was able to develop an image of elegance, exclusivity, and cultivation that provided the foundation for its repositioning, leveraging the *self-expressive human value* of *sophistication*. *Sophistication* has always been a value that consumers long for in their quest for self-enhancement and their personal *ideal self*. Consequently, it provided Schweppes with the necessary appeal to reach out to a larger target audience, while differentiating itself from key soft drink competition.

*Self-expressive human values* are a powerful tool to help brands form stronger and longer-lasting connections with their target audiences, the foundation for which is trust. Trust is one of the predispositions for brand selection and purchase. Most brand connections are entirely driven by emotional bonds and generally produce an extraordinary level of brand loyalty and advocacy. A brand that projects a *self-expressive human value* becomes quickly indispensable for a consumer seeking to approach their personal *ideal self*. However, these values also naturally generate a higher level of involvement with the brand, thus helping brand name and brand equity memorization, and it makes sense to actively push the value in communication messages as Nike does with *empowerment*. In addition, consumers generally prefer brands that reflect or share their personal values and beliefs. This may positively impact the purchase decision-making process and initiate some form of brand advocacy. Most likely, this is even more true for Generation Z audiences, who through the workings of social media have grown increasingly comfortable consuming noncontroversial content that conforms to their beliefs.

Now that we have discussed the nature and functionality of *self-expressive human values* in the branding process, the question is how to define them. Like for the Schweppes repositioning, a value with the potential to become self-expressive may just naturally impose itself by the brand's history or legacy. In most cases, however, these values must be defined using a strategic planning process. In this planning process, the *brand ladder* is a tool widely used in the industry. As a strategic brand planning tool, the *brand ladder* allows you to translate a functional product or service quality first into a relevant consumer benefit and ultimately into a transformative brand value with *self-expressive* properties. There are different versions of the brand ladder; however, this tool generally operates on four distinct strategic levels with a fifth one added sometimes in *purpose* branding.

As usual, in strategic brand positioning work, the starting point is the product or service reality. To create and own distinctiveness and relevance in the market, brands must first define a core product attribute or feature that they can leverage against competition. This attribute must be real and somewhat tangible, and it must enable the brand to make relevant claims attracting and convincing consumers to try the brand. One way to look at this attribute or feature is to define it as the *brand discriminator*, a term used in the *brand key* branding tool, which will be discussed in Chap. 8. The *discriminator* is a powerful word that suggests a strong sense of uniqueness and exclusivity for the feature or attribute you select. The *discriminator* becomes the foundation for your brand positioning. It is the attribute that *discriminates* your brand from all the other branded offers in the market.

While the *discriminator* sets your service or product feature apart from all competitors, it must simultaneously provide a clear set of functional and emotional benefits that are relevant to your target audience. The two benefits (functional and emotional) both refer to a core consumer or customer need. Once defined, these benefits then prescribe the route toward defining the potential self-expressive value. The *brand ladder* tool was first developed by the global Young & Rubicam advertising network and is shown in Fig. 6.2.

As already described above, the starting point is the physical reality of your brand: a unique or discriminating product or service feature, a particular attribute of a destination (place branding), a core competence of a corporate entity, a cause or a person. Virtually, anything may be turned into a brand and any brand may be defined by using the *brand ladder* tool.

The strategic planning exercise of your *brand ladder* always begins with the definition of your brand's core competence. This core competence or the

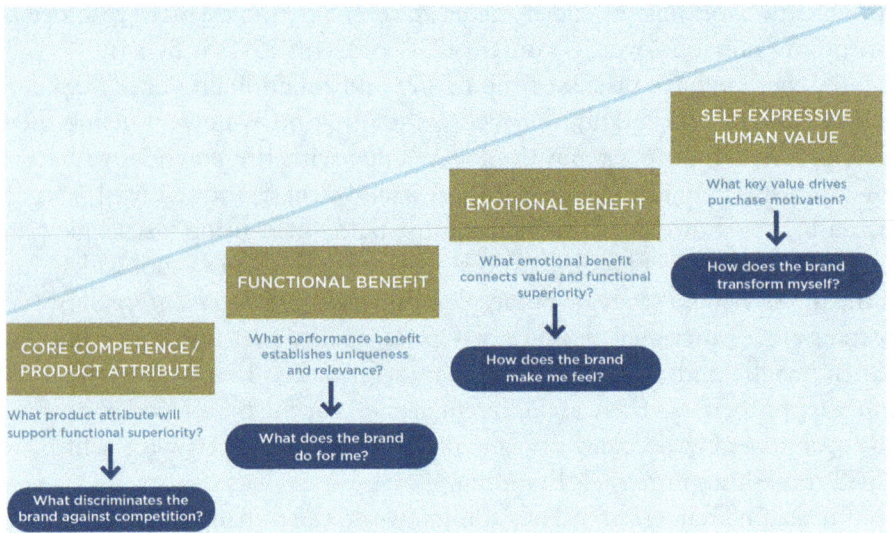

**Fig. 6.2** Four-step brand ladder tool. Author's own image

*discriminator* (see above) may be a product or service attribute or simply a know-how your brand owns throughout the manufacturing process or in the design of your service offer. This competence, attribute, or discriminator must give your brand a functional superiority that it can claim. This superiority must be real, tangible, and defendable. There is no point trying to stretch the truth or even make a false claim. Consumers will evaluate your brand's performance against the claims it makes and a mismatch at this point will inevitably lead to some form of deception, which is likely to damage your brand's image.

Once identified and confirmed, the next step up consists of translating your discriminator, competence, or attribute into a functional benefit. Functional benefits define what a brand does for its target consumers on a rational, tangible, or performance-related level. Again, the functional benefit must be seen as addressing your target audience's need. Otherwise, it will fail to produce relevance. From there, you proceed to defining the emotional benefit, which must be logically and credibly derived from the functional benefit you just defined. The emotional benefit defines how the *functional benefit*, which you have just defined in your *brand ladder*, makes consumers feel.

The last step of the ladder consists of the definition of the self-expressive brand value that your brand will stand for and own. This value represents an alternative way to define the brand essence, allowing you to inject an emotional dimension. This is the most complex step to take on the *brand ladder* and a process that requires a solid dose of discipline and creativity. It is where the choice of the perfect word matters the most. That word must fulfil several conditions, making this exercise the most complex part of the *brand laddering* process. First, the self-expressive brand value must evolve naturally and logically from the emotional benefit. The emotional benefit will be transformed into a value with *self-expressive* potential and qualities. Additionally, this value has a transformative function, suggesting that it may help the target audience to move from their *real self-* to their *ideal self-*perception. It is this self-defining dimension that lends the *value* its relevance and its power to establish strong and lasting emotional bonding, brand loyalty, and ultimately advocacy. The self-expressive value suggests how the brand may transform the target consumer from a purely perceptional point of view.

For instance, let us look at The North Face outdoor apparel brand used for illustration purposes only in Fig. 6.3.

The North Face, like Patagonia, Mammut, Millet, and other outdoor brands, has its roots in mountaineering, with their founders often coming from a professional or semiprofessional backgrounds. In some way, this fact has become a defining element for the product design, right from the start. Highly functional and performant, in many ways these apparel brands offer professional performance standards.

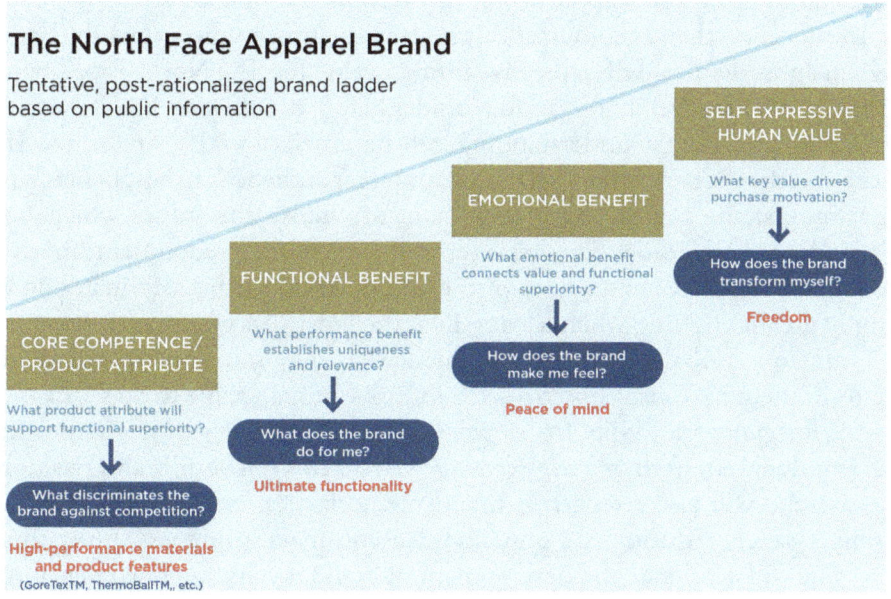

**Fig. 6.3** Use of the brand ladder tool illustrated by The North Face brand. Author's own image

To illustrate the logic of the brand ladder, let us look at The North Face by using relevant information available online concerning the brand. Of course, this is not the way you build the brand ladder in real life; however, it still serves our exercise. What stands out across the brand's entire iconic product line are claims about *high-performance materials and product features*. We may assume that this is the *discriminating* feature in The North Face's product reality (the discriminator). This is what the brand claims as its core competence, showcased by different product attributes that relate to its many iconic product references.

The next step consists of translating this *discriminator* into relevant consumer benefits, functionally and emotionally. Here, the choice of words can make a huge difference and the definition of the benefits must be done using concise and meaningful words. Each benefit is defined as single-minded, hence just one meaning. Ideally, using just one word. Doing so, the logic will lead to a functional or rational benefit that translates the discriminator (*high-performance materials and product features*) into a rational benefit claim of *ultimate functionality* (in the double sense of function and performance) and into an emotional benefit of *peace of mind* (supported by the rational benefit of *ultimate functionality*, which perception-wise makes these apparels worry-free). In other words, the high functionality of The North Face apparel goods leaves nothing to worry about when you are way out in nature.

The question then becomes: at this stage in the process, how does the brand logic help us define a self-expressive human value for The North Face brand? There are always several options to consider before deciding on the most powerful one, your target understanding will be crucial for this final step. The more and the deeper you understand your target audience's needs, beliefs, and motivations, the better you will be able to choose the value, which best responds to these needs. *Freedom* is certainly one of the predominant motivational patterns that incites people to explore nature in the way many do or simply dream of doing when leaving in a The North Face outfit.

Numerous global brands have defined what they stand for in one word. Many of them have also chosen a self-expressive human value to do so. L'Oréal stands for *glamorous*, Nike for *empowered*, and Oreo for *playful*. Leveraging the emotional strength of a *self-expressive human value* in your brand positioning exercise will also strengthen brand memorization and recall, leading to stronger salience during the purchase decision-making process. Over time, the value will accelerate the development of brand loyalty, as consumers more easily identify and engage with a brand that stands for a *self-expressive value* that not only corresponds to their needs but simultaneously becomes perceived as lifting their personal self-esteem.

# 7

# The Essential Role of Consumer Insights and How to Unlock them via Morphological Research?

To understand why consumers use a certain product or brand, you need to understand the underlying needs that drive them. These *consumer insights* are indispensable input into any brand positioning work. Insights provide a deep understanding of the true motivational patterns that drive consumer decision-making processes. They are of paramount importance in the world of brands. Motives for accessing brands may be managed by *tangible* factors such as material properties, performance, user-friendliness or usage convenience, sensory advantages, or price, which may be manipulated via innovation, messaging, or brand optimizations. Furthermore, consumers generally feel more confident judging and acting upon these factors by themselves. However, the more powerful brand factors are the unconscious, intangible ones. They combine real brand features with a solution to fundamental problems of everyday life.

Male shaving solutions provide a concrete illustration for this. For shaving brands such as Gilette, Wilkinson, or Braun, how should the contemporary man be portrayed today? In relation to shaving, there are only three possibilities to characterize a man: letting the beard grow, wet shaving, or electric shaving. Research reveals that a man who shaves wet is someone who acts and takes risks. The man who shaves electrically is perceived as someone who knows the right technology for taking care of himself. Both insights translate directly into solutions at the brand level. Gilette, expert in wet shaving, accentuates the brand image of the *vigorous man*. Here, a man's own vivacity is authenticated and strengthened by the heritage and tradition of wet shaving. While the Braun brand projects a similar vivacity, in this case it is directed onto the razor instead of the man. Here the right technology defines the Braun man.

Successful brands present their proposed solution so prominently that everyone knows these brands. This gives consumers a concrete choice. The prominent brands combine their *problem-solving* claim with the *brand's core competence*. This allows consumers to actually recall the solution messages of these brands. Nobody says, *I use Gillette because it makes me appear energetic and motivates me to tackle my duties right from my morning start* (referred to as the *insight impact story*). However, men tend to say that *Gillette is sharper than all other blades. You have to be able to deal with that* (referred to as the *declarative cover story*). Brands give consumers tangible orientation through arguments they may identify with and that are rationally legitimated in the *cover story*. However, these arguments should employ a second activity on a "deeper," unconscious level, which is triggered by the *impact story*. To truly unleash their power, brands must act on both levels and tell both stories. In the market context, this creates real positioning alternatives as demonstrated by the shaving brand example. If a brand that offers a solution to both the conscious and the unconscious *problem* (need) and if this solution is derived from the core feature of the brand or its core competence, the brand will be memorized for what it stands for.

Consumers may suppress their needs for some time; however, needs almost always lead to some sort of concise action, culminating in a purchase decision. When this happens, a consumer need has grown into something like a *problem* to which a product or service may provide a *solution*. In a purchase situation, all this happens in just a few seconds. Consumers do not notice the unconscious motives. They make decisions in seconds (except for high-priced purchases). Brand owners, however, should know what is going on in the mind of the consumer during those 3–4 s in front of the shelf at the point of sale (POS) or on the website of an online shop. Morphological research shows how both the conscious and unconscious motive structures work in this short time frame and make the decision seem so easy. If you know your brand's drivers and the mechanics behind them, you can influence them and steer the decision-making process in favor of your own brand.

Brands play a fundamental role in this problem/solution process as they provide orientation toward what consumers believe they stand for. The brand that is perceived as providing the most pertinent "*solution*" (benefit) to a consumer *problem* (need) will generate the highest level of attractiveness, hence deciding the purchase-decision-making process. While this is the case for all brands, global brands are built around *universal* needs for which they offer specific *solutions*.

Consumers experience different types of needs during any given day and not all require a complex selection process to satisfy them. In fact, brands help consumers quickly reduce their choices in the decision-making process, which may last less than 5 s at the shelf, leveraging their recognized brand competence. Brand positionings that rely on one word project a sharper and more memorable brand competence, which is associated with the brand solution to solve the consumer *problem*. In this context, morphological research, further discussed in this chapter, allows us to analyze and understand the cognitive processes that occur during this crucial moment in time, potentially providing the input brands need to impact these processes in their favor.

Unlocking the cognitive logic behind these processes offers brands the opportunity to position themselves more effectively as the ideal *solution* to a given consumer need (*problem*). Consequently, unlocking consumer insights is a crucial input into the brand positioning process. The deeper the understanding of the consumer motivations, the higher the pertinence of the branded answer.

There are multiple ways to identify and understand consumer insights that drive purchase motivations in any given product category. One such way is simple observations during purchase or usage situations. If you do not have particular budget, you may simply go to a grocery store and observe how consumers evaluate and finally decide on a given product or brand choice. Observations generally allow two levels of reading: the first is behavioral (how consumers approach, compare, and select their brand in a given category); the second is analytical and aims to decode what a specific behavior actually suggests, relative to a brand choice. Here commonsense reasoning might already provide initial clues for deeper lying motivational patterns.

When we worked on a German cat litter brand a few years ago, we consistently observed consumers rushing to and from the shelf, seemingly blindfolded and totally oblivious to any alternative litter choices on the shelf. Here the observation pointed to the fact that cat litter choices are usually formulated at a very early state of cat ownership and rarely revised thereafter. A fact that was later confirmed by consumer research and further analyzed using a morphological research approach.

Procter & Gamble (P&G), a globally leading consumer goods company headquartered in Cincinnati, operates a dedicated research facility to leverage behavioral insights obtained through observations on their innovation and marketing processes. The LifeLab facility has been designed to resemble typical apartments facilities, where consumers are invited to perform everyday cleaning tasks. The facility uses one-way mirrors, video cameras, and sensors to observe distinct cleaning habits, preferences, as well as pain points related to household chores and product usage. By studying consumers and the products or tools they use in these realistic settings, P&G gains valuable insights that are later leveraged in their product innovation, marketing, and branding processes.

If you take a closer look, you will see that most of the package goods we buy in grocery channels aim to make our lives more convenient. A frozen pizza responds to this goal as much as a power cleaner that eliminates grease with a simple swipe or the prewashed and precut fruits or vegetables that have recently found their way onto the shelves (even if the latter example may push the concept of convenience a bit too far). Apparently, P&G's Swiffer cleaning system, which has become a worldwide success, was chiefly developed with valuable consumer input from the LifeLab facility, helping P&G to stay ahead in the race of effectively addressing consumer needs.

Another way to unlock valuable consumer insights is through qualitative research methodologies, usually relying on focus groups or distinct forms of individual interviews (in a studio setting as personas (people interviews in a home setting) or more recently online). This can be done in a traditional setting, where a brand, a market, or a specific topic is discussed or in the context of a Usage & Attitude (U&A) study set-up, which might bring up some attitudinal insights. U&A studies provide input into how consumers use products, what attitudes they develop when doing so, and what intrinsic or extrinsic factors may influence their behavior. U&A studies may be fielded as qualitative or quantitative studies.

Qualitative research uses traditional interview techniques or group discussions to take a deeper look into how consumers relate to a certain product category or what motivates them to make their brand selections or purchase decisions. Most qualitative research offers use methodologies derived from sociology to research and analyze consumer reactions and opinions toward products and brands. While this might provide first insights into how consumers behave and feel toward a given market segment or the brands that operate in it, it also has its limitations.

The underlying principle of this research methodology (focus groups or individual interviews) is based on asking consumers to describe what they do, why they do what they do, and how this makes them feel. The problem here is that consumers are mostly unaware of what they really do and how they truly experience what they do. They tend to develop opinions as shortcuts for their personal usage self-perceptions. And this is what they mostly communicate in traditional qualitative research. In addition, these opinions are rarely neutral and most often influenced by societal conventions and beliefs. Many years ago, when we asked consumers in France about their daily oral care routine, most claimed a three-times-a-day teeth-brushing routine. Reality, however, tells a totally different story. Traditional qualitative research techniques sometimes struggle to reach beyond the declarative. However, while they might be effective to describe the "what," they have their limitations in explaining the "why" consumers do what they do.

Morphological research is different. Using the principles of Freudian psychoanalysis and the theory of *Gestalt*, morphological researchers formulate questions that help consumers describe their perceptions and experiences in a different and more cohesive way than what we are used to in qualitative research. This research methodology aims at making the invisible visible. It is designed to reveal the unconscious. The morphological process has nothing to do with hypnosis and it is not consumers who suddenly start talking about what unconsciously has motivated them toward a given decision or action. This research methodology has two underlying principles that allow it to dive deeper: more insisting consumer questioning techniques, where even small details or language slips are followed-up on and an extended capacity to listen, which is embedded in the methodology itself. Morphological psychology as a concept allows to circumscribe the soul of products and brands and the different forms consumers use to relate with them.

The concept of morphological psychology is based on Freud's theory and was developed by the German Psychologist Wilhelm Salber, Professor of the Psychological Institute of the Cologne University. The concept combines principles from Freud's psychology, *Gestalt-* and *holistic* psychology. The methodology describes consumer phenomena and renders the underlying conscious and unconscious workings visible. Imagine a bronze statue by the Italian artiste Giacometti sitting on top of a conference table with 12 participants around it. If you ask each of them to describe the statue, you will get answers from 12 slightly different viewpoints crossed over with personalized, highly individual descriptions of the statue itself. Some people might focus on shapes and forms, others will concentrate on details of specific statue parts, yet others might stress elements of texture, color, or surfaces, and so on. In the end, all descriptions combined establish a *Gestalt* of the statue with a high degree of detail and a complex set of subjective insights from the personalized points of view of each of the respondents. These multifaceted and detailed descriptions form the input for morphological psychology. In the mental state, all elements are interconnected, and these interconnections are what morphology decodes and transforms into an explicit and tangible model of actionable units, which can be leveraged in the branding process.

Brands and markets are also forms of *Gestalt*. They are linked by all their parts such as product formulas, brand history, packaging, and communications to form lively, only partially unconscious principles, obliged to provide continuity and change to remain attractive and alive. The goal of morphological research methodology is to produce models of actionable units where all parts can be described via their connections and interactions with each other.

This reveals true consumer needs and motivations and can even prognosticate directions brands should take to foster their market positions and enhance consumer relevance. We will see on the following pages how this actually works, the various benefits morphological research offers to brand owners and brand builders and how the insights it produces may be leveraged in the branding process.

Like with Giacometti's statue, morphological research decodes products and brands from multiple angles and points of view. Consumers in morphological groups or individual interviews are encouraged via specific techniques of deep questioning and discerning listening to describe their daily relationship with a given product or brand. In this process, morphological psychology relies on four distinct steps of understanding:

1. Tracking consumer descriptions to the very end
2. Differentiating base-tendencies in consumer behavior and beliefs.
3. Identifying relationships between base tendencies
4. Turning your brand into a solution provider

Let us look at this in more detail using some brand examples.

1. *Tracking consumer descriptions to the very end*

The direction traditional qualitative research usually takes is defined by the discussion guideline, which is conceived and validated prior to any project start. This is also the case for morphological research, however, with a decisive difference: the openness and willingness to follow consumers in their description of how they use a certain product, service, or brand, even or especially if this implies leaving the discussion guide for a little while. The way consumers see products, handle, or use them and what they feel when doing so? What meaning is a person giving these usage forms and the product attributes? Morphological researchers follow every trace. This particular willingness to follow the stories that are being told is one aspect of what makes morphological research special.

Product usage might evolve throughout an ordinary consumer day depending on moments of consumption or the context of a given situation. As a result, related consumer experiences are rarely static, predefined, or the same for all users of a given product, brand, or service offer. In morphological research, every detail counts even a "Freudian-slip" might draw their attention, pursuing it up to a certain point. The objective is to understand a market, product, service, or brand from the consumer's perspective by following the various usage and attitude turns and directions products or brands may trigger in consumers daily lives, consciously and unconsciously. This willingness and flexibility to follow the flow of consumer descriptions in a conversational setting allows us to unlock and understand the unconscious side of the consumer declarative data. Most often the real tendencies only start to emerge later in the process and after the obvious has already been discussed. The questions asked in morphological research help consumers describe their perceptions and experiences in more detail. This way the unconscious often emerges all by itself.

Morphological research listens to the stories consumers tell about products and brands, looking for relevant tendencies to emerge and to confirm. At first, consumer storytelling (the description of their personal perceptions and experiences) often develops a unique and distinct atmosphere in the group or reveals a certain mood in individual interviews. This atmosphere or mood is considered as first input for analysis. Take a group of male beer drinkers for example. After a quick round of personal introductions, the group's input toward the motivation of beer drinking swiftly hones in on taste, refreshment, and on a description about how beer drinking is performed in an atmosphere of civilized behavior, preset standards, and etiquette. As participants elaborate on these civilized forms of beer consumption, they each start leaning back in their chairs, one after the other, loosening or taking off their ties and rolling up their sleeves. This group behavior provides initial clues about the true motivations behind beer consumption. Rather than the claimed civilized, refreshing, and taste-driven world, beer drinking is about the *liquification* of the drinker's state of mind. Social barriers are lifted, conversations become more carefree, and the general atmosphere more relaxed. Observing insights in this seemingly innocent group behavior not only reveals a first paradox but also hints at a hidden route to be explored. Only later in the process does the discussion shift to the fact that beer consumption usually leads to the celebration of heavy drinking.

Morphological research allows us to understand what truly matters from the viewpoint of the consumer, how he, she (or they) wants his, her (their) opinions to be understood and how these findings might be transposed onto the definition or management of a given brand. This research tool listens to all sorts of consumers descriptions, word choices, gestures and body language, and later sorts out their interrelated meaning.

When you ask consumers about their daily shower routine,[1] you may hear stories about how overwhelming it is to get out of bed and start a new day,

---

[1] Illustrations for showering, snacking, yoghurt, and make-up provided by Wiesmann Forschen & Beraten, Cologne, Germany.

about the futile and usually less flattering first look in the mirror, the pain of choosing the day's appropriate outfit, and so on. This sluggish and discouraged mood suddenly evolves once under the shower. The warm water somehow favors the lingering in a world of dreams and ultimately washes the sleep away. The initial tension is now experienced as a lift-up, the mood becomes more invigorated and energetic. For example, people who talk about singing in the shower testify to this. This brief example demonstrates how storytelling, which is given the room to delve down into deeper levels of consumer behavior, has the power to provide insights that might unlock valuable input for the positioning of any product, service, or brand.

Deeper questioning and a more discerning approach to listening provide a more fertile ground for analysis. Here researchers and consumers embark on a journey where they both learn something new through the questions asked and the answers provided. Typical questions asked in this process are: *What comes spontaneously to mind?*, *What exactly do you mean by that?*, *How did you feel about that?*, *Could you describe this in more detail?*, *To what extent is this linked to the product you used?*, *What must the brand do to generate this kind of feeling?*, and so on. The underlying principle always is to follow the thread offered by a given answer and to spin it further, as long as it produces additional meaning and while it remains closely related to what consumers experience in their daily life and within the product category in question.

The storytelling logic leveraged in morphological research can also provide discerning details even within a same product category. In salty snacks, for instance, the consumption of pretzels versus chips reveals opposing motivations. The stories consumers tell indicate that pretzels with their bakery legacy, the baked dough, and salty crust are preferred in more formal settings because fingers stay clean and personal appearance counts. Chips, however, with their greasy texture, yummy spices, and irregular crumbling shapes become the preferred choice in moments of transgression and uninhibited socializing.

In a similar way, cat owners spontaneously embark on detailed descriptions of the intimate relationships they have with their cats. The opposite is the case when you ask the same consumers about their use and relation to shower gels, which touch upon similar intimate dimensions. Cat owners talk about their cats like partners, children, or their own alter-ego. Here, intimate relationships are formed that lead to anthropomorphic connections, which may entirely block out the animal side of a cat (independence, hygiene, etc.). Obviously, the above understanding becomes indispensable in the positioning process of any pet brand targeting cat owners.

By now, you may ask why all this focus on the emotional side of consumer usage and attitudes and how about the rational elements that make a product or brand? A jam has a texture and sweetness, salami has a fat or cholesterol content, a service brand may entitle you to certain privileges, and so on. Of course, these rational or functional product attributes deserve the same amount of attention. They, too, are discussed in the context of the stories that surround their usage in consumers' daily lives. However, consumers form lasting relationships with brands mostly through emotions. Rational or functional brand attributes are predominantly used to underpin an emotionally driven purchase decision. A fact that marketeers sometimes tend to overlook or neglect.

2. *Differentiating tendencies in consumer behavior and beliefs*

In the process of morphological research, the different directions or tendencies that emerge from the discussion or interviews are already organized during the research itself. Along the journey into the deeper layers of a market or brand, several directions may open up. Let us take another look at the cat owner example and their generalized enthusiasm at the beginning of the group discussion. You will quickly realize that even their widely described admiration for the cat's legendary independence quickly comes to an end when you approach the topic of hygiene and excrements. The all-loving cat owner suddenly turns into a keeper of law and order who has set clear rules for the cleanliness and hygiene expected from the beloved cat. This becomes visible in their stories on the cat litter box and its daily management. We can now already see the first two diverging directions cat ownership defines: the unconditional love for the cat and its character and the limit-setting rules established to deal with its hygiene. Another paradox, like the one referred to above in relation to beer consumption.

Natural yogurt provides another set of interesting insights. Consumers see natural yogurt as a living substance (live yogurt cultures) capable of vitalizing the entire body, and particularly the gut. This is why natural yogurt is consumed often after an illness or during springtime. However, consumers also attribute a certain *cleaning function* to natural yogurt, which is imagined from the virgin-white color and the slightly sour taste. In this sense, natural yogurt transcends a status quo, which consumers wish to reattribute for themselves (cleansed). Finally, a third direction or tendency emerges in consumer research: the fact that the white color stimulates creative processes by adding colored ingrediencies like jam, chocolate, or fruits, which become imaginative forms drawn in the white mass, just like on a white sheet of paper. With these three different directions or tendencies for exploring a brand's positioning exercise, marketeers have gained substantial meaning and understanding.

In all qualitative consumer research, there is one main story that is always told—and that all your competitors also know. However, there are also other stories that are harder to unlock when told simultaneously with the main one. Morphology as a methodology has developed ways to slip under the skin of the main story and to uncover and understand the others, too. As already mentioned, this is done in part with more discerning questions, designed to go deeper. However, the methodology also commands a solid dose of curiosity, interest, and the capacity to listen and insist.

You may ask, how is all this achievable within the timeframe of an average group or individual interview? That is a legitimate question. Diving deeper and exploring naturally requires time. However, the time in morphological research is just used differently and trained researchers know how to ask the right questions to get to the psychological realities and connections that are lying under the obvious.

### 3. *Identifying relationships between base tendencies*

Once the different base tendencies have been identified, you could simply imagine working with them one by one within the scope of your branding project. However, morphological psychology always assumes a direct and meaningful connectivity between these base tendencies or directions of any given market or brand. This connectivity further assumes a paradox, two seemingly opposing, or polarizing tendencies.

We have seen that cat owners have two souls: submission (to the nature of cats) and dominance (imposing human hygiene standards). The same applies to makeup. Applying makeup is generally felt like a metamorphosis where women aim to bring out the individual beauty of their faces. Yet they also aspire to follow a leading makeup trend to look like other women. Natural yogurt is enjoyed for its particular pureness and *virginity*, while few resist the temptation to mix in fruit, chocolate, or jam. The pursuit of these tendencies via detailed consumer descriptions allows us to identify the connections between them. And as we will see, it is these connections that will nourish the branding process the most.

### 4. *Turning your brand into a solution provider*

Brands present offers to consumers. They provide a guided and focused shortcut during the purchasing process. Brands translate the much-discussed tendencies into attractive formats, allowing consumers to recognize them. This is what makes brands attractive and desirable. However, in order to identify and organize these base tendencies inherent to a market or a brand, you must first match them with your brand reality (attributes), then prioritize and organize them.

In a certain sense, brands function like people who own a core competence and a general know-how. This competence might answer different consumer need dimensions. However, it is the lead tendency that will determine the format a brand has to take. This format must be single-minded, built on a designated brand competence, i.e., an attribute that produces a high level of saliency during the purchase decision-making process.

Weihenstephan, a premium German yogurt brand, strongly insists on its proximity to the pure, alpine milk used to make its products, as well as a background of happy grazing cows. Differentiating its brand via the platform of "purity" naturally limits a consumer's desire for mixing. Private label brands, on the other hand, which also claim *purity*, fail to provide sufficient codes to support this claim with their less directive pack designs and exclusive distribution channels. These latter *brands* may stimulate the desire to mix, while Weihenstephan with its prescriptive *pure nature* universe, restricts it (see Figs. 7.1, 7.2, 7.3, and 7.4). Yogurt is traditionally sold in round containers, unlike the German dairy brand Müller. Müller launched a square snacking yogurt format in 1998 called Müller Corner proposing a square bi-compartment container where a corner filled with jam or other sweets can be whopped over into the white yogurt base in the other, larger portion of the packaging. The Müller Corner directly leverages the play factor embedded in natural yogurt consumption to differentiate its brand from the highly competitive European dairy market. On yet another angle, Actimel, a yogurt drink from the Danone Group, stresses the vitalizing side of yogurt (natural defenses) and

**Fig. 7.1** Yogurt as essential food, suggesting pure consumption. Author's own image

**Fig. 7.2** M&S private label brand without consumption clues. Author's own image

**Fig. 7.3** Müller Corner yogurt with yogurt base and corner to mix providing stimuli for deeper consumption experiences. Author's own image

neglects the dimensions of purity and creative liberty. Be that as it may, Actimel is prescriptive of daytime and seasonal usage moments (one shot a day, keeps the doctor away).

**Fig. 7.4** Actimel yogurt drink prescribing a ritualized consumption—a shot per day. Author's own image

A precondition of successful brand positioning is the understanding of how to weigh and leverage the multiple tendencies in a distinct market or a brand. For those interested, I will still descend one level lower into morphological research: the concept of functional layers. Morphology differentiates between six functional levels that both guide the analysis of the findings and condition the research process as shown in Fig. 7.5.

To illustrate these functional levels and the way they mutually interact, let us take another look at beer drinkers.[2] This glimpse into the beer drinking market only shows certain aspects of the research process, but enough to illustrate the concept and the underlying dynamics that organize motivational effects in this product category.

We have seen that beer-drinking is motivated by a mood changer effect (liquification of a state of mind) that transforms the ordinary working day. It makes people more relaxed, more open, more sociable, and talkative. The constraints of daily life start to slip away and evaporate—obviously a desired effect of alcohol consumption in general (*Transformation*).

---

[2] Source: Gruppen Diskussionen in der Marktforschung - Rheingold Verlag 2008, p.60-61, Rheingold Research Institute in Cologne, Germany.

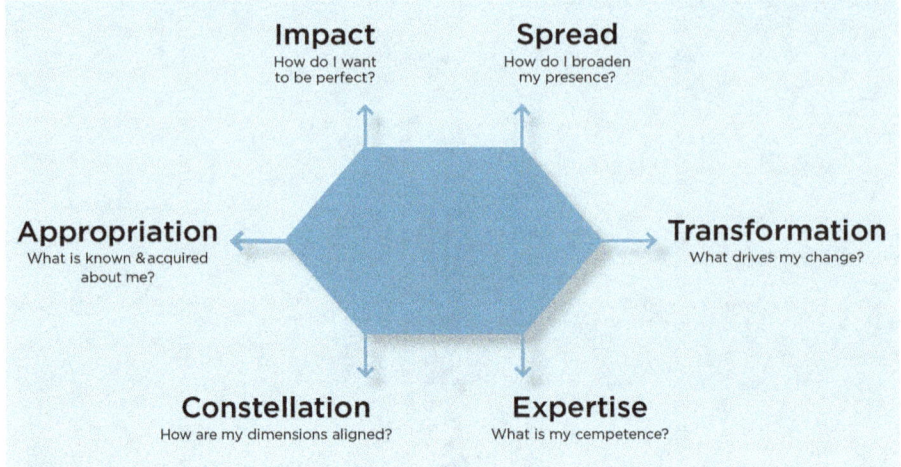

**Fig. 7.5** The six functional layers of access motives analyzed in morphological research. Author's own image

These drinking rituals entail certain forms of beer drinking preparations. People may drink their beer informally directly from the bottle or may celebrate each new glass that is being filled by reproducing a foam crown like barmen do with draft (*Appropriation*). To prevent excesses that become visible through well-established behavioral patterns such as slurring or staggering, beer drinkers also set themselves self-imposed rules to limit their consumption. *No more than three bottles tonight, … only until the movie ends, …*, or drinking rituals and other forms of regulation (*Expertise*).

In parallel, certain beer drinking formats or rules serve as pillars of a socially acceptable drinking culture, such as taking small sips (*Constellation*).

Despite this transformation, the reality of tomorrow's work day remains present in the background and somewhat regulates the desire to transform. This helps to avoid excesses, because you must get up and go to work the next morning (*Impact*). Simultaneously, the pleasures related to a feeling of *lightness* as a tangible consequence from the *liquification* process motivate the continuation of the drinking process (*Spread*).

This little example highlights how much individual facets of the beer drinking behavior are related and functionally connected: *Liquification* of the state of mind, background rules for limitations of excess drinking, preparation and staging of beer drinking rituals within the social context. A branding expert who gains access to these consumer insights receives various input for defining what a given brand should stand for. This is why morphological research is an indispensable tool in the *one-word* branding process. It allows you to reveal and decode the invisible, thus opening new venues for successful brand differentiation and most importantly, brand relevance.

Overall, morphological research might appear somewhat complex or difficult to access. Rest assured, it is not. Any marketing or branding expert will quickly find a personalized way into this remarkable methodology, which provides significantly more food for thought than any traditional qualitative research. There is of course a deeper theory based on psychology and the work of Wilhelm Salber, the father of morphological research. And this is what you need to watch out for. Today, only few institutes are capable of delivering a truly morphological methodology in praxis, even if a fairly sizeable amount of institutes claim that they do. Researchers working in this field should have a psychological background and not come from sociology. Also, this methodology is not confined to Germany, but available in research institutes in most developed markets.

What you need to keep in mind when you consider morphological research is that this methodology like other qualitative research formats also uses the principle of consumer storytelling. Only morphological research pushes storytelling to much deeper levels, driven by a methodological curiosity and desire to discover the whole story, including its underlying connections and not just parts of it.

Here are two final examples from the Rheingold Institute in Cologne, Germany,[3] that help to illustrate this point:

*Example: Brand preferences in full flavor cigarettes*

Smokers generally claim brand preferences based on flavor. However, in blind testing, few can distinguish their brand from other full flavor cigarettes. This may suggest that brand preferences are formed through other elements of the brand mix than the actual product performance (flavor). For consumers, their real motivations remain inaccessible, tucked away in the unconscious, not only in cigarettes. Once you enter the deep-telling process suggested by morphology, you quickly realize that brand preferences in full flavor cigarettes are not formulated by the flavor, but the universe proposed by the brand.

However, even the brand world is difficult for consumers to talk about. In discussions with loyal Marlboro smokers, respondents quickly revert to the idealized, somewhat old-fashioned Marlboro world of freedom and adventures illustrated in Marlboro communication. While this world is admired, it also generates a certain dose of criticism. Once you push the group to a more

---

[3] Source: Gruppen Diskussionen in der Marktforschung—Rheingold Verlag, 2008, pp. 60–61, Rheingold Research Institute in Cologne, Germany.

detailed description of the world of freedom and adventure, you quickly realize that this world only exists on the surface. Deeper down there is a totally different Marlboro world, one of a regulated working day where the Marlboro man is busy hording grazing horses into confining gates. Instead of living a life of freedom, he is focused on limiting the freedom of the animals he is paid to look after. Only in the evening, once the job is done, may he sit down at his campfire and enjoy a cigarette and coffee with his horse looking on. The world of the Marlboro man leaves little room for important deeds, and it is characterized by the search for perfection in his working day filled with constraints and limitations. His vision for life is summed up by *work before pleasure*, *do what you do well*, and *find your greatness* in what you do.

This attitude is stereotypical of a career-oriented blue-collar worker, which explains the worldwide success this brand has had and still enjoys today. The paradox of freedom and restriction inherent in the Marlboro brand is further expressed by its logo or brand block, where the overstretched *l* and *b* in the Marlboro name evoke the dimensions of the unlimited, while the red color refers to the campfire and the white triangle represents the roof that keeps the Marlboro world confined and together. Like any successful global brand, Marlboro offers a *solution* for a universal consumer need: a rewarding structured and organized life.

*Example: household cleaners*

The stories told by consumers of household cleaning products mostly circle around the fact that cleaning leaves the house spotless. The shiny result of the cleaning process appears to be the focus of their motivations and ultimately their brand choices. However, once you request a detailed description of the actual cleaning process, it becomes clear that it is not the cleaning process itself that generates the motivation, but the drama included inside the process. Here consumers develop detailed and often ritualized processes to deal with dirt and hygiene. Entire strategies surface in the stories by which dirt is attacked and eliminated, while few objects remain in their place during the household clean-up campaign.

Here is where the genuine motivational forces are located and not in the generally mentioned desire for cleanliness. For house cleaner brands, this means it is not enough to simply promise product performance (cleaning). They must also provide the screenplay of a drama for the cleaning process. Brands like the German brand *Der General*, which used the recurring character of a woman in advertising whose white blouse became decorated with shoulder pads and chest medals once the product was put to use, illustrates this category understanding. P&G's global brand *Mr. Clean* also leverages this insight (see Figs. 7.6 and 7.7).

**Fig. 7.6** Vintage advertising poster *Der General*. Permission Henkel AG & Co. KGaA, Düsseldorf, Germany

**Fig. 7.7** French packaging label Mr. Clean household cleaner. Author's own image

*Deep-telling* is what makes the real difference, while the psychological analysis simultaneously runs in the background. To what extent you may understand the detailed mechanisms of this research tool is not of real importance in the end. What really matters are the findings, the insights, and the meaningful connections it delivers. Morphological research not only makes them visible, but also renders them operational for your brand positioning process. This methodology is by no means limited to product, brand, or market research. You may use morphological research to analyze and understand any topic explored during qualitative research from packing to communication materials and from service to destination, people, or corporate brands.

# 8

## Simplicity on the Other Side of Complexity: Identifying the One Word that Defines your Brand

Developing a powerful brand positioning is a delicate and complex affair.

There are lots of things to consider and massive amounts of information to process. All this adds complexity to a process that, to become successful, requires utmost simplicity in the final definition of what your brand will stand for. Numerous cases from the past have shown that real power of branding is unleashed once you can define with just *one word* what your brand stands for.

The level of complexity may vary from brand to brand and from market to market. In crowded and fragmented markets, the ones that many FMCG brands operate in, complexity increases due to a multitude of competitive offers and claims, while in luxury goods or destination branding the competitive set might be somewhat more limited. The scope of competitive alternatives always raises the challenges for brand differentiation. Another important aspect to consider is brand heritage. In settled market segments, many brands benefit from a long branding history with a well-defined brand equity and strong image perceptions locked into consumers' minds. This is the case for any brand that has been introduced at some point to its respective target audience, but it becomes increasingly so as brands accumulate years of consistent and persistent messaging. Obviously, the longer a brand has been around, the more its image perceptions will be engrained in its target consumers' minds. Once a certain image dimension is installed, it will be very hard to change, unless your brand has some sort of scandal or a perduring quality problem. Therefore, understanding what your brand currently stands for is paramount to finding a successful way to project it into the future and to reposition it. On the other hand, positioning a new brand alleviates some of the complexity, since the brand equity has not been developed yet.

Whether you are considering the positioning of a new brand, let us assume for a start-up, the repositioning of an existing brand, or the revival of a *vintage* brand, which has lost some of its traction with consumers, the same basic principles apply. The objective is to filter through every bit of information available, distilling it down to what we refer to as the *simplicity on the other side of complexity*: defining your brand by just *one word*. The following methodology is designed to do just that.

A powerful brand positioning is all about identifying one magic word that will define what your brand stands for and will ultimately drive your entire go-to-market effort, providing clear and tangible guidance for your entire organization, at any level of responsibility. One-word brand positionings point every single person in the organization in the exact same direction, providing a clear and actionable roadmap and channeling your staff's energy, creativity, and inventiveness toward one single-minded superior objective. This not only generates higher productivity in the branding and brand management processes but also assures more consistency in brand messaging at all levels of brand activity and brand communication.

Too many organizations are still organized in silos, where different departments with different tasks operate in parallel rather than in synergy. Providing a mono-dimensional direction for the brand that represents the organization or its products, service offers, or destination helps to create an intellectual synergy, which will by no means be restrictive. As a matter of fact, it is this single-minded focus that provides a world of freedom to fully capture individual competencies and talents. A single-minded, one-word brand positioning provides a common brief for everybody to follow … and all the freedom that comes with a tightly defined strategic direction. In practice, the one-word brand positioning is leveraged as a sort of prism that functions as a strategic guide for initiatives, ideas, and concrete product or service features and as a measurement to evaluate these initiatives, ideas, and features at an early stage of the development or executional process. If a brand like BMW stands for *driving pleasure*, then the key contribution of every employee in the company should be to maximize driving pleasure by any means at their disposal and within their respective domain of responsibility or when networking across responsibility domains.

Admittedly, the one-word concept does not always translate into just *one word*; however, it always delivers one single-minded angle of attack. It does not really matter if driving pleasure is composed of two words rather than just one. The meaning remains as sharp and clear as if expressed in just one word. There is absolutely no ambiguity regarding the final customer experience that

## 8 Simplicity on the Other Side of Complexity: Identifying the One...

everybody who works at or for BMW as a supplier must produce. Even the tiniest and seemingly insignificant individual contribution to the whole will be geared toward producing *driving pleasure*. As we will see later, the one-word branding process applies to all types of brands, from product to destination brands and from corporate to service brands. A cause, a person, a movement, and so on anything that can be turned into a brand. Every single brand may be defined by just one word.

The American 2016 elections are just one example of this. *Make America Great Again* (MAGA) effectively summarized what the Republican Party as a brand stood and still stands for: *greatness*. It gathered over half of the American population to vote for Donald Trump, because it provided a universally meaningful, relevant, and single-minded Republican brand positioning message. The Tory's approach during the UK election in 2019 leveraged the same principle with the claim *Get Brexit Done*, positioning the party on a value proposition that also suggested swift and *tangible action* (versus empty promises). Just like Obama in 2008 with *yes, we can* positioned the Democrats as an *actionable and dynamic* political movement that promised *change*.

The process to define a brand in one word follows four distinct steps, called the *brand positioning funnel* as shown in Fig. 8.1.

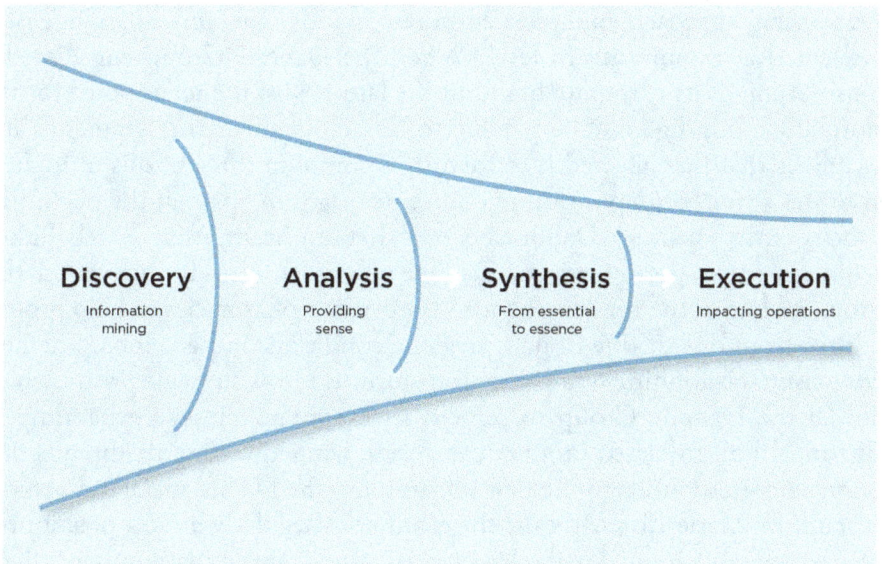

**Fig. 8.1** Four-step brand positioning funnel. Author's own image

## Information Mining

The discovery phase has a single-minded objective: to gather as much information about the brand, the product, the target audiences, and the market environment as possible. The discovery step is structured and designed to dive deep. The starting point is the *product* and there are many aspects to consider: the formulation and composition, the origin and quality of the raw materials, the intrinsic functional attributes or service features, the production process, the customer experience, the potential benefits, distribution and logistics, and so on. Every tiny detail counts. You should strive to become the uncontested expert of your product or service in all its facets. Reading all about it and discussing it with everybody down the chain responsible for producing or designing it, the engineers, product, and service designers, production and supply chain managers, quality controllers and purchasing. We always visit at least one factory as part of the *information mining* or *discovery* step. Not surprisingly, it is often the most seasoned people in an organization who truly hold valuable pieces of information, as they have known the brand in its peak years or when things were less obscured by excessive information complexity. When it comes to rebranding, the answers on how to fit your brand for the future are mostly found in its past.

An analog approach applies to corporate brands. The only difference is, it is executed at a more macro level. When the Danone Group considered a repositioning of its corporate brand in the late 1990s, the focus point for the information mining was the product offer across all market segments and disciplines that first allowed it to identify a common thread. This ultimately led to the *active health* positioning. Since its origin in Spain at the beginning of the twentieth century, Danone believes that our health is intimately linked to our nutrition. Issac Carasso, Danone's founder, already incarnated this vision and had at the time introduced yogurt into pharmacies to help protect children from disease due to poor hygiene conditions in Barcelona. The new *active health* positioning was swiftly transformed into a strategic prism, which allowed the Danone Group to refocus its corporate strategy expanding in nutritional health-related product categories, while divesting the brands that no longer corresponded to the new positioning (the LU biscuit brand, Amora mustard, or Marie frozen meals, for example). Regularly, brand positioning provides valuable input for the larger corporate strategic development direction, too.

Danone at the time and still today believed in a *glocal* management approach, referring to a global strategy being executed locally with some level of executional freedom to count for cultural and market maturity differences.

The corporate *active health* positioning literally transformed how the corporation functioned at many levels. Marketing teams repositioned existing brands to stress nutritional health (e.g., calcium for bone strength, proteins, or vitamins), even in dessert dairy products. This also impacted the product development process and encouraged Danone to expand worldwide, introducing two of its first functional food brands: Actimel and Activia. These brands became the most literal interpretation of the new *active health* positioning with Actimel promising a *strengthened immune system* and Activia promising an improved *digestive transit*. Both claimed a unique yogurt culture to justify the respective effects and both brands became global power brands with multibillion dollars in annual sales. As a side note, these functional claims may require serious scientific evidence to get approved by local regulatory institutions, as was the case for both Actimel and Activia, which established and provided evidence for their claim through research studies, later documented in scientific monographs.

The *active health* positioning also enabled the sales teams around the world who leveraged the new positioning and its differentiation in generally highly fragmented local dairy markets, facilitating and improving key parameters in distribution and tariff negotiations against fierce defense actions from local competitors. The new corporate positioning also impacted the Danone employer brand. Selling *nutritional health* provided a sense of *purpose* for Millennials and GenZs, which turned out to be way more attractive than selling yogurt and dairy desserts.

But the corporate repositioning also had an important side effect. It combined the energy, creativity, and inventive power of the entire organization and directed it into one single-minded direction. The Danone Group was now selling *active health* instead of dairy, cookies, frozen meals, water, or mustard from before the corporate repositioning. It is easy to see how a health-claiming yogurt or dessert generates a different value perception with consumers, significantly impacting product margins. Yogurt is made from milk, and that milk is bought at a certain cost from local farmers. Transforming it into yogurt or other dairy products generates value, which can be leveraged in the price positioning. Here, a plain natural yogurt generally generated a margin factor of 1, while selling the same *milk* under the Activia brand raised the factor to roughly 1.9, and generated a factor of roughly 2.3 for Actimel, 230% higher than for plain yogurt.

It would be a blatant exaggeration to say that it was the corporate repositioning that allowed the Danone Group to grow from a strong regional player to become the worldwide leader in dairy. However, there is no doubt that it strongly contributed to its rise. *Active health* has given the Danone Group a true differentiation against other corporate dairy brands and has provided stronger distinction as a publicly traded company. The positioning has also helped to increase productivity by pointing everyone in the same direction, hence creating a greater sense of synergy between different departments and operative functions. And *active health* made Danone a more interesting place to work, providing purpose: a place, where what employees do really matters.

Danone's active health positioning provided fresh orientation for both its existing brands and new ones to be launched. As such, it helped to refocus the Activia brand (formerly introduced in 1987 under the name of *BIO*) on the digestive transit regulation function, addressing a tangible consumer need, especially in female target audiences. Actimel was launched in 1998 as the first new brand under the new corporate *active health* positioning umbrella. Danone has since maintained a constant flow of innovative product and brand launches, entering market segments such as infant milk, medical nutrition, and their recently introduced *GetPro* high-protein dairy range.

Also, service brands such as hospitality facilities, transportation companies, insurances, or any other service provider offer vast amounts of information that need to be mined, scrutinized, and processed in this first phase of the brand positioning development. Like tangible products, their offers have attributes and features that translate into consumer benefits. The same holds for destination brands that claim natural, cultural, or historical features and attributes that are unique and can be leveraged in the place brand positioning process later.

Independent of the brand type and the *product* reality, this first phase of the branding process requires thorough investigative work to collect and organize all data and information about the brand, even those elements that may seem less relevant at first.

Once the product, corporate or service reality has been fully researched, attention should be focused on the brand and its repositioning exercise.

Product or service features are only one side of the brand reality, while brand heritage and consumer perceptions are equally important to understand. Existing brands own equity, no matter how important they have become throughout their existence and independent of how well they are known to their target audiences. A brand's equity is never forgotten or lost, and it may always be revived in a well-prepared repositioning process. Getting to know and to understand the implications of the brand equity is an important component of the branding or the rebranding exercise. Product and advertising history, package design and format evolutions, brand signatures may have evolved over the lifetime of a brand, and so on. You need to take a deep look at any signal your brand may have sent out to its targets over time and to understand why decisions that led to a message evolution were made.

Sometimes, brands run legendary advertising campaigns or launch an iconic product that becomes part of our collective memory. Advertising refers to all forms of branded communication, offline, online, packaging, PR, or product placement, and so on. These different types of communication or products are of particular interest as they may have had a disproportional impact on the brand equity. It may therefore be useful to research and understand how they may have fashioned the brand image. Working on a brand that was part of the Chanel group, we spent a full day at the Chanel Conservatory in Paris, looking at hundreds of fashion items and accessories that had been created throughout the brand's over 140 years of fashion history. This helped us to better understand the brand's personality and unique style. In branding, thorough observation sometimes is worth more than a 1000 words.

The next area to analyze is the competitive set. To achieve proper differentiation for your brand, you must understand how your competitors are positioned and what the market segment competes on, too. Valuable information on what competitive brands stand for may be found on their websites: the *about* section, or the *vision and mission* statements, for example. Also, the actual brand slogan may provide some leads to identify a competitor's brand positioning. A slogan generally summarizes the brand positioning into a catchy and memorable phrase. If all this still does not provide a clear enough understanding of what a competitive brand stands for, read through its storytelling or research the brand on Google or via an AI tool such as ChatGPT, Gemini, or CoPilot. But be careful because information from chatbots is not always reliable or correct.

Once you have identified and paraphrased the respective positioning statements of each of your brand's competitors, you may start to compare these with the hypothetical positioning of your brand. For this, we generally use a specific branding tool, called the *Competitive Brand Map* (CBM). A CBM allows you to visualize how a given brand is perceived in a market segment relative to its direct and immediate competitors, essentially those who compete for the same consumer. The tool functions with two axes (a horizontal and a vertical axes) and uses attribute clusters to describe the four prevailing positioning dimensions present in any given market and as illustrated by the axes as shown in Fig. 8.2.

For a competitive brand map to provide sensitive intelligence on any given market, the market definition and the corresponding competitive set must be tight. For example, it is virtually impossible to analyze the entire car market in one brand map. Although exceptions may apply, buyers of luxury limousines generally do not shop in the subcompact car category and vice versa. SUV buyers do not necessarily shop for two-seater sports cars, and if they do, they are generally driven with totally different motivations and needs.

**Fig. 8.2** Competitive brand map showing the four prevailing positioning clusters in make-up. Author's own image

Only the direct competitors who compete for precisely the same target consumer should be analyzed and the sole focus of the analysis is not the *product* or *service* offer but the *brand*. In order to use this tool the right way, you need to develop your interpretation of the positioning statement for each of the competitive brands. List them all on one page and then try and see whether you can identify some similarities. Competitive brand positionings may be very distinctive and differentiating while they are still inspired by one and the same overarching user vision.

Let us take a closer look at masstige (mass & prestige) makeup brands, predominantly sold in grocery stores or at beauty specialist outlets such as Sephora. Here, we have Rimmel that claims to give women the *London look*, Maybelline that promises the *New York look*, Bourjois stands for the *Parisian look*, and Yves Rocher that differentiates itself with the *natural look*. All four makeup brands are sharply positioned, each claiming a unique point of difference. At the same time, they all follow a similar *overarching user vision*. All four sell a *lifestyle* look. This means that one dimension of the masstige makeup market is defined by *lifestyle* brands, which all own a discerningly differentiated positioning with supposedly high relevance to its target consumers, as each one offers a look inspired by a different lifestyle. From a business perspective, this means that "lifestyle" is one of the positioning dimensions under which the market currently operates and competes and where significant sales are being generated.

Accordingly, the analysis of the European makeup market allowed us to identify three additional positioning clusters. Opposite to the *lifestyle* dimension, there is the *fashion* brand cluster. Here, all major competitors come from a fashion/haute couture background that legitimizes their makeup competence. Yet each of them differentiates on a distinctive brand positioning in the high-end fashion market. *Expertise* designates the third cluster, as all these competitors come with a distinct makeup or beauty know-how or expertise: either as makeup artists (MAC, Max Factor, Bobby Brown), as color experts (OPI, Essie), as hair stylists (Dessange), or as specialists of sensitive skin (Clinique). Finally, the *glamor* dimension regroups makeup competitors that position themselves around the dimensions of catwalk beauty and elegance (L'Oréal Paris, Revlon, Lancôme). Brands that are positioned toward the center of the map are in no distinct *positioning* position and generally lack differentiation. The placement of the individual brand logos on the map is of course somewhat subjective. It is only meant as an indication and the exact placement may be subject to endless debate, while, at the end of the day, it does not really matter. What does matter, however, are the axes and the brand clusters that constitute them. This is what provides valuable insights and understanding. In this example the makeup market competes on lifestyle, fashion, expertise, and glamor. All four dimensions have proven relevance for consumers, demonstrated by the fact that they already buy from makeup brands that correlate with these dimensions. This information provides a first hint at where your brand might position itself within this market context, considering its own brand choice dynamics. The map also highlights potential white spots, where you see reduced competition. These *white spots* may indicate potential positioning alternatives available to your brand. You now need to check these positioning alternatives against the reality of your product or service brand to see whether you find an attribute that allows you to claim a white spot position on the map.

Competitive brand maps for other than product brands are established in the same way and by the same processes. Besides providing useful market intelligence on the competitive set and the market dimensions in general, the map also exposes areas of opportunity for a future brand positioning. These are the *white spots* that are not yet claimed by any brand. While they do not necessarily suggest that a given brand should position itself in one of these spots, they are worth considering. If a brand's product or service reality offers the features and attributes to claim a position that fits a *white spot*, this positioning might become a serious option.

The profound and detailed understanding of the *product* reality, the way it is sourced, designed, and manufactured, brand heritage and brand equity, the deep understanding of the competitive brand set, all provide important input into the brand positioning exercise. You have got to do your homework first, making sure all relevant data has been sourced and organized for the structured and methodological analysis to follow. This may quite resemble an investigation, where detail after detail is examined and pasted together to create meaning and to map out a potential path toward your future brand positioning.

However, unquestionably the most important data source to consider and to analyze is the target audience. Ultimately, your brand must be highly appealing to it. To assure that this is the case you must understand your customers' needs, beliefs, attitudes, and motivations. As mentioned earlier and seen from a simplified perspective, needs are like problems for which brands are perceived to offer a solution. Brands propose shortcuts for consumers in their decision-making processes by incorporating a given problem/solution equation.

There are multiple ways to find relevant information on your target audience, much of which might already be available in-house. In general, companies possess sociodemographic data about their brand's target audiences. While sociodemographics provide a good basis for a start and the media planning task at a later stage, target information that provides insights on a more behavioral and psychological level is your most valuable asset. Within the actual brand positioning exercise, consumer beliefs, attitudes, preferences, and motivations are more important than age, income, education, or occupation. To understand your target audience in a holistic way, you need to slip into your target's shoes or even better, slip into their skin.

This sociodemographic target data provides a first filter to narrow down the target audience and then approach other more behavioral and psychographic target definitions through generational targeting in a second step. Each generation has been born into a unique social and economic context, which will inevitably have a formative impact on how that generation acts as consumers. Each generation has its own shared values, beliefs, and attitudes toward the world they live in. While Millennials (1985–1998)[1] are considered to be the first generation to consume with a view on the future, GenZ (1999–2010) has never seen a world without the internet and connectivity. Both have grown up

---
[1] Note: There is no unanimous definition for generational target cluster brackets.

in a world considerably different from the one experienced by baby boomers (1945–1964), who were born and raised in the aftermath of WWII period, which was marked by economic growth and radically improving living conditions, but also by great conservatism in many parts of the world. In a certain way, each generation is the product of the events, values, attitudes, and beliefs they experienced during their childhood and teenage years.

There is plenty of information available online to research any of the generational targets still alive and behaving as consumers. From a market perspective, these target definitions present huge potential. In the United States, baby boomers account for roughly 20% of the population, but they own 50% of the wealth. Even at an advanced age, they are in much better shape than any other generation before them and they continue to live to their fullest. Roughly, 10,000 baby boomers currently reach retirement age every day in the United States alone, adding up to 3.65 million new retirees in 2023. They possess great wealth and have plenty of discretionary money to spent. An in-depth understanding of how, for example, baby boomers behave as consumers and what really motivates them will help any brand that aims to target them.

Yet with all the available data, generational targeting remains somewhat generic and anecdotical. Also, it generally is not relatable to any specific product category or brand and therefore provides only transversal insights into broader consumer clusters that are tied together by certain beliefs, attitudes, and behaviors. A way to gain more quantifiable target insights is through psychographic research such as data collected by the globally operating VALS Group. VALS (Values and Lifestyles) assumes that psychological traits in combination with demographics are more powerful for predicting consumer behavior. The research institute defines the following eight profiles: Innovators, Thinkers, Believers, Achievers, Strivers, Experiencers, Makers, Survivors. VALS looks at a given product category with the aim of identifying the prevalent psychological consumer profiles of that category, let us say premium skin care. The methodology then uses a set of 35 tailored questions to research actual and potential consumers of the category. The profiles obtained are then matched against the VALS cluster lifestyle choices, attitudes, values, and beliefs, thus providing deep insights on how each cluster behaves as consumers. Not everyone agrees with this methodology, but there is no doubt that it has its merits in the quest for deeper target understanding, and it provides quantitative information, which many marketing departments prefer over qualitative data, often seen as less reliable. Psychographic insights into target groups simply allow you to gain deeper knowledge that may be leveraged to increase your brand's general appeal.

However, from my experience the most powerful target research methodology is morphological research, first developed by the German Psychologist Wilhelm Salber, Professor at the Psychological Institute of Cologne University. This holistic psychology methodology is founded on Freud's psychology and the theory of Gestalt. The goal of the morphological research methodology is to produce a model of actionable units and functions where all parts can be described according to their connections and interactions with each other (holistic view). It reveals true consumer needs and motivations and allows brands to prognosticate directions they should take in their near future to strengthen market positions and to enhance consumer relevance. This qualitative research method is affordable, quick to implement, and highly efficient in generating deep consumer insights. It has already been discussed in more detail in Chap. 7.

But how about the positioning of an entirely new brand, a start-up company, or a product or service development imagined by internal innovation processes? Unfortunately, little or no target audience information might be available. In this case, a way to gain a first understanding is by looking into the target data of existing brands (your future competitors) in the same category. This can be done by buying scanner data from grocery stores who leverage fidelity cards, for example. These schemes are widely used, and consumers are incentivized to handover their card each time they shop gaining points or dollars for later purchases. Payback, which has a loyalty program in Germany, Austria, and Poland, operates with a similar system. It is independent of any major retailer and can be used in different retail chains. The Payback card allows consumers to accumulate points with each purchase, which can later be exchanged for products from the Payback catalog. Payback is free of charge and the system allows you to register and collect information with an item's barcode.

For the target definition, this loyalty platform offers brands two distinctive advantages. First, the database provides relevant sociographic data on the owner of the Payback card. This information is requested at each opening of a Payback account. Second, the program also allows you to correlate purchases in one product category with other categories where the same shopper also shops. Crisscrossing these different datasets allows you to carve out a fairly solid target definition for any FMCG brand. The same holds true for any kind of proprietary retail loyalty program, except the database to tap into for your target definition will be smaller.

Things are slightly more complex for service brands or destination brands, while B2B and corporate brands define their targets based on a business proposition rather than sociodemographic or psychographic data. Nevertheless, target data for B2C service brands may be obtained from household panel data. Household panels exist in nearly all developed markets around the globe. They allow you to research what products or services consumers buy, in what quantity and frequency, and at which retail channels. The panel contracts consumers from representative households generally for a duration of 2 years. People get paid a certain fee for their participation over this period. Participants are then requested to fill in a detailed personal profile, mainly covering sociodemographics and they are required to scan or manually report any product or service purchase, such as a streaming service subscription or a food delivery. Identifying the households that subscribed or used these services in a given period of time allows you to scan the households and its members based on the initial consumer profile data provided at the start of the program. Once you have pinned down the demographics, you can then follow up with generational data or psychographics just like for product brands.

There are many other sources that hold specific potential for a brand's target definition. Social media and social media listening tools like Brandwatch may provide target information related to a certain product or service category or on the discussions that revolve around specific products, categories, or brands. Google, Statista, or payment service providers such as Square and Stripe also hold data sources to be crossed with others. There are many sources that can be tapped to retrieve target information for brands, if not directly, then indirectly. By crisscrossing data, the user profile of any brand will become quite visible and produce enough leads to commission further research to go even deeper. Sentiment analysis, powered by AI tools, may provide deeper target understanding. It is important to note, however, that all of these sources must be ethical and do not infringe on consumers' privacy rights. Unfortunately, this has not always been the case in the past, especially with leading social media companies.

The importance of truly understanding your target audience is demonstrated with the Bud Light case in the United States. On April 1, 2023, Bud Light ran a brief social media campaign on Instagram using a video produced by the transgender actress and social media personality Dylan Mulvaney. Having recently lost market share, Bud Light attempted to attract a younger audience to the brand. The video highlighted an edition of the Bud Light can with a photograph of Mulvaney printed on it and announced her partnership with the Bud Light brand.

While Bud Light's effort as a brand to recruit younger consumers seems like general practice, its marketing team appears to have worked either in target silos or lacked a thorough understanding of its core target audience (*bull's eye*). The result of this social media campaign turned out to be quite disastrous.

Initial protests came from conservative, anti-transgender groups, quickly followed by several videos posted by influential personalities, showing Bud Light cans being crushed or destroyed. One video showed country singer Kid Rock shooting at Bud Light cans with a MP5 submachine gun, calling for a boycott of not just Bud Light but also AB InBev, Bud Light's parent company. The video quickly went viral and generated over 11 million views in just a few days, bringing more and more people into the conversation around Bud Light. By then, many Bud Light consumers had joined the boycott, leading to devastating effects. By early May, off premise sales were down 26% and volume had decreased by almost 30% toward the end of May. By then the boycott had also affected other Anheuser Busch brands with Bud down 11%.

Deeper insights into their target consumer clearly would have helped protect Bud Light from the events following the initial Instagram post. Psychographics, in particular, would have provided valuable attitudinal insights into Bud Light's core target audience, which might have protected this brand from running a program that went out of control. Clearly, understanding how your core target audience always allows you to make sub-targeting decisions in a more sensitive manner.

## Providing Meaning

Now that most of the relevant data has been sourced, organized, and analyzed, the branding process is at its peak of complexity. The key challenge now is to sort through the data complexity and to start selecting the information that holds the highest potential for brand differentiation: a unique ingredient, a difference in the manufacturing process, a unique recipe, or a special product formulation. If you cannot find uniqueness in the obvious, investigate the details. From experience, there is always something that sets your brand apart. However, this something must be relevant to your target audience or it must allow you to formulate a claim that strongly suggests this relevance. Branding is never an exact science and requires a large dose of creativity and imagination. Often, it is not the detail itself that commands uniqueness and relevance, but the way you refer to it or what you make out of it—ethics preserved.

The main objective in this second phase of the branding funnel is to identify and define your brand's core competence. The one expertise that your brand will become known for and what it will stand for in your specific market segment. Brands must also develop this competence before considering stretching into other market segments using line extensions, for example.

Product attributes or service features, historical milestones in the form of products or campaigns, unique compositions or ingredients, exclusive ingredients, or proprietary production processes, and so on. Anything may provide the input and proof for claiming a unique brand competence. There always is the one element of information that will do the job. However, you must constantly keep all the main balls up in the air: target audience needs, competitive claims, product or service realities, and brand equity.

## From Essential to Essence

This far down the process, a first or maybe even several hypotheses for the future brand positioning will have emerged. This is the time when the new brand positioning options will be tested and tried out with the help of the *brand key* tool (see Fig. 8.3). The brand key has two basic functions. It is a strategic planning tool to define the key dimensions of your brand's DNA and a sort of safe place to keep the brand DNA for yourself or future generations of brand managers. The brand key was initially developed by the Saatchi & Saatchi advertising agency in the United Kingdom. Today, it has become a widely used tool in the branding and rebranding processes. The primary objective of the *brand key*, similar to the *brand ladder* discussed in Chap. 6, is to define the brand essence, which spells out what a brand should stand for. It does so in just one word or one *angle of attack*.

Work on the *brand key* always starts bottom-up, although you may also fill in individual boxes as you move along. However, to develop the final correlations of the *brand key* elements with each other and define your brand logic, the tool is used starting with the root strength, working your way up to the circular part, which is developed by crisscrossing, defining the discriminator, then the benefits followed by the reason to believe and the brand personality and values. The choice of the brand essence comes last and is the logical consequence of all the information included in the *brand key*.

The root strength, as the term suggests, refers to your brand's initial strong point and competence; the one thing that was primarily responsible for its initial success. The original Cadum formula was conceived to counter skin problems like eczema or similar skin irritations. Cadum soap contained cade oil as an ingredient, which was known for its skin soothing properties. Every brand that has been around for a while did build its success on some tangible element: a unique product attribute, a recipe, a geographic origin, a service feature. Initial success, as moderate as it might have been, always comes from one element that set the brand apart and made it attractive to its target audience. Often, that one element turned into the brand competence or a characteristic for which the brand has become known and considered as "best in class."

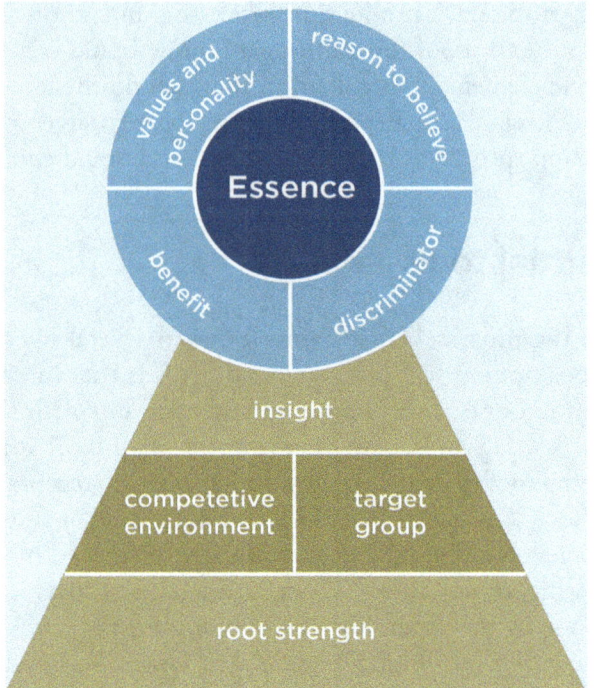

**Fig. 8.3** Standard brand key model. Author's own image

The root strength or core brand competence may not always be built on tangibles. Sometimes a brand's root strength may tap into stereotypes to evoke uniqueness. This is the case for Milka brand that claims authentic Suisse origins. While this is true, the Milka family-owned business was indeed based in Switzerland prior to being acquired by today's Mondelez group; however, this does not make Milka in any way unique. There were and still are many other Swiss chocolate brands that compete against Milka, although maybe not on a global scale. However, the reference of *authentic Swiss made* provided a powerful root strength for the brand. It gave Milka high relevance and universal reach as it allowed the brand to capture and leverage the imagery of Switzerland and the Swiss Alps as a stereotype that comes with very positive imagery. From an operational point of view, Milka's root strength is actively used in its brand universe or territory, which refers to the place or world where or in which a brand lives. Consequently, any brand advertising for Milka is always set in the Swiss Alps.

The next box in the *brand key* is the competitive set. What goes here is a sharp and concise description of your brand's core competitors. This is defined as narrowly as possible according to the competitive brand map exercise discussed above. Only brands that compete directly and frontally with your brand should be considered for this field of the brand key. You either list them all by name or you characterize them by a short description that is to the point.

The target audience comes next. What you use for the brand key is the definition of your core target audience, the *bull's eye* as it is often referred to in branding. This expression generally refers to the most valuable consumer segment for your brand. Those heavy consumers are at the center of each market segment. Your target definition here restates briefly what your target analysis turned up in terms of sociodemographic, generational, and, if possible, psychographic information.

The *insight* box is reserved for behavioral target information. As discussed in Chap. 7, insights refer to needs, aspirations, attitudes, or beliefs commonly shared by your target audience and here, in particular, the *bull's eye*. For example, chocolate is considered a daily *dose of luxury*. Oreo leverages the fact that you do not play with food, thus legitimizing a certain form of transgression via a voluntarily ritualized Oreo consumption. Insights are hard to get by, and often the ones that are visible at the surface of a consumer interface are leveraged by everybody in the category. Nevertheless, these insights are valuable and may serve their purpose. Any competitor is aware of the fact that women believe soap dries out their skin. This has not kept Dove from leveraging this rather banalized insight to build a power brand.

Having defined root strength, competitive set, *bull's eye* target, and consumer insight now allows you to define the brand's *discriminator*. The *discriminator*, as the name suggests, sets the brand apart from all its competitors. It allows the brand to discriminate itself in the market. While this term might sound somewhat awkward, in branding it has by no means any racial connotations. *Discriminator* is undeniably a bit of a harsh word, but it is very precise and focused at the same time, and forces you to really think hard about the one argument your brand will leverage to distinguish itself in the market against all competitors and by offering the highest possible relevance to the target consumer. The discriminator may be a fact or a claim that can be made with the backing of the product's reality. In that sense, it may be tangible or intangible, concrete, or entirely abstract.

The *discriminator* somewhat relates to your brand's unique selling proposition (USP); however, it forces you to push further. Deciding on the discriminator is a challenge and requires a high dose of synthesis. This is the moment where you must mentally run through everything you researched and learned about your brand. The *discriminator* may be a product attribute, a service feature, an element from your brand's heritage or from the brand equity. It may be a simple reference to an origin or a constituent of the recipe. It may be the play factor Oreo has leveraged to ritualize consumption of its sandwich cookies. At times, the discriminator may be similar or even identical to a brand's root strength. This is mostly the case for new brands or those in the process of being created from scratch.

The discriminator is a crucial piece of the brand puzzle. Together with the benefits, it will feed directly into the definition of the brand essence—the one word your brand will stand for. Getting the discriminator right is paramount and, as always, there will be many options. Sometimes it takes several shots before you feel comfortable and reassured that you are building your brand on the right discriminating fact or claim. As always, the best way to choose is by toying with several options to see how they fit with the other elements of the brand key. By the end, all the boxes must communicate among another in perfect logic and coherence: like a little piece of music without false notes.

The reason to believe (RTB) is meant to provide proof of evidence for the discriminator. With all the information gathered and analyzed in the first phase of the *brand positioning funnel*, the RTB is generally rather easy to define. However, in certain cases, you may find that the discriminator and the reason to believe are quite close. This is the case with Milka chocolate, which uses *Alpine milk* as a discriminator and as part of its reason to believe, referring to the claim of using genuine Alpine milk in its authentic Swiss chocolate recipe. However, these cases are rare, and as long as all boxes of the *brand key* remain coherent, this is not really a problem.

The *benefit* box is the next one to be defined. Like in the *brand ladder*, we distinguish between the rational benefit (what the brand does for me) and the emotional benefit (how the brand makes me feel). If you have already worked on the *brand ladder*, you may simply transfer your benefit definitions to the *brand key*. If not, you will need to define your benefits based on the discriminator, and in some cases also the reason to believe.

To make it easier to project yourself into this exercise, you may regard the discriminator as a foundation from where to build your brand promise. The brand promise then translates more easily into the benefits. The brand discriminator of the Dove brand is that it creams your skin while you wash. When the brand was launched by the Unilever parent company back in 1957, this was quite a revolutionary innovation. Never before had soap had the ability to clean and cream at once. Dove achieved this prowess through an entirely new formula, unlike soap. This is also the reason why Dove is referred to as a *beauty bar*. As a matter of fact, from a formulation point of view, it is not a soap and must not pretend to be one. However, given its shape and its utility, this becomes just a detail, which most likely has little relevance with consumers, who continue to perceive Dove as a *soap*.

If Dove discriminates on the *cream while clean* dimension, then its benefits are defined quite easily. Rationally, Dove softens the skin and emotionally this makes women feel more beautiful. By the way, the fact that women feel more beautiful is a consumers insight Dove leveraged at the time of its launch and still does today. Indeed, Dove's brand positioning has not changed over a period of close to 70 years and neither has its advertising for the brand, which still follows the principles of the 1957 launch commercial. As such, the Dove brand is a strong proof of evidence that consistency pays off in branding. Beauty has also become Dove's core competence, which it leverages in its much talked about charitable effort referred to as the *campaign for real beauty*. Indeed, global research commissioned by Dove in the early 2000s had revealed that only 4% of women perceived themselves as beautiful. A devastating finding, pointing finger at the beauty industry, which had over decades set the beauty standards with heavily photoshopped beauty imagery.

Before we look at the brand essence, which defines what the brand stands for, let's look at *brand personality* and *brand values*. These are the only branding dimensions that are a bit less strategic than the others. The brand personality refers to the character and behavioral traits you want to assign to your brand. It defines how the brand expresses itself, interacts with, and relates to its target audience. Brand personality is a way to look at a brand from a human perspective. The role of the brand personality is to create an emotional platform from which consumers or customers can more easily connect and interact with the brand, a bit like if the brand were a person.

To decide on the brand personality, you must imagine how your brand should relate and interact with its target audience and what it will take to make that interaction interesting and lasting. The brand personality will very much depend on the product category your brand competes in. If you sell a pharmaceutical product, your brand should be perceived as knowledgeable and sincere. On the other hand, if you are promoting a soft drink, your brand may assume a more entertaining or even humorous and fun personality, like Pepsi does. The brand personality is defined by two to three adjectives to remain sharp and concise, such as *sophisticated*, sincere, *knowledgeable, humorous, lighthearted, playful, positive*, trustful, and so on.

Defining the brand personality is somewhat subjective. You must just make sure that it stays coherent with the other dimensions of your brand definition in the *brand key* and that it does not contradict them. It must be fully aligned with what your brand stands for. Be that as it may, this exercise is projective, meaning it defines how you want your brand to be perceived from a human perspective in relation to your future brand positioning. Once defined, the brand personality will have an executional impact on all brand communications, including the brand identity. In particular, the brand personality provides the strategic brief for the development of the brand identity (ID) codes such as colors, fonts, signs and symbols, iconography, and the logo. It will also set the tone for all brand communication such as advertising and promotion, storytelling, RP efforts, CSR messaging, employer communication, web design, and wording, all the way to packaging design.

On the other hand, the brand values define what your brand believes in and what it acts upon. Brand values are not empty words and brands must be seen as living up to them in what they say and what they do. There is no exception for this, and the younger consumers in particular are increasingly sensitive to how brands do what they say and say what they do. Transparency, trust, and honesty in branding will no doubt become more relevant in the short- to mid-term, as the recent proliferation of greenwashing strategies has shaped an increasingly critical consumer who uses social media networks to laud or sanction.

The definition of the brand values is strategic and must also be considered in the context of the brand's parent company. Like for the brand personality traits, the values a brand adopts should be limited to three to four. Any higher number would reduce the brand's focus and is likely to make the values less actionable. Within the value mix, there might be one value that connects with the parent company and the other three that are specific to the brand itself. Typical values that brands adopt are *authenticity, respect, caring, people or customer centric, friendliness, reliability, humility, transparency, integrity, inclusiveness, diversity (the latter ones being mostly from the corporate world)*, and so on. The list is endless and the values you pick will in some way define the code of conduct of your brand but also of your company.

Like for the brand personality traits, the values you define for your brand must be coherent with its positioning, reflective of what matters to consumers in the market where your brand competes and achievable in terms of the product or service reality.

Remember that consumers relate and connect with a brand using values (see Chap. 6) and in that sense, there is no difference between a self-expressive value that defines what your brand stands for and the values your brand believes in and acts upon.

Consumers simply bond with brands more easily if they feel closer to them. And what better way to connect and bond than by sharing the same values and beliefs.

The centerpiece of the *brand key* tool is the *brand essence*. It defines what your brand stands for and it does so in just one word or precise and unambiguous angle. The more words you use to spell out the value proposition of your brand, the less sharp and concise it will become and the less direction it will provide to everybody, who at one point will have an impact on the management or your brand. The whole brand key is an exercise of sharpness where less words means more, and the brand essence is the king's way where you should aim to bring the meaning down to just *one word*.

The *brand essence* is the one single, intangible attribute that differentiates the brand from competitors as perceived by its target audiences. It is the brand's fundamental nature or quality and one *constant* across all product categories and throughout the world.

The *brand essence* is what a brand truly owns in its market and against all other competitors. It also defines the brand's competence. The *brand essence* is expressed in one word. It is infinite (the brand essence is sacrosanct, unless you have striking proof and evidence of its weakness).

By now, the brand ladder should have provided valuable input for defining the brand essence. If this is not the case, the essence will be defined in similar steps as prescribed by the brand ladder. The starting point for this is, as already discussed, the product or service reality and here, in particular, the product attribute or the service feature that defined the discriminator and, by extension, also the brand competence. The attribute or feature by itself or translated into a performance claim will establish the discriminator and from there you distill the brand meaning further down, identifying the one word for which the brand will stand and become known to its target audiences over time. As the word suggests, the brand essence defines your brand in its purest sense.

The brand essence becomes most powerful when it is free of any complexity or any thought that pollutes its singular meaning. What differentiates an Oreo cookie (see Fig. 8.4) is that its consumption is ritualized. As a connoisseur, you will not simply take a bite or put the entire sandwich cookie into your mouth but perform certain rituals that the brand and its community have defined and established over time. These rituals seem even more attractive to consumers, as they validate a certain form of transgression in which all Oreo fans unite. Ritualized consumption may take you down several routes in search of the brand essence. It may be *connoisseurship* or *cultivation* because consumers are aware. Or another route may be skillfulness, because you need to showcase your dexterity to properly master and perform everything the Oreo cookie allows you to do. The brand decided on *playfulness*, which appears the most coherent of the above options, as it connects with Oreo's consumer insight. *Playfulness* allows the brand to build tangible, emotional ties with its consumers and since *play* has few limits, it keeps them involved in forever exploring new ones, thus helping keep the brand up-to-date and contemporary.

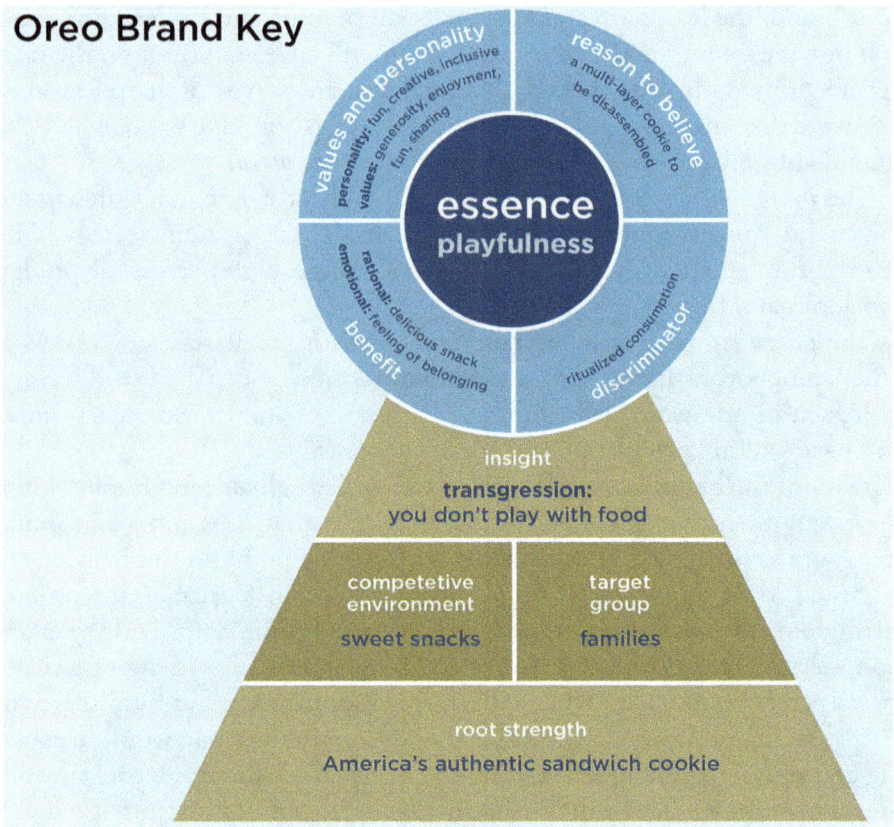

**Fig. 8.4** Post-rationalized Oreo brand key model without original brand input for illustration purposes only. Author's own image

Defining a brand with one word requires three consecutive steps: information mining, analyzing and providing meaning, and then focusing on what is essential to select the brand essence. A massive amount of information is involved in this process, and you need to look at it all. At the start, there is no way of telling which piece of information will be the most valuable one, the one that will allow you to formulate the brand essence in a single word.

As it happens, the biggest challenge brands face is prioritizing the information they have and the claims they can make. The brand positioning consists of isolating the one thing to say that becomes the striker claim to attract consumers. None of the other messages will be lost and, in the process, referred to as brand behavior, all relevant brand claims will be properly addressed, evaluated, and placed or prioritized according to the newly established brand logic.

It does not make a difference if your work on a product or a service brand, a corporate, people, or place brand. The exact same brand positioning funnel methodology and the exact intellectual principles on how to deal with them apply in the same way. Here, success lies in doing your homework, developing curiosity, and applying rigor during the data analysis phase and then connecting the dots until first potential positioning axes emerge. Brand positioning work is not an exact science. No doubt, it relies on proven tools, but these must be used with discipline and creativity to find the best wording that provides the most sense and culminates in a brand logic where everything you have defined so far converges. Again, like a piece of music without false notes.

At the end, and once your brand has been successfully positioned, everything will appear obvious. However, it is the obvious that is hardest to achieve and the best way to look for it is aiming for *the simplicity on the other side of complexity*. And then as always, when you think you are there, the next challenge waits just around the corner. Even well-defined brand positionings, which have been boiled down to a *one-word brand essence*, will still feel somewhat abstract—and quite frankly they are. Everybody can easily see and experience the way Disney stands for *magic*, BMW for *driving pleasure*, or Oreo for *playfulness*. The reason for this is that the positioning of these brands has already been translated into ample communication messages and marketing action.

The brand behavior process always follows the brand positioning exercise and is designed to make the still fledgling and somewhat abstract brand essence actionable and operational. This is a job for the brand owner, who best knows and understands the brand. The process requires a good dose of creativity and demands bringing people on board and behind the positioning. It will be discussed in more detail in Chap. 10.

However, unless you have gathered enough evidence from initial research and before you are sure that all other brand elements also converge to confirm the new positioning, you might want to validate it through an appropriate research process. A first *torture test* always consists in translating your new positioning into a vision and mission statement and to write a brand signature. If this can be done naturally and without great effort, your brand positioning will be suitable to direct the entire marketing, sales, and innovation processes now and in the future. It also indicates that your new brand positioning is clear and understandable. This *operative* capacity is essential—too many brand positioning platforms simply do not live up to these initial performance indicators and, as a result, end up unused and filed away in in the parent company's archives.

In addition, internal feedback is another source for validation. Exposing your work to colleagues in your office and in selected branch offices may provide valuable input on how the brand positioning is perceived and received and whether people can easily follow the new brand logic imposed by it on their individual operative level.

Measuring the relevance of the new brand positioning can be best done through qualitative or quantitative research methodologies. It is important to not only focus on the *what* but also on the *why* during this process. Brand validation research should be designed to reveal what is strong or weak, attractive, clear, and differentiating, but also provide understanding on why the designated target audience perceives it like this.

This far down in the process, differentiation and the logical link between positioning and product or service reality have been checked and approved along the way and as part of the positioning funnel exercise. That being so, any process implying consumer research should focus on verifying that the new positioning has high relevance with your target audiences. This applies to any brand: product or service, people or destination, and corporate or employer brands.

Generally, the *why* is more easily understood in qualitative research and in particular by the morphological methodology. Besides testing a short brand positioning statement, you may formulate a positioning concept for testing. A brand concept generally consists of three short paragraphs and a representative image that helps to illustrate the main brand proposition or promise. The first paragraph states the category insight, a problem your brand will help to solve, or a need it will satisfy. Example: *Everyday, living a modern life exposes all of us to multiple health risks like viruses and bacteria, which challenge our immune defenses.*

Next comes the brand promise and the reason to believe as defined by the new brand positioning. Example: *Actimel helps to strengthen your immune defenses, because each little bottle contains billions of active L. Casei yoghurt cultures, vitamin B6 and D.* The third and last paragraph of the concept states the benefit for the target audience. Example: *One Actimel a day supports your natural immune defenses.*

It is common practice to test up to four alternative qualitative concepts in these research set-ups and besides concepts, you may also use other stimuli like the vision or mission statement, the brand signature, and even a logo or a model packaging for example, in case you have already pushed the brand platform that far.

The development of the brand positioning or the definition of a repositioning platform is a complex exercise. It must be given the appropriate resources and time to perform to professional standards. Its strategic goal is not to run an intellectual exercise but to render brands more differentiated and relevant in their respective market segments and for their designated target audiences. Once finalized and defined by a form of the brand essence, brand positionings must be operative, easy to translate into marketing and sales action. Only then will a brand positioning produce tangible results as measured by lowered costs and increased sales.

# 9

# *One Word* Positioning and Brand Vision, Mission, and Purpose

As already discussed in the previous chapters, consumers engage with brands primarily on an emotional level. While the concrete and tangible performance benefits of any given product or service also play a central role, the latter are rarely evaluated objectively since consumers generally lack the competence to do so. The way a product or service is evaluated holistically by consumers may depend on many factors. Loyal consumers generally express a more favorable opinion toward their brand's performance versus consumers who use the brand only randomly, presumably because loyal consumers are more engaged with their brand. Brand image, previous brand experiences, hearsay, or stereotyped opinions, beliefs, or convictions related to brand symbols or brand messaging may all impact the performance perception of any brand in one way or the other. We have further seen that brand connections may be strengthened by values and beliefs. Brands that appear to share certain consumer values and beliefs may be evaluated more favorably and become preferred over others.

Brand vision, mission, and purpose are brand dimensions that are closely related to values and beliefs that consumers and brands assume alike. They are derived directly from the brand essence. The brand essence, being the purest and sharpest definition of what a brand stands for, becomes the commanding element of all subsequent branding work—vision, mission, and purpose included. Each of them must be conceived in full coherence with the brand essence. Vision, mission, and purpose are all branding parameters that relate to the emotional dimensions of a brand. While vision and purpose may be worked somewhat independently from each other, the brand mission is correlated to the brand vision and spells out how the brand considers acting upon its defined vision.

The brand vision statement expresses in what a brand believes in relation to its field of activity, while the brand mission statement lays out how the brands will transform these beliefs into action. The brand purpose statement is somewhat treated apart, as it generally refers to the larger contribution a brand may be making to better society, using its unique brand competence. The French construction company Saint Gobain defines its corporate brand purpose as *making the world a better home*. To sustain this purpose, the brand leverages its 350-year-old expertise and competence in the construction industry to propose more sustainable and comfortable homes and office spaces, which address pressing environmental issues of today and tomorrow and aim to improve the overall quality of life of people who will be living in the spaces the company builds. Saint Gobain's *purpose* statement is formulated in a clear and meaningful manner to its target audiences. At the same time, it provides strategic direction for the company as a whole and for everybody working inside but also for suppliers and external service providers.

Looking at a wider number of brands, no matter what type or what industry they operate in, you quickly realize that brand vision, mission, and purpose are often used interchangeably, and in a way that is not quite clear-cut. There is ample evidence of some confusion about the concept of these branding dimensions, and you may repeatedly find a presumed *vision statement* that refers to the *brand mission* instead.

There are two ways to look at brand vision, either to express a brand's view on the future of its field of expertise, or by defining *its philosophical* view on its target audience's life. Both generate a visionary message that offers consumers a platform for identification. Over time, the Swedish furniture brand IKEA employed both definitions toward its brand vision. At its very beginnings, IKEA was built on the vision of its founder Ingvar Kamprad who believed that nice furniture design should be affordable. The opposite is true in the furniture business still today and genuine designer furniture generally commands prices that makes it inaccessible to average income households.

IKEA lived by its vision designing, manufacturing, and selling its furniture in a revolutionary new way. Strictly speaking, IKEA is a private label brand that does not sell any other branded furniture or accessories in any of its worldwide store outlets but IKEA. IKEA designs furniture for its functionality and style, eliminating a huge portion of the costs by adopting what is generally referred to as *flat packaging*. This manufacturing concept automatically shifts the responsibility for the assembly of a piece of furniture to the customer. This clever idea helped IKEA to keep manufacturing, transportation, and warehousing costs low, a cost saving that IKEA partly hands over to its target audiences. However, price is not the only motivational driver in the

IKEA business model. Recognition and pride for putting their newly purchased furniture together on their own is another nonmonetary value, which is actively leveraged by the brand: a phenomenon also widely used in Home Depot DIY brands.

Clever product but also service design caters to a consistently excellent shopping, assembling, and usage experience. Building on its original brand vision of *designer furniture made affordable*, IKEA has since evolved toward a new, restated brand vision statement: *to create a better everyday life for the many people*. While somewhat related to the original statement, the actual one feels more like a *mission* or *purpose* statement. It describes what IKEA strives for on a day-by-day basis, but it no longer expresses a belief or philosophical thought like the original *brand vision* statement. IKEA is not an exception. When you look at corporate websites, you will find many other examples and it quickly becomes evident that in daily praxis the definition of brand vision, mission, and purpose are not as sharp as they could be.

In the one-word branding process, everything a brand claims is derived and connected to the brand essence. Once the brand essence is defined, it commands all the other core brand dimensions: values, personality, the visual identity, all forms of messaging, including the brand vision and mission. Deriving the brand *vision* directly from the brand essence helps to keep it simple and fully consistent with the latter. A brand essence translated directly into a brand vision provides a much stronger emotional push to connect with the brand's target audience. If the IKEA brand, as most likely is still the case, stands for affordable design (not just furniture but by now also home accessories), then defining a brand *vision* in which IKEA claims to believe that designer furniture should be accessible to everybody makes for a much more tangible *vision* statement, which is meaningful and relevant for IKEA's target audience. It also offers another dimension for target audiences to connect and bond with the brand.

By defining and using a *vision* statement, a brand claims and defends its own view on the market that helps to underscore its differentiation in relation to its competitive set. Simultaneously, it signals a strong engagement by the brand to provide a tangible overall benefit to its target audience. Consequently, any brand *vision* statement should be derived directly from the brand essence and formulated as a philosophical expression of what the brand believes rather than stressing its larger business *purpose*. A brand vision built on the brand's beliefs is mostly emotional, while the one that is built on how the brand sees its future is primarily rational. In this sense, the IKEA brand would also benefit from rethinking its current vision statement. *Creating a better everyday life for the many people* just feels less sharp and less differentiating than its original brand vision of *design should be affordable,* which also imbeds a slight dose of militantism.

In the end, it may also be for this subtle militant tonality that employees and consumers alike engage and bond easier with a brand. Brand tonality, by definition, is an emotional driver in branding, too. As a matter of fact, other successful brands such as Walmart in the United States or the French retailer Leclerc, which both claim and defend everyday low prices (EDLP) in their grocery stores, have developed a somewhat similar brand vision like IKEA did at its roots. Today Walmart still claims everyday low prices as its corporate strategy, while defining its brand vision as creating a better world. Now, how differentiating is that? On the other hand, Leclerc has remained faithful to its original brand vision and with a particular outspoken tonality of militantism, it still defends *everything that is important to you*—a vision that in praxis has gone beyond everyday low prices to now also include societal topics. This shows that a sharply defined brand vision is by no means narrow and limiting but it does offer plenty of scope for stretch. We talked earlier about the freedom provided by a tightly defined strategy. It applies equally to the brand vision statement.

The brand mission statement simply translates the brand vision into a brand *action* statement. IKEA believes that designer furniture should be affordable (brand vision) and acts everyday to provide well-designed furniture and accessories to its target audiences at affordable prices (brand mission). The vision states what the brand believes, the mission what the brand does. On a *philosophical* level, Nike believes that if *you have a body, you are an athlete* (*brand vision*) while operationally Nike focuses its efforts on *bringing inspiration and innovation to every athlete* (brand mission). Zoom, the video conferencing service platform, believes *that human connections should be limitless.* It defines its mission as *helping people to connect, collaborate, and get more work done, together.* Google's brand vision falls into the category of vision statements that represent a brand's view of the future. Contrary to Nike, its brand vision is less about a *philosophical* belief. From the outset, Google aimed to *organize the world's information and to make it universally accessible and useable.* Formulated like this, the original brand vision becomes almost interchangeable with the *mission* statement. Like many big and successful brands, Google does not seem to distinguish brand vision and mission, and has opted to just focus on one of them. IBM's vision is to *make the world work better,* while IBM defines its mission as *bringing together all the necessary technology and services to help our clients solve their business problems.*

*Making the world work better,* formulation-wise, also gets close to being considered as a brand *purpose* statement. It refers to IBM's societal contribution, and it leverages the brand's core competence as the reason to believe. This is just another example of the subtle differences between these three brand dimensions. In praxis, the lines are fine indeed, and it will be up to you to decide for your brand and yourself what makes most sense related to the context and its complexity in which you are operating.

By now, the above examples have provided some illustration for meaningful and actionable vision and mission statements as part of the branding process. Both are not just *nice to haves*, but essential elements of any brand definition. They are instrumental in verifying that a brand essence lends itself to be translated into action and are a first torture test for taking your newly positioned brand from the strategic level to a more operational one. In particular, the brand vision statement, like the brand essence, will provide tangible input for the development of the corporate strategy and provides orientation to internal audiences. Correctly defined and formulated, both the vision and the mission statements provide a theme or motto that brings people together and behind one and the same idea.

To develop these statements in a meaningful and effective manner, there are several things to consider:

- They must be written in a short and concise sentence. Evian believes in living a *young life*—all life. This is best expressed by its brand signature *live young*, which by itself feels like a vision statement. Saint Gobain defines its brand purpose as *making the world a better home*. Both statements are simple and straight to the point.
- They should be single-minded, proposing just one claim or thought. The brand vision statement will be derived from the brand essence, the brand purpose statement from the brand competence. Nike stands for *empowerment*. This brand essence is closely related to Nike's vision in which the brand claims to believe that *everyone with a body is an athlete*. There is total intellectual coherence between Nike's brand essence (empowerment) and its vision statement. The brand has succeeded to translate its brand vision into an arresting and memorable statement, which has become a central pillar of the brand's narrative and storytelling. Its mission statement picks up on the same single-minded logic. *Bringing inspiration and innovation to every athlete* simply describes how Nike empowers people.
- Make sure the vision, mission, and purpose statements are actionable. There is no point in claiming something your brand or your organization cannot deliver. A simple claim without follow-through action might backfire and ultimately hurt your brand. Google *organizes information and makes it accessible and useable* by constantly perfecting its Panda search

algorithm. The brand has been focusing on this right from the start and holds on it until today.
- In that same sense, stay away from overambitious claims. What your vision or mission statement claims must be perceived as credible and realistic in daily operations. Your brand's vision or purpose statements should reflect what your brand stands for and this must be honest and credible.
- Make sure all three statements are relevant to your target audiences. A brand essence that is perceived as irrelevant to its target audience is not worth much. The same holds true for the vision, mission, and purpose statements directly derived from it. Their job is to connect your brand with its targets, and to get them involved and over time engaged with the brand. With many brands vying for consumers' attention every day, only those that have something relevant to say may be noticed and considered.
- Write your vision, mission, and purpose statements to reflect your brand personality. Most consumers will evaluate them as messages coming from your brand, and the way they sound and the feelings they produce will engage your target emotionally. With a little dose of militantism, your brand might be perceived as more determined and engaged. This may further motivate your target consumers and contribute to federating them behind the brand.

*Brand vision, mission, and purpose* statements are a central part of the strategic brand messaging. They are instrumental in getting consumers to relate and bond with brands. Not by themselves but through brand communication where *vision, mission, and purpose* provide sensitive input and direction for your brand's storytelling efforts. Storytelling is as old as branding itself; however, it has only been recently rediscovered and since turned into a marketing hype. Remember, we have all grown up listening to stories and still use stories for most of interactions in our social lives. Social media platforms have created the perfect channels to cater to people's desire for storytelling in words, images, and sounds. Personal and highly emotionalized storytelling produces effective brand reach and has become a key lever in the development of brand awareness.

# 10

# Brand Positioning and Brand Behavior: Successfully Translating Brand Positioning into Marketing Action

Now that the brand essence has been defined and translated into a brand vision, mission, and/or purpose statement, the next step consists of taking the new brand positioning to the operational level. This indispensable step englobes all brand activities that are referred to as *brand behavior*. The brand behavior phase is about transferring the meaning of the brand essence into every single action taken by the brand now and in the future: marketing, advertising, promotion, sales, innovation, CSR programs, to quote just a few. Every activity and interaction between the newly defined brand and its target audiences will be guided by what the brand now stands for with its *one-word brand essence*.

In the process of defining the brand essence, we have leveraged deep consumer insights from sociological or morphological research sources. This has provided a highly relevant understanding of the needs, beliefs, and preferences of the brand's designated target audiences. And we have applied powerful branding tools such as the *brand map*, the *brand ladder*, and the *brand key* to define the brand positioning by a razor-sharp brand essence, distilling the brand meaning down to *one single word* or angle of attack. This single word will now become the *prism* through which all brand activities will be seen, evaluated, and enacted. The brand essence functions like a road map and measurement stick at the same time, guiding and directing all operational activities surrounding the brand. Every idea or initiative is matched with and evaluated against the brand essence and only those that fully strategically conform are turned into action.

At first sight, this may seem like a major constraint. This is not the case, and the approach simply leverages the *freedom provided by a tightly defined strategy*.

The essence defines the brand's single-minded meaning, from which you must shape all communication messages or other forms of brand expression. Seen as a concept in branding, the *one-word* brand positioning may seem like a methodology; however, it is foremost a way of reasoning where facts and logic, focus, and the quest for simplicity converge. Through the distillation process, which runs in the background of any brand positioning project, the meaning of a brand is successively reduced to its most essential denominator where one single-minded claim is sufficient to differentiate the brand in a relevant and pertinent way for its target audiences. In the *one-word* branding process, we look for the biggest denominator and not the smallest common one.

The *one-word* brand essence is by no means reductive. It simply prioritizes the *one* brand message that counts the most over all others with the objective of positively impacting the purchase decision-making process; no matter how impulsive or reflected, simple or complex, light or scrutinizing it may be. Throughout the distillation phase of the *brand positioning funnel*, every potential brand message is considered and assigned its distinctive place within the brand's message hierarchy, and nothing is lost. This approach provides a fluid brand narrative, which is coherent and tailored to the defined brand logic. In such a brand narrative, each relevant message finds its designated place in the overall message mix.

Unlike some brands those defined by one single word function with a holistic concept that facilitates shortcuts in consumer decision-making processes. As such, brands are cognitive facilitators where the brand equity or, in other words, the sum of opinions consumers hold about the brand may significantly direct and shorten the evaluation and decision-making process. For impulse purchases or complex high-involvement purchases alike. As research has shown time and time again, most of our decision-making is triggered by emotions. A well-defined brand essence translates the brand reality into an emotional claim to which the target audience may easily relate or identify with, leading to an emotional bond with the brand. There is no better decision-making *shortcut* than the one triggered by emotions.

Brand preferences, engagement, or even bonding are generated by emotional factors, even if these may have partly been formed by rational input and seemingly objective experiences. However, all these effects are rarely the result of the brand essence itself, but of its strict and precise application in the brand messaging over time. It is the brand essence that produces this consistency, as every message and every action a brand takes becomes strategically aligned. Each time a new communication tool is conceived, the sense of the brand essence, and not necessarily the actual word, is captured and transcribed. BMW stands for *driving pleasure* but rarely claims this outrightly. However, its brand essence is well captured in its brand signature: *the ultimate driving machine*. Most of the time, BMW's only plays off its brand essence but does not refer to it literally.

Translating the brand positioning into brand behavior is a creative process, and in a certain way the brand essence becomes the *creative brief*. It is the brand essence that steers the form and format of every single brand message or brand activity to produce a totally coherent and consistent mix. Writing the brand vision, mission, and/or purpose statements represents a first torture test to see whether the brand essence can be turned into a tangible *brand behavior*. I have come across many branding and rebranding projects where the final and validated essence remained too abstract and was never acted upon. Defining the brand positioning is a high stakes process, which makes it complex, and sadly also often political. The brand positioning statement that emerges from these processes or the brand essence itself are anything else than *essential*. The problem is that this makes them *non-actionable*, and many of them end up filed away in the company archives. Developing a brand positioning under these circumstances is clearly unproductive. Significant internal resources will have been tied up over months and important sums have been paid out to external service providers, all without producing a workable result.

This is not really a surprise. In traditional branding processes, many hands get involved. Most frequently run by the marketing team or the human resource department in the case of corporate, employer, or B2B branding, often too many other important decision-makers within the parent company also get involved: from the management board to the sales team, from divisional leaders to legal departments, from central structures to regional or local ones. The bigger the organizations, the more complexity it generates. Things are even worse when Mergers and Acquisitions (M&A) have been a company's lifeline for multiple years. All too frequently acquired corporate entities are integrated mainly on financial and productive grounds while company culture and cross market branding strategies frequently take much longer to converge. While this is understandable because of fear of losing the grip on local market positions, or local talent that might turn away if the inherent cultural shock is too severe or if liberties at the local level get reduced in more significant ways. There are hundreds of these highly fragmented holding companies or groups, predominantly B2B, and they frequently struggle to agree on a commonly defined brand positioning for the above reasons.

These are lost opportunities because any corporation, no matter what the size or organizational structure, would benefit from a sharply defined essence for the group or the corporate brands. Danone's active health umbrella brand positioning is a standing proof for this. Any company, small or large, gains from curating an internal company culture to foster loyalty, motivation, and productivity. A well-defined brand essence perfectly translates into a theme or motto that helps to do just that. *Active health* provided the corporate philosophy and theme that gave everybody at Danone a reason to believe in the company and its values, identify with a common and honorable higher goal, much more attractive than just producing and selling dairy. The embedded purpose in *active health* certainly had a positive impact on employee motivation and productivity. The corporate brand essence serves as a foundation to also define the employer brand, as we will see in Chap. 15.

Complexity in the brand development process is counterproductive. Strong brands have opted for the *simplicity on the other side of complexity* to define what they stand for. However, complexity has another awkward side effect. It stands in the way of sense and meaning. Complexity obscures what direction a brand should take and, by the same token, it stands in the way of formulating clear, coherent, and relevant brand messages to recruit or bond with new target audiences. In complex set-ups, everything is free-ranging, and ego-driven opinions may often prevail over input, which is solely motivated by the quality and the efficacy of final result … to strengthen the brand equity and increase sales. There is a term for this particular and frequent mindset: the *not invented here syndrome* (NIH). Regardless of its benefits, an idea that is not generated inside the organization or even inside a particular department or team is rejected. Often, NIH inflicted companies work in silo structures with different levels of team isolation. It is easy to understand how these structures miss out on efficiency and productivity.

And there is yet another downside to corporate complexity in branding. Many people get involved, many more opinions are listened to, and everybody, sometimes only for political reasons, has something to say in the process. Needless to say, this makes things again more complex, and it lowers the chances of the data distillation process succeeding. This is why branding agencies repeatedly struggle to provide meaning and why, more than once, the final and approved corporate brand positioning statement is a long shot from being simple, sharp, and actionable. Crafted to please everyone that counts, these positionings become impossible to execute and to transcribe into brand behavior actions. Of course, all decision-makers must be brought on board, but you should do so once you have been through a large portion of the brand positioning funnel. Their input is valuable for any branding expert, but it is even more so after the initial brand positioning routes have been identified and distilled down.

Too much complexity surrounds corporate, place, and political branding projects and things are generally easier for brand positioning work on products, services, and personal branding. This helps the brand behavior process, too. Not only are there fewer minds to listen to and to consider, but the brand essence also is often more tangible and concrete. Nevertheless, the *brand behavior* process remains challenging and the risk that the new brand positioning might be watered down in the attempt to take it to the brand behavior level remains real.

To successfully define the brand behavior from the brand essence, the best way to succeed is to start with the brand identity (ID). The brand identity defines the visual codes your brand will use under all circumstances in its efforts to build awareness and equity with its defined target audiences. Depending on the brand, these codes may be straightforward or very diversified; however, they must all be defined in total coherence with the brand essence, the brand values, and the brand personality, as laid out in the validated *brand key*. Remember, the brand key holds your brand's DNA, and it represents the best point of reference for the definition of each step in the *brand behavior* process.

Your brand's essence, values, and personality provide tangible guidance to develop the brand identity: primary and secondary colors, fonts, symbols, signs, or pictograms, the key visual, the logo, the brand signature, the brand iconography, and territory. It is easy to imagine that these ID codes may differ substantially if you work from a brand essence of *empowerment* (Nike) versus one that refers to *glamor* (L'Oréal Paris). A second indicator is your brand personality, also defined by the brand key tool. It has an impact on colors and shades, on the fonts you chose, and on the iconography that defines your brand's universe and its mood or ambiance. While remaining coherent with the brand essence, the brand ID codes also reflect the brand personality. Once established, the brand identity is generally summarized and laid out in detail by what we call the *brand book* or the *brand guidelines*. This brand guidebook provides precise directions for the strategic role of the brand ID and how it must be applied.

Defining the brand ID is a subjective exercise and requires some interpretation. Fonts, signs, and symbols are conceived in line with the definition of the brand personality as defined in the brand key. These elements may seem of minor importance; however, they all contribute to bringing the brand to life. A bold, square font evokes different emotions than an elegant light font, inspired by a handwritten style. Organic shapes for symbols and signs produce different feelings than rectangular or square ones.

Colors also have a meaning and there is ample research on color theory to help you make the right decisions. The meaning of colors might not be identical in all cultures. Especially when you consider building an international or even global brand, color and words matter in the individual cultural context of each market you plan to target. In general, red is associated with energy, passion, and strength. In the occidental world, red is also associated with alerts and warnings. It easily stands out and has strong impact, probably one reason why it is used in traffic signage around the world. In China, red is associated with prosperity and luck. On the opposite scale, blue is an appeasing color, seen as more conservative and associated with reliability and trust. Light blue has become established as the male gender color code or as the dominant color of the reduced fat dairy market or personal care for sensitive skin. White is associated with purity and innocence in most Western cultures, while in oriental cultures, white is the color associated with death and grief.

Wordings are also important. Brand names and words might provoke different meanings from what was initially intended—sometimes with heavy consequences. Initially introduced as the Honda Fit, this passenger car steered up some turmoil in Scandinavia and was quickly rebranded Honda Jazz. Fit being associated with *fitta*, Scandinavian slang for female gentiles. Electrolux, the Swedish vacuum cleaner brand, launched its brand in the United States by using a literal translation of its local slogan: *nothing sucks like an Electrolux*. While grammatically correct, it did not quite communicate the intended message. Motel One Group, a striving German budget hotel chain, just expanded to the United States. Motel One hotels offer great value rooms in central city locations. When the company decided to launch its first US hotel in New York, the brand name was adapted to *Cloud One*. The company was afraid that potential clients might simply expect a parking slot right at the hotel's doorsteps had they launched in the United States under *Motel One*.

The on-street car rental service *MILES* in Germany recently experienced a nationwide vandalism campaign, originating in the German capital Berlin. Wherever a car or van was parked on a quiet street, people rubbed off the lower horizontal line of the letter *E* to transform the *MILES* brand name into the word *MILFS* as shown in Figs. 10.1 and 10.2. Admittingly, this is a tough one to foresee during the naming process. Given the speed and reach of communications today, a creative initiative like this one may spread and scale up faster than any brand can counteract. Also imagine what AI-powered tools are already capable of realizing today or in a few years from now. This makes you want to run your brand name through these AI-powered chat platforms before deciding on its final shape.

MILES reacted swiftly and turned this apparent weakness into a strength. Instead of sitting out the social media buzz gone viral that had indeed quickly gained all major cities in Germany, with more and more MILFS cars turning up in the urban landscape, MILES asked its LinkedIn community for

**Fig. 10.1** MILES rental vans with the official logo. Permission: .fount/Anthony Molina

**Fig. 10.2** MILES rental vans with the vandalized logo. Permission: .fount/Anthony Molina

comments and ideas. Rather than fighting this form of vandalism or brand logo tempering, the brand embraced it and turned it into a significant communication campaign, which did a great job to build awareness for the MILES brand. Lots of ideas were posted on MILES social media accounts and for many, the *vandalized* brand name has become what customers now use when they refer to a mobility rental. Besides demonstrating a sense of humor, which helped to further emotionalize the MILES brand, its attitude toward this form of vandalism mobilized many people to actively engage with the brand as the examples in Figs. 10.3, 10.4 and 10.5 illustrate.

Beware of local brand signature adaptations. Translated too literally, they often miss their point, and it is wiser to allow the local version to translate freely, by insisting on preserving the signature's sense and conceptual meaning. Pepsi's *come alive with the Pepsi generation* campaign signature ended up naïvely translated into Chinese as *Pepsi brings your ancestors back from the grave*. Today, powerful translation software partly driven by AI may have become an effective protection shield; however, glitches still happen in

**Fig. 10.3** Idea from the MILES LinkedIn community proposing tangible solutions to respond to the logo vandalism. Permission: Miles GmbH, Berlin, Germany. Author: Nick Denecke

**Fig. 10.4** Idea from the MILES LinkedIn community proposing tangible solutions to respond to the logo vandalism. Permission: Miles GmbH, Berlin, Germany. Author: Michael Pfeiffer-Belli

international branding and the adaptation processes. It is all too human to look the other way after a beloved brand name or slogan has been approved instead of having it turned down by some cultural issue in some place far away. In today's global world, no place is far enough away anymore.

Other brand clues like key visuals may also bear risks of being culturally offensive. A while back, Gerber launched its baby food in African markets, using the original US label featuring the iconized Gerber baby on the label. At the time, common local package goods predominantly featured the product ingredients on their labels… I leave you to your own conclusions. There are many cultural traps to watch out for when you work in international or global branding, even today and with all the possibilities you have to double-check.

**Fig. 10.5** Idea from the MILES LinkedIn community proposing tangible solutions to respond to the logo vandalism. Permission: Miles GmbH, Berlin, Germany. Author: Gostaf Mandel

At this stage, brand signature, iconography, and brand universe deserve some more detailed attention to define their precise role in the brand universe. The brand signature or alternatively the brand slogan translates the brand essence into a catchy advertising phrase, which is both easy to understand and to recall. However, this does not necessarily mean that a large percentage of your target audience will ever memorize your brand signature or slogan. If you do the test yourself, you will see it is hard to even cite ten brand slogans of any brands you might know spontaneously.

The true role of the brand signature is multifaceted. As creative interpretation of the brand essence, it will over time contribute to developing the brand equity. It may also help to build brand awareness, as it adds meaning to the brand name. Meaning contextualizes otherwise abstract messages and makes them more memorable. However, the foremost role of the brand slogan is to serve as a *jumping board* in your brand story. It is here where it is most effective. Sticking with Nike as an illustration, its brand slogan *just do it* connects directly with the brand's *vision (everybody with a body is an athlete)*. It also relates to the brand mission that claims that Nike *provides inspiration and innovation to all athletes to find their own, personal greatness*. In this example, brand slogan, brand vision, and mission all logically tie together to tell a consistent and coherent story—like a little music without false notes.

*Brand territory* and *iconography style* define the *living space* that a brand aims to occupy and through which differentiation is communicated visually. You may understand *the brand territory* like the *place where the brand lives* and the iconography style as the brand's dominant visual signature. The Rolex brand *lives* in the territory of luxury sports (see Fig. 10.6), while Red Bull leverages the *world* of adrenaline and extreme sports (see Fig. 10.7) for its brand territory. Apple has decided on a white tech space (see Fig. 10.8).

**Fig. 10.6** Rolex luxury sports brand territory. Permission: Rolex, Geneva, Switzerland, @Rolex/Ashley Neuhof

**Fig. 10.7** Red Bull extreme sports brand territory. Permission: David Sodomka, www.davidsodomka.com

The brand territory is always defined together with the iconography style. This englobes not only photography but also illustrative styles for signage, symbols, or pictograms, which all are part of the brand identity. Brand territory and iconography style are primarily defined by the brand personality. However, both will also be checked against the brand essence and brand

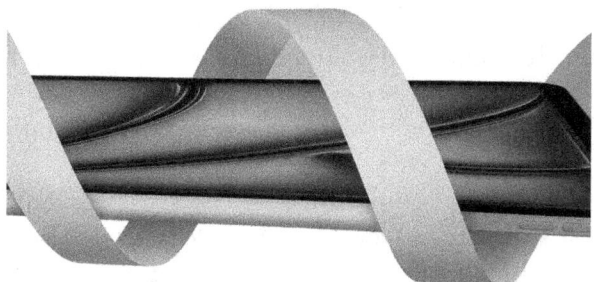

**Fig. 10.8** Apple tech white space. Author's own image

values. As visual elements of the brand identity, they support the brand memorization. This makes brand territory and iconography an important pillar of the brand behavior process.

The *brand universe* refers to the *ecosystem* that a brand develops with the goal to engage its target audiences. It includes all communication tools, messages, channels, and target audience touch points, and may also cover partnerships and cooperations. This *ecosystem* forms the structural tissue of the brand behavior exercise. As mentioned before, the brand equity is no longer exclusively shaped by what brand owners want it to be. Increasingly, consumers contribute to the brand equity with their opinions and experiences. This represents an important paradigm shift that any brand universe must account for. It also implies that the *consumer experience* both offline and online assumes a much more holistic role in today's branding. Personal opinions about a respective brand are increasingly leveraged to influence others, mostly randomly but on larger scale through social media conversations. The dimensions of the consumer experience have also evolved. Initially confined to the product or service reality, it now extends well beyond to include social, environmental, ethical, philanthropic, and even economic responsibilities. These ethical and moral aspects required for a sustainable approach to branding will be discussed further in Chap. 18.

The above elements of the brand identity are the first to be defined in the brand behavior process. They are straightforward and relatively easy to conceive and are all informed by the brand key. In the process of developing and defining them, you have probably turned your design agency into an ambassador of the newly defined brand. A first important ally who intimately understands the new brand positioning and is capable of transforming it into the first workable tools. Training the people who will work on the brand, internally and externally, is important to build a community of experts, who fully understand and internalize the brand positioning. They are the ones skilled enough to provide meaningful contributions, fully aligned with what the brand stands for. To build the new brand positioning into a powerful federating tool, everybody on the inner or the outer working circle should be converted into a brand ambassador who consciously imagines, decides, and acts by leveraging the *brand essence* as a *prism*.

Nevertheless, the brand ID is just the tip of the iceberg. Following the successful definition of the brand identity, other communication messages must be conceived: your brand narrative and storytelling concepts, advertising, and promotion campaigns. Again, your role as a brand guardian will be to manage these creative processes and to make sure every member of your team genuinely understands what your brand stands for. Even at this advanced stage, the brand positioning, although well-defined, might still feel somewhat abstract, not only to the others but also to yourself. This is totally normal and nothing to worry about. These perceptions will naturally fade over time as the brand continues to express itself with a growing array of communication tools, feedback, and fresh creative input for future actions. In sum, this brand activity constantly challenges the core brand message that naturally nourishes the process of interpreting it.

In the *one-word* brand positioning methodology, every building brick of the brand universe must be defined relating back to the brand essence. This is a creative process and the challenge is to find the words that genuinely describe the sense of the brand essence, looking at it from different angles and working on it for different objectives.

Step by step, new experiences produced by this process will provide more reassurance and serenity for the evaluation of new ideas or developments in domains of activity that have not been touched or managed before.

For this to happen swiftly, developing some kind of advertising format is the right thing to do. Advertising will oblige you to push out the new positioning directly to the target audience. This should significantly help you render the brand positioning more concrete and tangible. It will also bring on board more creative talent, experienced to work with the concept of the brand essence and skilled to translate it into impactful and relevant messages that will hit a nerve with the target audience.

The objective here is to develop and produce an *organizing brand idea*. A creative concept with transversal potential to be used across the brand's entire marketing activities—online and offline. A sort of *motto* or *theme* that may be used prominently on all communication tools and is selected to shape the marketing plan. By means of an *organizing brand idea*, every single *consumer touch point* identified in the communication mix carries the same identical message in visuals and words, thus simultaneously delivering message frequency and absolute message consistency.

Identifying these touch points is the job of the *journey map*. The journey map is conceived through research, observation, and with common sense. It aims to identify the decisive phases within the consumer or customer decision-making process. It looks at gain points (positive experiences) and pain points (negative ones) and generally provides a contemporary (real) and future (ideal) perspective. Some journey phases may be common across all products, services, or industries while others are case specific. Journey maps distinguish between phases such as awareness, consideration, evaluation, purchase, trail, and post-trail. They concentrate on the moments of truth, those decisive decision-making moments inside the journey and track consumer behavior and perceptions for every journey step. Journey maps are best built by service designers, generally highly specialized product designers. Like so many aspects in branding, journey maps are, by definition, consumer/customer-centric and heavily reliant on research to identify corelated needs and motivations.

*Design thinking* is a branding discipline that is commonly associated with the journey map. While this was possibly the case in the early days when the California design agency IDEO and one of its founders, David Kelly, developed and popularized the concept. Since design thinking has proliferated beyond the design competence where many service providers claiming it are not always fully skilled to deliver it. This is not to suggest that all agencies specializing in *design thinking* deliver poor results, but I recommend you take a closer look before hiring one to work on your projects.

The journey map might be particularly useful for service brands, where the actual journey on which consumers embark to place an insurance claim, for example, or to make an online purchase is analyzed and evaluated to identify key pain points and areas for improvement. A well-designed journey map may deliver detailed input to develop and ensure a positive user experience that may extend well beyond the initial product or service usage. Not just for the purchase-decision-making process but also covering core phases of the post-purchase experience.

Integrated marketing communications (IMC) is an effective concept to build brands more quickly than more fragmented marketing techniques. Not only does IMC help to save costs, but it also assures optimum message consistency. Brand awareness and brand equity develop through message consistency and repetition. As marketers have little choice but to hand part of their brand control over to highly connected and increasingly influential consumer communities, preserving the remaining control and vying for strict consistency regarding all *push* messages is becoming more critical.

The brand behavior process expands well beyond brand identity and brand communication to also include sales and innovation. Promotional messages and offers all contribute to the consumer journey and require the same message consistency, derived from the brand essences. The Milka chocolate brand, owned by the US-based Mondelez Group, stands for *tenderness*. Milka's brand essence is anchored in its product reality, a recipe with Alpine milk. While milk sourced from one place, or another might not have a perceivable impact on the mouthfeel of a chocolate, the stereotyped imagery that consumers hold for the Swiss Alps nourished by its preserved and lush landscapes supports the claim or *tenderness*. *Tenderness* is what Milka stands for the Swiss Alps brand territory and the Lila cow is what makes the Milka brand recognizable.

In an effort to target young adults, less open to assume and express tenderness, Milka launched a European integrated marketing campaign (IMC) in 2013 where Milka's *tenderness* brand essence was translated into an organizing brand idea to span across advertising, promotion, and press relations. *Dare to be tender* became the motto that was also adapted to a massive in-store promotion effort. For this, Milka again leveraged a stereotyped consumer insight, playing off the belief that the best piece of chocolate always is the last one. In a challenging industrial process, Milka cut the legendary last piece of chocolate out of millions of chocolate bars, allowing consumers to claim it back via the promotion website or alternatively have it sent to a loved one as a gesture of *tenderness*. This highly successful IMC campaign literally translated the Milka brand essence into an organizing brand idea, allowing the brand to act in total consistency while projecting a contemporary and innovative brand image.

Every single innovation project and all continuous research and development (R&D) activities are also bound to conform with the strategic lead of the brand essence. For in-house and outsourced assignments alike. Over the years, Milka has line extended its chocolate offer, entering many new market segments from ice cream to salty snacks and from confectionary to cookies. Each new category has offered Milka a new source of business, selling its unique brand experience to many new consumers or offering already acquainted consumers alternative options for consumption. The food category frequently alludes to *share of stomach* that refers to the quantity of a certain product type consumers are willing to consume. People may only eat so much of anything in a given day, and at one point everybody simply craves for change. Milka's clever line extension strategy has provided many options to satisfy this desire for change, allowing its target consumers to alternate within the overall Milka branded product offer. Being present in all these different market segments, also offers Milka the opportunity to increase its consumer touch points and to further develop its brand awareness, especially in less developed Milka markets.

Nevertheless, throughout this diversified and multilayered innovation process, *tenderness* has consistently remained Milka's point of differentiation. Any one of Milka's new product formats, no matter what market segment it addressed, leverages Milka's core brand competence of providing the most *tender* chocolate taste. Tenderness refers to Milka's core brand competence and it is the brand's single-minded essence. All Milka's R&D and innovation efforts are guided by this angle and no new product must enter the market unless it offers some form of a *tender* taste experience.

Brand positioning and brand behavior must work hand in hand to build strong and successful brands. The first defines the meaning, and the second provides ongoing direction for what a brand may and must not do. Ideally, the brand positioning is defined by one single word or one single-minded angle of attack, the brand essence. Once properly defined and validated, the brand essence is somewhat immortal. Its role is to provide consistency in everything a brand communicates and offers through its brand experience. Every detail counts and the brand essence provides the ultimate guidance for getting every detail right.

Once the brand essence has successfully been translated into executional behavioral tools such as brand ID, advertising and promotion, and product or service innovation, it continues as the natural threat or prism to steer your marketing decision-making. Consequently, the time and energy you invest into defining what your brand will stand for takes this definition toward tangible action, which will pay off swiftly and render every marketing program more effective, as it helps to reduce costs and improve results.

There are various reasons why the *one-word* branding methodology might help your company reduce costs. First, it gives brands a sharper focus, eliminating multifaceted messaging and ambiguity in terms of what a brand stands for. Brands that are defined with thought consistency throughout the entire consumer or customer experience develop more quickly and require less resources—human and financial alike. The methodology is highly effective in simplifying the entire brand development and management process, making it concrete and tangible. It allows you to put every staff member into the driver's seat. Nobody is left behind and everybody can make sensitive contributions. This is highly motivational not only for your own staff and across your entire organization but also for outside partners and suppliers. At the corporate brand level, this might provide the direction for a new and engaging corporate culture, including the employer's brands. Missteps in the development of marketing and promotion programs become more limited and the brand essence may invigorate the future product or service innovation process.

Channeling creativity and human energy this way produces a highly motivational work environment, which significantly improves productivity. And it is easy to see how such focus also contributes to reduce costs.

# 11

## The Revival of Vintage Brands

There has been much talk about whether brands have life cycles like products do. Personally, I do not subscribe to that point of view. Having worked on the revival of numerous vintage brands, they all fought back and regained a vigorous position in their respective market. Even brands whose products or services had fallen out of favor with consumers. There is almost always a way to resuscitate a tired brand and to bring it back to renewed attractiveness. The equity of a once well-known and powerful brand is indestructible, unless it got involved in a major and widely communicated health or safety scandal, which still lingers around. Even bankruptcy or changing consumer needs will not prevent a brand from coming back, as long as it can rebuild itself on a once strong and recognized equity.

There are many examples of *vintage* brands that have made comebacks. Triumph or Royal Enfield motorcycles, Champion Sports Apparel or Adidas's Stan Smith Tennis shoe, Polaroid, Dr. Martens that went from Punk niche to mainstream or the German Birkenstock brand. All of these were brands or niche players that have successfully staged their comeback as vintage brands. Known for its premium quality and comfortable sandals, Birkenstocks were initially confined to the German medical corps. Wider appeal came in the 1990s, with a renewed interest for minimalistic and functional styles. The brand cleverly sized the opportunity and continuously gained new traction way beyond its original appeal and target reach. After several years collaborating with luxury fashion brands, Birkenstock recently integrated LVMH, the world's largest luxury goods group.

There is no miracle at work. All of these brands recognized the signs of their times and were able to leverage their reminiscent brand equity. Any brand reconnects with success for a reason and money alone does not do the job. To redefine a vintage brand, you must go back to its roots or *root strength* as it is called in the *brand key*. The root strength always reveals the brand's original competence, which allowed it to be seen as differentiated and relevant to its target audiences. However, rarely the original root strength will allow you to directly revitalize a tired brand. In most cases, waking up a sleeping brand requires reinterpreting the root strength, placing it the current social and market context. Consumer needs and preferences evolve over time and so must brands, in order to stay up-to-date and attractive. Vintage brands have often failed to do so, losing energy and attracting less and less investment over time. A vicious cycle that can only be broken with a solid brand repositioning.

The methodology, tools, and discipline are the same as described in the previous chapters. You can work with the brand positioning funnel to walk step by step through the repositioning process. Here, truly understanding the brand's root strength is critical.

You must research what exactly brought the brand to fame. Looking at historical files may be of great help and might offer inspiration. Generally, the early communication messages such as brand slogans, package designs, and advertisements offer interesting clues on how the original brand positioning was understood and allows to hypothesize why it was relevant to the brand's target audiences at the time. The combination of revolving teams with changing views and competences often waters the brand positioning down over time. This is a slow process, and nobody notices at first when the brand starts losing its appeal, consumers' trust, and eventually its marketing support.

Launching an entirely new brand seems so much more attractive than revitalizing an existing one and few people appear to be bothered by the long-term costs of such a decision. It seems that as businesses in the hyper-global economy have come to adopt quarterly performance horizons, the long-term investment of building a brand has become somewhat obscured. In fact, it takes years longer and costs millions of dollars more to build a new brand that even remotely equals the strength of a vintage brand, even if the latter appears to have lost most of its traction.

Decisions to launch a new brand are often made too quickly and light-heartedly, no doubt partially because most marketing professionals are passionate about brands and more inclined to launch a new brand than revitalize an old one. This particularity applies to the innovation process. Oftentimes, the initial reflex of transforming an innovation into a business proposition will be to create and launch a new brand. It is impossible to put an exact number on this marketing phenomenon, but apart from very few exceptions, these innovations could be more easily and more efficiently marketed under the umbrella of an already established brand. And there is another unfortunate side effect to this. As innovation feeds into the creation of new brands, existing brands will progressively receive less funding and have trouble renewing themselves. Remember, to remain successful, brands must manage the paradox between *consistency* and *change*.

Strategic innovation, fully aligned with the brand essence, is the only effective way for brands to enact *change*. Any *change* that compromises the perception of consistency is risky and might backfire. By the same token, innovation can become a great booster for a sleepy vintage brand if it conforms with the brand essence.

In any case, redefining the true meaning of a vintage brand is an indispensable first step to getting it back onto the road for fame. Chapter 8 has outlined the steps and tools to do so in detail. However, vintage brands may deserve an even more profound investigation of their *root strength*, to truly grasp the element responsible for their initial success. Every evolutionary step of the brand at its peak performance is worth analyzing. many cases, a *true and deep* understanding of the problem will reveal the solution, something Albert Einstein suggested with his 55/5 rule. The wisdom behind this rule was that if he was given 1 h to solve a problem, he would allow himself 55 min to analyze and understand the problem and 5 min to find the solution. It is a great rule to use when working in branding.

The moment you understand what exactly differentiated the brand at the time and what made it relevant and desirable to its target audiences, you can match these findings against findings from today's consumer research regarding the respective product or service category. Also, researching what opinions and beliefs consumers still hold for the brand holds a lot of potential. If possible, you can use morphological research (see Chap. 7). The competitive environment may have evolved, and it is wise to establish a competitive brand map to see how your vintage brand fits into today's market context.

A thorough root strength analysis, morphological consumer research, and a courageous innovation process brought back the CADUM personal hygiene brand in France. CADUM was one of the first brands introduced in the French market at the dawn of the twentieth century, using modern marketing techniques recently imported from the United States. Michael Winburn, general manager of the Omega Chemical Company in New York, in association with Louis Nathan, a pharmacist in Levallois-Perret, a suburb of Paris, had developed the CADUM Cade oil-based soap formula in 1907. It was designed to sooth irritated skin. By the mid-1920s, CADUM had become a staple not only in Parisian stores but also in the streets on roofs and on the fronts of entire buildings. The brand owed part of its success to massive outdoor

**Fig. 11.1** Giant Cadum billboard at the hotel Scribe in Paris. Permission: L'Oréal Group

advertising for the first time in advertising history covering entire facades like the famous hotel Scribe near the Parisian Garnier opera house. At the time, this billboard was the biggest poster in the world, measuring 1072 m² with the head of the baby alone being 17 m height. At one point the campaign became so intrusive that Parisians signed a petition asking city hall to take all the billboards down (see Fig. 11.1).

In fact, clever branding and massive advertising had turned CADUM into the leading soap brand in France. Positioned as a beauty brand (see Figs. 11.2 and 11.3), it advertised using movie stars and other celebrities claiming *a skin soft like the skin of a baby*. The claim was visually underlined by the brand logo showing the portrait of a laughing baby, also visible on the soap's pink packaging. Over the years, CADUM had not only grown into France's favorite personal hygiene brand, but it had also entered the collective memory. Generation after generation of families had adopted CADUM, and the *bébé* CADUM had become a popular phrase people addressed to whining children in French schoolyards. *Oh, quel bébé CADUM (Oh what a CADUM baby)* can still be frequently heard in kindergartens and at home today (Fig. 11.3).

During the 1950s, CADUM merged with the Palmolive brand to eventually integrate the Colgate-Palmolive group in 1964. Things continued going well for CADUM until a significant shift in the market took place: the arrival of shower gels. A more modern form of personal hygiene considered more convenient (soap gets soggy when wet), shower gels started to first erode the market share of soap in France and across Europe and eventually gained a leadership position, further pushing soap sales down throughout the 1990s and early 2000s. By then, soap had turned into a product with one of the oldest median user bases.

**Fig. 11.2** Cadum advertising poster, 1920s. Permission: L'Oréal Group

**Fig. 11.3** Cadum beauty brand poster. Permission: L'Oréal Group

Be that as it may, the Colgate-Palmolive parent company probably no longer considered CADUM a strategic brand with global potential. Sales were restricted to a few international markets, generally with some kind of francophone linguistic backgrounds, including France, Belgium, Morocco, and Algeria. In this overall context, Cadum was considered a tactical brand inside the Colgate-Palmolive brand portfolio and marketing support started to decline. As a result, the brand image strongly associated with the CADUM *baby*, which was once evocative of female beauty, slowly drifted toward *baby care*. At that time, the CADUM baby was still being used for the brand's logo and key visual.

In absence of a clear *beauty* message, the *baby* logo started to overshadow consumer brand perceptions. This comes as no surprise as visual elements generally dominate. The baby being omnipresent in CADUM's advertising and on its packaging for decades, perpetually cannibalized the brand's original beauty image perception redirecting it toward an image for baby care. By the early 2000s, with only two soap formats (125 g and 200 g) left on grocery shelves next to a dedicated baby product line, CADUM had lost its original brand equity, transforming itself successively into a personal hygiene brand for babies.

At this point, Colgate-Palmolive divested itself of the brand, selling it to a private equity fund who under a new business model relaunched the brand by introducing a new line of shower gels. The new owners essentially focused on marketing, sales, and logistics, while product development and manufacturing were outsourced to specialized suppliers. However, despite major efforts in distribution and strong marketing support including TV, sales did not materialize as expected. Efforts so far had focused mainly on the development of a new product line of shower gels, as well as distribution and marketing actions, with the aim of compensating for fading sales from the two CADUM soap bar formats still on the market. The brand as such had not been analyzed and was assumed to have the necessary equity to appeal to consumers in a radically changed market environment, compared with CADUM's glory days. However, as research showed, it was the brand that was the problem.

CADUM became mostly perceived as an ageing brand of personal hygiene products for babies. Simultaneously, shower gels were predominantly seen as products used indiscriminately by all members of the family. At the same time, consumers also perceived them as noncompatible with babies. CADUM was caught in between its brand equity, firmly anchored in the baby universe and its product offer targeted to families. It was this perception gap that turned out to be responsible for the disappointing sales performance. According to consumer research results in France, it became obvious that CADUM first had to bridge the perception gap before the brand could expect to be seen as a relevant alternative for consumers in the shower gel market.

A solution to CADUM's branding problem required a 55/5 approach. A true and deep understanding of the problem that would suggest the solution. Consumers buy brands for their features and attributes that give them a certain performance. However, they relate to them via emotional bonding. At this stage, CADUM was missing both, the right emotional values and the corresponding product attributes. The brand logic was off balance and lacked substance and coherence. While the soap bars were still considered for babies, they offered somewhat outdated product attributes and while the shower gels were offering attractive and differentiated product attributes (the new CADUM shower gels differentiated with unique ingredients), they did not project the right values, in line with the CADUM brand.

It quickly became clear that the solution was to be found in the identification of a value, capable of uniting the brand, its new product offer, and the needs and beliefs of the family target audience. Despite significant progress in gender equality, numbers show that women still do most of the household purchases. Women were also CADUM's historical target audience for over 100 years. CADUM's brand identity codes reflected this and there was no point calling that into question. In branding, you cannot work *against* perceptions, you must work *with* them.

Women are not only the ones who continue to do most of the family grocery shopping, they also continue to dominate in their role as the family caretaker, at least from an emotional point of view. Things are certainly evolving, and exceptions do apply, but for the average blue collar or middle-class household this is still the case. The glue that holds families together is *love*. Love is the predominant undercurrent in a mother's relationship with her baby and with other family members. *Love* was a value that CADUM, as a *baby brand*, could legitimately claim. However, *love* by itself remained too abstract and too generic to be effective in CADUM's brand positioning effort. The value of *love* had to be directed toward claiming a competence that CADUM could legitimately own.

From the start, CADUM had been a skin care brand, claiming competence in making skin soft like the skin of a baby. This competence was an integral part of the CADUM brand equity and its original brand roots. As a brand, CADUM owned both *skin* and *love*. Hence, *Love for the skin* offered a potential to be leveraged in the repositioning process as being unique, differentiating and highly relevant to the target audience. It was a value, which was not limited to soaps and shower gels, but could be used to differentiate in almost any other segment of personal hygiene market, from shampoo to deodorant and from skin care to an extensive baby care line. The new positioning was clearly open to stretch.

However, there was one last problem to solve. CADUM's products did anything else than love consumers' skin. Like most of its competitors, the new shower gels were composed of several black-listed ingredients. This was a serious issue, since the new value for which the CADUM brand would stand in the future was not coherent with its product reality. The CADUM management team now made a very brave decision and overhauled the entire product line. Prior to a second relaunch, all shower gels were reformulated, replacing questionable ingredients and chemical agents. By redefining its strategic brand positioning, CADUM also became one of the first personal hygiene brands to be recognized by Greenpeace's Cosmetox Guide as avoiding toxic ingredients such as preservatives, EDTA, or BHT. This was not a minor detail, since it showed that the brand walked its talk and not only promised *love for the skin* but also delivered it through its revamped product formula. The new positioning was expressed via the new brand slogan: *your skin needs so much love*, which is still used today.

During the development of the new positioning of the CADUM brand, other product categories served as benchmarks and precedents. For instance, fabric softeners capitalize on the caretaker's desire to express love and consideration for the other members of the family, too. Searching inspiration in other, unrelated product categories is an effective way to inspire the brand positioning process.

At the time when CADUM was repositioned, the brand had lost most of its traction with consumers. Without a doubt, the brand had entered the collective memory in France with its *Oh, what a CADUM Baby* expression, yet it only randomly made it onto consumers' shopping lists. However, CADUM still owned a solid brand equity, with plenty of positive imagery. Even so, these image elements were no longer relevant for the consumer targets the brand aimed to reach. Nevertheless, the remaining equity provided a solid foundation on which the repositioned brand could be newly built. Investigating and understanding the brand's root strength and matching it against target consumers' needs and beliefs allowed us to bring it back, at one point reclaiming the number 3 position in the French personal hygiene market. Interestingly enough, this was not exclusively the merit of the revamped line of shower gels, but also the result of well-researched line extensions such as shampoo, deodorant, body care, and a revisited baby care line. It was the new positioning that not only invigorated the brand and made it relevant and attractive to French consumers but also the repositioning's capacity to provide freedom for stretch. A brand's capacity to stretch and line extend into other market segments with a differentiating and relevant proposition is a low-risk way of growing your business.

Speed of change is another reason why vintage brands offer great potential, not only in today's context but also for years to come. It is only a hypothesis; however, I believe that consumers increasingly feel they are losing ground under their feet. One of my very bright young students recently remarked dispiritedly that *at only 21, she already feels left behind.* Speed of change prevents most of us from staying on top of major developments that happen around us, affecting how we live and how we feel. Humanity is currently going through the Third Industrial Revolution, with fossil fuel generated energy being replaced by sustainable electricity and with AI quickly transitioning our economies from production to knowledge-driven ones. These periods have always been times of great instability. Instability for which brands may offer some relief. Vintage brands, in particular, are often reminiscent of times when the world and life were somewhat more predictable and under control. By referring to something in the past, they provide *meaning*.

This perception is not unique and from what we see in consumer research, many people share a similar perception of the world they live in. Not surprisingly, this generates anxieties and even existential fears (see GenZ). Yet this worldwide context of perceived instability and accelerated change offers great opportunities especially for vintage brands. It is no surprise that vinyl records outsold CDs in the United States in 2020, while music in general and fashion or object design in particular increasingly draw inspiration from the 1960s, 1970s, and 1980s. Retro design is celebrating a great come back in bicycles, scooters, or the very successful Smeg household appliances brand. The golden 1980s are perceived as a time when life was more under control and the world was more easily understood. Objects and brands that are reminiscent of those times may offer psychological comfort and reference points for today's context and this is what makes them highly attractive. This trend goes much deeper than the simple quest for nostalgia, and it serves a need for protection from a world that is outpacing most of us.

Brands in general, and vintage brands in particular, provide these reference points that project a certain sense of *protection* or least at a sense of stability. A brand that stands for something meaningful provides this meaning in a consistent way over time, offering something to hold on to mentally, something to rely on. By their history and established brand equity, vintage brands generally offer a rich narrative for connections. While this is definitely an asset, it is clearly not enough to bring back a vintage brand. Vintage brands must also provide relevance and differentiation to stay up-to-date and engage consumers over time. Just bringing a vintage back in a refreshed design might not do the trick. Like with the CADUM example, to be successful, these brands must reconnect with its target audiences, leveraging a need for which the brand offers a relevant proposition. This almost always requires a repositioning process and the identification of a self-expressive human value or a single-minded brand essence that directly relates to the brand's service or product reality. Most importantly, vintage brands rarely succeed with their old and sometimes outdated product formulations and frequently require a significant effort in innovation and development to stage a successful comeback.

On rare occasions and through a visionary repositioning process, vintage brands may even offer a way larger potential for development and growth.

This is the case for the TAG Heuer brand of luxury watches, which belongs to the French LVMH Group. TAG (Technologies Avant Garde), a private holding company based in Luxemburg City and whose sectors of activity include aviation, motorsports, and hospitality, acquired the Swiss Heuer watchmaking brand in 1985. The Heuer brand, founded in 1860 by Eduard Heuer, a watchmaker in St. Imier, Switzerland, is considered one of the fathers of time keeping. He had patented his first chronograph in 1882. By 1916, the company produced time keeping pieces capable of measuring up 1/100 of a second. While Heuer did not actually invent timekeeping, he was one of the key figures contributing to the evolution of this technology in the late nineteenth and early twentieth centuries.

However, when the TAG Group acquired the brand, it had no significant market position and limited target reach. Heuer certainly owned many technological innovations, patents, and know-how in watchmaking, but the brand did not really appeal to a wider target audience and, at the time, was considered a niche player. The obvious way to invigorate the brand would have been to reposition it, giving it a sharper meaning and a renewed brand identity. However, the TAG Group saw a larger potential and opted for a higher risk approach.

In the late 80s, TAG Heuer was not the only one selling chronographs in the premium or luxury watchmaking market segment. Most of the established brands all offered their own models, mostly inspired by the world of diving or aviation, as was the case for Breitling. Nonetheless, the market strove for luxury timepieces whose main focus was to offer men a *legitimate piece of jewelry*. There was no subsegment for functional watches with a sporty look. This is where the Heuer brand differed. With its *root strength* in professional timekeeping, a long history of chronograph innovation and the official timekeeper of many high-level sport competitions, Heuer also owned an entire range of watches with a recognizable signature design and sporty looks.

Here, laid the potential for differentiation, and instead of searching in the brand's roots for a platform to reposition the brand itself, TAG Heuer ambitioned to create a whole new subsegment in the luxury watch market in which the TAG Heuer brand could claim a dominant leadership position. Positioned as *the professional sports watch*, TAG Heuer promised its target audience a certain form of *empowerment*, rationally underpinned by product features offering professional standard functionalities. This claim of *professional functionality* was well anchored in the brand's product reality.

Every TAG Heuer watch came with six functional product features, which, if not necessarily unique individually in the industry, were exclusive in terms of its presence as features across all TAG Heuer watches. These features included a watertight single piece steel-case body, a scratch-resistant crystal watch glass, a screw-in crown, a unidirectional diving ring, a double-click wrist band and a waterproof guarantee up to 200 m. A depth few leisure divers would ever reach, but a feature that made the watch a professional time keeping piece.

Offering a full range of these sports watches at different price levels, from the accessible F1 series to the premium 6000 series, helped to make TAG Heuer's claim for an entire new market segment credible. Soon after, the traditional players of the luxury watchmaking market began introducing their own sports watch models, helping spur the growth of this nascent subsegment and bring it to life.

This visionary repositioning effort appears even more remarkable in the context of the depressed traditional watch market at the time. Brands like Hamilton, Casio, Seiko, or Timex had staged a major assault on the low to medium price watch category in the 1970s with a new generation of digital watches, using liquid crystal displays (LCD) rather than regular watch hands to tell time. Many of the big traditional watchmakers suffered. At the time, buying a watch or owning one was still considered a once in a lifetime affair. In those days, watches were mostly purchased to commemorate an important moment in peoples' lives, such as round number birthdays, graduations, weddings, retirement, and so on.

When times get tough the tough get going. In the early 1980s, when LCD watches had reached high popularity, ETA Manufacture Horlogère in close collaboration with a small group of outside talent in branding and design leveraged the *commemoration* consumer insight related to watch purchasing and ownership to develop and launch its Swatch brand. Swatch, the contraction *second watch*, was a clever idea that designed to revive interest in watches by turning a timepiece into a fashion item and a lifestyle statement that would appeal to the masses. Luxury watches may contain more than 1000 individual parts, a Swatch was uniquely designed to function with only 50. This made the watch way more affordable and allowed the brand to sell at under $50 a piece. With fun and constantly changing designs and affordable prices, Swatch had all the right ingredients to make its watches a fashion accessory. The concept motivated multiple watch ownership, worn to match any outfit.

The Swatch concept not only created a big business opportunity for ETA, but it also contributed to changing consumers' view on watches, hence playing an important part in revitalizing the market and making watch ownership less exclusive and more democratic. Swatch was later acquired by Société Suisse pour l'Industrie Horlogère (SSIH), which also owned the Omega brand. Apart from being an important watchmaker and marketeer, SSIH was also one of the largest manufacturers of Swiss watch movements, who had also suffered under the pressure of the LCD models. As another proof of consumers' need for reference points, LCD watches are currently staging a limited comeback. While Swatch was a purebred brand creation, TAG Heuer serves as an example for a vintage brand that helped to reposition an entire market injecting fresh vision into the watch industry. A vision that still powers it today.

Yet another example for a successful rebranding of a vintage brand is Procter & Gamble's (P&G) Old Spice. Originally launched in 1937 by the Shulton Company as the *Early American Old Spice* fragrance for women and quickly extended in 1938 to propose a male aftershave, Old Spice was acquired by P&G in the early 1990s with the goal of rejuvenating the brand and countering Unilever's highly successful AXE brand. Only marginally successful during the 2000s, Old Spice staged a new, consumer insight-driven approach in 2010 that paid off.

This example shows that you do not always need to field a major research project to come up with a workable consumer insight. In the case of Old Spice, the way a well-known consumer insight was leveraged was certainly more important than the knowledge of the insight itself. When it comes to shampoo and body wash, men generally use whatever is in the shower. Since women still do most of the grocery shopping, they are the ones who make most of the brand and product choices in this category. Here is where Old Spice saw its point of differentiation. Soon after its initial introduction in the 1940s, Old Spice's successful male hygiene line dominated the male grooming market. The brand owned its root strength in scents and its male target perception. This allowed P&G to swiftly build its relaunch strategy around the stereotyped personal hygiene behavior of men. Executed in a humorous way, the now legendary *the man your man could smell like* campaign was developed by the San Francisco-based agency Wieden & Kennedy, featuring the American football star Isaiah Mustafa. It repositioned Old Spice as a brand for men that would allow them to no longer smell *like lady scented body wash*. Perfectly timed to air during the Super Bowl and on social media platforms thereafter, the campaign quickly gained traction and became viral, eventually generating over 50 million views on YouTube and delivering the brand a sales uplift of 27%. This insight-driven campaign approach represents yet another technique that can be used to revitalize a vintage brand. Old Spice now ranks second in the US bodywash market.

A brand never fully loses its equity, and any vintage brand can be revived. Consumer insights, market vision, or self-expressive human values defining the brand essence are only some of the options to be considered for a successful relaunch. However, words and meaning are not the only things that need to change, and product formulations might also need a revamp. All vintage brand repositioning efforts should converge in the same starting point, taking a thorough look at the brand's root strength and its brand equity. In vintage branding, the answer for the brand's future is almost always embedded in its past.

# 12

## Sharpening Established Brands (Product and Service Brands)

There are several reasons why established and even successful brands may require a redefinition of their value proposition or brand positioning. It may simply be beneficial or in other cases a real necessity. It may be strategic and fundamental, redefining or clarifying what a given brand stands for or tactical, aiming to improve the brand's messaging or refreshing its identity codes. However, a repositioning exercise should never be considered a cost but an investment in the future of the business. Strong and well-defined brands always recover the investment that went into building them, attracting new consumers and fostering loyalty, generating payback through higher margins and equity over many years to come and developing more resilience toward competition.

A brand repositioning exercise may also generate greater buy-in and ownership from brand managers, leading to higher motivation and productivity.

However, repositioning an existing brand might also rhyme with taking a certain risk, especially when the brand already performs successfully. Therefore, such a move might be considered only if what the brand is supposed to stand for is not really clear. Brands that already define themselves with a sharp angle or in just one word might first consider redefining its messaging, rather than attempting to reinvent the wheel.

There are multiple reasons why a brand might benefit from a repositioning. Among the most frequent ones is a change in the corporate strategy or the consequences that come with Mergers and Acquisitions (M&A). Also, a changed competitive environment or evolving consumer needs might make a repositioning indispensable to keeping the brand relevant to its target audiences. Through outside influences or their own, brands sometimes experience a negative image evolution. This may result from a scandal, a product quality issue or a conscious decision to change the product formulation, which might trigger a real or perceived deterioration of the product performance. Finally, a brand may require a repositioning effort to stimulate renewed consumer interest, leveraging the power of emotional messaging.

Regardless of the reasons, the redefinition of an established brand positioning generally has two main purposes: to verify that the actual brand positioning is at its optimum and to find a way to express it in the sharpest and most relevant way. As we have seen in the previous chapters, the exact word or single-minded angle of attack, by which your brand will ultimately be defined, has a fundamental impact on how your brand will be perceived by its target audiences. This is not a self-fulfilling intellectual exercise but a basic condition for any brand's operational efficacy. For everybody involved in its creation and management, a razor-sharp and meaningful (relevant) positioning will clarify what your brand really stands for, thus providing a clear roadmap for concrete marketing and sales action.

The positioning, for example, will provide a straightforward and unambiguous brief for the design team to imagine a new brand identity. In many cases, a refreshed identity will do a great job of updating a brand. Many corporate and service brands have succeeded in attracting new customers, not by completely redefining what they stand for but by clarifying it and by leveraging this clarification in the process of redefining the brand's essential visual codes and messages.

Federal Express repositioned itself in the mid-1990s as a provider of global delivery services; motivated in part by the undesired image associations inherent in the word *federal* but also recognizing their target's actual behavior. As a matter of fact, many customers already referred to *Federal Express* simply as FEDEX. Under such circumstances, it is relatively easy for any brand to adopt a new (already commonly used) name and a new identity. This allowed FEDEX to move individually branded services, acquired through years of M&A activities under one identical brand umbrella, adopting what we refer to as the concept of a *unitary brand system*. Unitary brand systems are capable of functioning with just one brand, in addition to product and/or service descriptors that highlight the particular expertise of the branded offer. By adopting a unitary brand system, FEDEX transformed itself from a *house of brands* to a *branded house*, focusing all efforts on one single brand, saving marketing costs and, ultimately improving results.

Positioned as a global delivery service provider, with a holistic service portfolio, covering all relevant service offers for customers with shipping needs, FEDEX had a sharp and single-minded brand positioning. *Speed* is what

## 12 Sharpening Established Brands (Product and Service Brands)

counts in delivery services (and what produces relevance), *speed* is what the word *Express* already suggested in its original brand name. And *speed* is what FEDEX was able to deliver through its many designated services, its knowhow and performance standards (product reality), and its global reach. *Speed* is what FEDEX stands for. If you take a closer look at the FEDEX brand logo, speed has two forms of creative expressions. First, it leveraged orange as a color of *energy and dynamics* and second the brand chose a font that suggests an arrow symbol between the *E* and the *X* in the FEDEX brand name (see Fig. 12.1). At the time, FEDEX was already an established and successful brand in the delivery service industry. However, the organization had grown through an M&A corporate strategy and the decision to challenge its positioning helped FEDEX sharpen it, producing fresh understanding and initiating a revamped creative concept to express it.

To redefine any established brand, follow the methodology and steps suggested in the brand positioning funnel (Chap. 8). If your brand continues to perform well and you just want to double-check its positioning and find a sharper focus, you may start by using the competitive map and the brand key. Both tools, if used with consideration, will provide a first tangible indication of how sound your brand's positioning really is. If this exercise is conclusive, you may proceed directly to working on the paraphrased brand essence to enter the brand behavior phase. If both the competitive map and brand key do not provide certainty on your brand's capacity to differentiate in a highly relevant way, you must start from scratch and work through the entire positioning funnel.

However, in either case there is an additional challenge you will face. Established brands come with a lot of baggage and an already defined brand

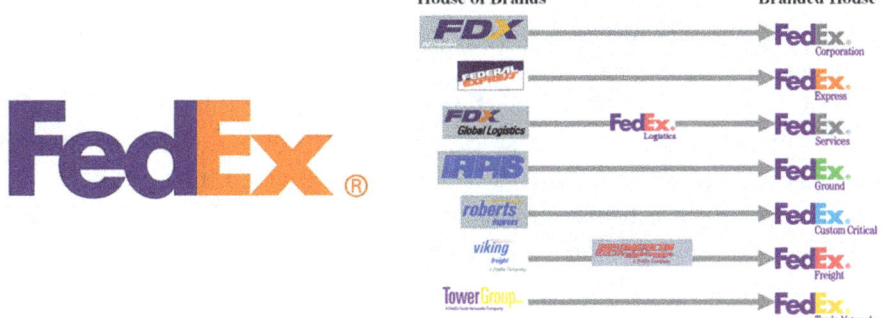

**Fig. 12.1** FEDEX house of brands illustration. Permission: Ivanov Consulting in cooperation with Mark Ritson MBA—https://www.business-games.ai/brand-architecture-primer/

essence. This is what makes the exercise harder. To properly reposition these brands, you must attempt to put aside what you already know and what the brand currently stands for, essentially starting with a blank sheet of paper. This implies questioning everything that has been defined in the past and avoiding the assumption that certain elements are set in stone. Starting with a blank sheet of paper is critical. To identify a product attribute that might improve your brand's potential for differentiation, you must truly embrace it and push it through all the steps of the positioning funnel to see what kind of brand essence it may suggest. Only at this point will you be able to really challenge the actual positioning, ultimately deciding on a strategic positioning change or simply opting for improved focus and wording.

France Telecom, the state-owned French telecommunication provider, which was partly privatized in the late 1990s, was pushed by EU regulations to open national markets to outside competition. In 2000, France Telecom acquired *Orange*, a well-established telecommunication brand from the United Kingdom. Owning a much stronger and less public service-related brand ID, Orange offered France Telecom significantly more potential and scope to build a global telecommunication business. The decision was quickly reached to rebrand France Telecom into Orange. This happened over time and in a well-planned process. Initially, the Orange brand was only applied to mobile services.

This makes sense, as this business division was likely to reach the broadest consumer base. Once the brand was established for this target audience, all other sectors of activity could easily follow, building on Orange's newly established brand equity. The last element of the original France Telecom brand universe to convert to Orange was the corporation itself. It took over 10 years after the mobile service division to finally transition the France Telecom corporate brand to Orange.

Today, Orange is one of the leading global telecommunications service providers with strong market positions in Europe, Africa, and the Middle East. However, France Telecom's rebranding did much more than building a globally recognized brand. The repositioning also introduced a new set of brand values and helped to rejuvenate the corporate culture. In the process, Orange made a major shift to become more customer-centric, insisting on its technological advancement and premium quality in hardware and services. Its minimalistic brand ID, leveraging the intrinsic strength of a bright orange color code against a mostly black background, now inspires strength, modernity, and state-of-the-art innovation.

The higher the risk, the higher the return. Sometimes, established brands that make a bold decision reap bigger awards. To do so takes courage and

## 12 Sharpening Established Brands (Product and Service Brands)

most importantly a lot of investigative work into the brand equity, the product or service reality, and the competitive landscape. You must do your *homework*, investigating all these sources to keep the risk down and to secure a positive outcome. In the early 1980s, Apple was a small and unknown tech brand only faintly known to IT nerds. It had no relevant market position even in the United States, and consumers were mostly unaware of the brand. This changed radically when Apple decided to reposition itself as a lifestyle brand, offering a totally new vision for IT technology and computing in general. Strategically, Apple did something brilliant. Instead of simply positioning itself as an alternative to IBM, the leading PC brand at the time or any other PC competitor, Apple took on the entire PC industry, proposing a radical change supported by the products' user-friendliness. In essence, Apple proposed an entirely new and alternative standard for an industry that was controlled by a small club of established competitors. This, a highly effective approach, was also used by Lipton to position tea as an alternative in markets where hot beverage consumption was historically dominated by coffee.

Apple's repositioning effort hit the market with a big bang at the 1984 Superbowl. The famous 1984 TV commercial, inspired by George Orwell's novel *1984* and directed by Ridley Scott, only aired once at a giant media cost of $3 million at the time. This communication strategy put Apple on the map and laid the foundation for the brand's rise to become the most valued company on the NASDAQ stock index. The strategic decision to reposition itself as a lifestyle brand was also reflected in Apple's brand slogan still in use today. *Think different* has since served as Apple's *brand prism*, driving messaging, brand ID, and innovation. Just for the record, Apple's *think different* was a playoff of IMB's *think IBM* slogan of the times. It cleverly summarizes what Apple stands for, supported by its highly user-friendly product and service reality.

The legendary British Burberry fashion brand transformed itself from a functional clothing brand in the premium segment of the market to a fashion luxury brand. The brand's root strength lay in the invention of a new fabric called Gaberdine, which was light and waterproof and a favorite of soldiers engaged in France during the First World War. Contrary to FEDEX or Apple, Burberry's repositioning did not happen instantaneously, but over time. The brand evolved in several successive steps, all following a previously established brand logic. What often drives luxury fashion brands are origin and creative direction, and Burberry is no exception. First, under the general leadership of Angela Ahrend, who refocused the brand on its British roots and then under the creative leadership of Ricardo Tisci, the brand successfully extended its product portfolio to include streetwear and accessories. The new creative edge introduced by Tosci later gave Burberry a more democratic appeal and extended its target audience to include younger generations. Furthermore, inspired by the new positioning, the brand started to communicate differently, becoming one of the first luxury fashion brands to make heavy use of social media communications, reaching out to 10 million followers. This brand evolution also pushed the brand to rejuvenate its messaging and brand identity codes. In 2023, Burberry had over 20 million followers on Instagram alone.

Burberry's initial social media strategy included hereto unseen techniques in the luxury fashion industry such as live-streamed fashion shows and a *see-now, buy-now* marketing effort, where fashion could be bought online the instant it was introduced on the catwalk. In a rather light repositioning effort, Burberry managed to preserve its brand equity essentials by translating them into rejuvenated brand appeal that was attractive to younger consumers around the world, especially in the rising Asian market, with China alone accounting for 15% of the global market in 2023.

Sometimes, brands may fall victim to poor management decision-making, or a lack of corporate ethics. This happens much more frequently than you may think, and many important global brands, such as Siemens and Crédit Lyonnais, have suffered from such incidents. In most of these cases, a repositioning becomes inevitable and the quicker an affected brand reacts, the better the prospects for a brighter future.

Back in the 2000s Siemens, a German leader in the global engineering industry got entangled in a major bribery scheme. As a contractor, Siemens lacked the ethical codes of conduct to successfully prevent corrupt sales practices. Starting in the early 1990s and over a period of 16 years, Siemens had illegally paid out $1.4 billion to ensure lucrative contracts, mostly in telecommunications, transportation, medical equipment, and power generation. The scandal had global ramifications and eventually broke into the open in 2006, when German authorities raided Siemens' Munich offices and found ample evidence, including a corporate process, facilitating payments made *off the record*.

In B2B, business ethics are as important as product and service performance, and simply repositioning the brand will not be enough. Siemens had no choice but to enact a major management shakeout and a radical overhaul of the company's compliance procedures. And the company did just that. The scandal, which gained global coverage for months, had not affected the product or service quality of the Siemens brand, but the corporate image took a hard hit. It is easy to imagine how a stained image of this sort will impact business in the world of public contracting. However, swift action, renewed

## 12 Sharpening Established Brands (Product and Service Brands) 179

transparency, and adequate corporate messaging helped to contain the damage and served the purpose of repositioning the Siemens brand as a trustworthy business partner in engineering technologies. Simultaneously, the repositioning of the Siemens brand introduced a new set of values and had a significant impact on the corporate culture of the entire organization, transforming its image as an employer brand and infusing new credibility and trust into Siemens branded B2B operations.

A more radical way of making a scandal go away is rebranding, the replacement of the actual brand name with a new one. This repositioning methodology was applied by Crédit Lyonnais, France's oldest banking institution, founded in 1863. In 2006, Crédit Lyonnais got caught in the crossfire during one of France's biggest financial scandals, which eventually cost the government €403 million in damages and the bank its reputation. Compliance again played a role in this mishap and Crédit Lyonnais decided to radically change its name into LCL, a short form for *Le Crédit Lyonnais*. The rebranding move was the right thing to do, and it came with a redefined brand positioning, including a new set of values, improved compliance procedures, and a modernized, punchier brand identity. While the talk about the financial scandal is still in the media today, the LCL brand stays clear of it and has recovered most of its customers. Luckily for brands, peoples' collective memory is short-lived.

Rebranding Crédit Lyonnais was probably the only way to salvage the brand. However, like any major overhaul, the process imposed change also in other strategic areas. The new LCL brand came with a well-defined brand positioning that imposed tangible service attributes to match customer expectations and needs: newly designed services, significant progress in the digitalization of online banking services, and a new CRM program at staff level. Intensive training programs and restyled branch offices all across France contributed to making the new brand positioning visible and transforming the customer experience. LCL's new positioning became a success story, also because it was built on a revisited product or service reality. No brand ambitions for consistency, but sometimes change may help to challenge the status quo and to gain new vigor and efficiencies.

Scandals, although quite frequent, are not the only reason to justify a rebranding. In the early 1990s, the European Commission passed a law that obliged all brands using the word *bio* to conform with the official standards and regulations newly established for organically produced products. This obliged the Danone Group to rebrand its highly popular *Bio* yogurt brand. After several years of deliberation and after having explored and tested thousands of alternative names, Danone finally settled on *Activia*, a name that hinted at the activity of the live yogurt culture used to differentiate this functional yogurt. The stakes were high, as the brand globally supported a multibillion-dollar business for the Danone Group. Surprisingly, few consumers consciously noted the change. *Bio*'s distinctive green color-coded packaging dominated the name change in consumer perceptions, and for many the name change went mostly unnoticed. Brand packaging is mostly remembered holistically, and it is memorized a bit like a *jpg* image. Rarely, a brand name or logo is decoded in detail.

Marketeers may also consider reevaluating the actual brand positioning because of evolving consumer preferences. These preferences may be influenced by a variety of factors that might come into play at any given time, potentially diminishing a brand's attractiveness. The most frequent factors, which concern many of us, are events that provoke a lifestyle change: getting married, starting a family, making a career move that offers a higher income, or simply ageing. All of these events and circumstances may have an impact on consumer preferences that might require adapting the brand positioning to ensure continued relevance for its target audiences.

Some years ago, the Dreft detergent brand found itself in an uncomfortable position, having lost its potential for growth. Certain consumers considered the brand less effective against tough stains than Tide and less gentle for baby skin than Ivory Snow. While others considered Dreft gentler for the skin than Tide and superior in stain release in comparison to Ivory Snow. With part of Dreft's target consumers going through lifestyle changes, getting married or founding a family, the brand was losing some of its consumers to either Tide or Ivory Snow. Dreft found itself stuck in the middle, neither fully delivering on tough cleaning nor gentleness.

From a product formula point of view, Dreft contained Borax, a natural bleach. This product feature allowed it to claim gentler, yet still efficient cleaning properties, which were perceived as less aggressive for the skin than detergent-based formulas. However, natural lifestyle changes may impact consumer preferences. This was the case for Dreft. In households with strong preferences for tough cleaning, the arrival of a newborn was less likely to overturn the need for cleanliness. However, the contrary was true for consumers who were already aware of sensitive skin conditions. They were more likely to switch to the gentlest laundry cleaning formula when their first child was born, possibly replacing Dreft by Ivory Snow. While mothers were unlikely to abandon Ivory Snow for their babies, gentleness remained highly relevant to them for the other family members and also their babies as they grew up. It was against this target segment that Dreft could leverage its formula. Dreft's decision to reposition itself as a *gentle extension* of Ivory Snow allowed the brand to hold on to part of its original consumer base and attract new consumers with a preference for *gentleness*, often triggered by a recent lifestyle change.

Environmental awareness has become a major factor for changing consumer preferences. Concerns about the environment, animal well-being, biodiversity, local sourcing, fair trade, and many others have served as a powerful agent of change for consumer preferences in the past 10–20 years and will continue to do so in the future. Brands that operate in such an environment must stay on top of things to remain relevant. In this context, taking a close look at the actual brand positioning is the right thing to do. In Germany, one of Europe's most environmentally advanced countries, the market share of organic produce was roughly 7% in 2022, and only an average of 3% of consumers buy exclusively organic, a surprisingly small percentage for what one would expect from such an informed and environmentally conscious society.

Environmental concerns are among the key motivators for organic food purchases, with 84% of consumers declaring climate and environment protection as their key motivator to switch to organic produce. On the other hand, the cost perception of organically grown goods remains the biggest barrier to purchase. However, this is much less the case for organically produced eggs, which command a share of close to 16% in the German market. Here, consumer preferences have continued to shift over recent years, chiefly motivated by animal well-being, which seemingly outweighs price concerns.

Another factor in changing consumer preferences is the trend for *holistic health*, currently the most influential trend worldwide. In the past, health often became defined by the absence of illness. While this is still the case today, the notion of *health* extends to also include mental and spiritual dimensions next to physical health. Consumers around the world no longer only aim to add more years to their lives, they strive to add more life to their years. Staying healthy physically, mentally, and spiritually has become a key motivator and change agent for consumer preferences on a wide range of product categories from food and personal care to clothing and leisure activities, health and fitness-related services, and media content choices.

The list is seemingly endless and, in one way or another, any mass consumption brand is to some extent affected by the *holistic health* trend. In the 1970s and 1980s, bicycles had to be foldable to fit into a trunk, since cars were what demonstrated status. Today, ever more fancy models are proudly showcased on the bike rack at the rear of the car. The explosive growth of e-bikes in Europe is another tangible sign for shifting consumer preferences, impacting even distant product categories, far beyond biking and fitness. Most importantly, this kind of trend always reveals a change in the consumer's state of mind. A changing attitude comes with changing consumption preferences. Brands that fail to recognize these preference shifts might get into rough waters in the years ahead. Hence, reevaluating a brand's positioning in the context of an emerging trend is a must-do affair and should not be put off, even if the brand is in full swing today.

Trends introduce movement and change into any market segment, which current competitors and newcomers are quick to explore. This can lead to lasting consequences for your brand and business, in the blink of an eye. In the late 1980s, ConAgra, a US food conglomerate, introduced *Healthy Choice*, which differentiated itself from competitors with recipes lower in fat, sodium, and cholesterol. Mike Harper, the chairman of the time had suffered from a heart attack and after returning from his rehabilitation program, worked together with the FDA to develop a range of affordable foods based on healthier recipes, while refusing to compromise on taste, the No. 1 consumer choice criteria in food.

The timing of this launch was sensitive, as the healthy eating niche market was just about to go mainstream. An example being the *Whole Foods* supermarket chain, which had quickly expanded across the United States. First introduced with a small assortment of frozen meals and cold cuts, Healthy Choice quickly extended its product portfolio to offer a wide range of prepared meals, constantly adapting to evolving consumer taste preferences. With its extensive R&D capacity and powerful trade relationships, ConAgra certainly had the muscles to quickly gain listings and market penetration. Weight Watchers and Stouffer's, two major players in the prepared meal market at the time and still today, did not see things coming early enough. With comfortable market positions, they were slow to recognize the nascent healthy eating trend and became paralyzed in their own brand positioning.

Built around the brand competence of weight management, neither Weight Watcher's nor Stouffer's felt threatened by the arrival of Healthy Choice. However, most people with a weight problem will at some point encounter a health issue, needing treatment. This made this consumer segment highly educated on and sensitive to health and food consumption. Naturally, they were a core target of Healthy Choice's brand value proposition. Not surprisingly, sales started to shift in ConAgra's favor, allowing Healthy Choice to quickly establish itself in the market.

Unlike the global holistic health trend, Healthy Choice recognized a nascent change in consumer preferences early on and seized the opportunity. Both market leaders failed to identify the changes in their established market environment and were too slow to respond. The Weight Watcher and Stouffer's brands both competed on weight management, Healthy Choice on healthy eating and taste. Very likely, this made Healthy Choice look less like a threat.

## 12 Sharpening Established Brands (Product and Service Brands)

Extending market reach may be another good reason to take a fresh look at the brand positioning and the entire brand key. Established brands with a clearly defined and recognized competence in their core markets may gain from extending into new market segments. The key for this to succeed is their *core competence*, which might be leveraged to develop a differentiated offer in an existing but not yet explored market segment. Nivea was able to launch its iconic brand into makeup because Nivea's core competence of *care* provided relevant differentiation against mass market competitors, who were mainly beauty and style focused and who did not explicitly offer skin care as a side benefit of makeup and beauty. Brands capable of growing not just through market share but also through line extensions generate a higher return faster.

The correct identification and definition of the brand's core competence (often equivalent to the root strength) is a key success factor in a brand's strategy that relies on stretching the brand offer into new subsegments of the market. Milka started to build its brand competence on the chocolate bar. First, the line extended from the original milk chocolate product into chocolate bars with add-on ingredients such as nuts, caramel, and so on and then stretching the brand portfolio into chocolate-related categories such as cake, cookies, ice cream, confectionary, and treats before even entering salty snacks. Milka's brand strength and its recognized core brand competence also allowed the brand to venture into temporary or long-term co-branding activities, such as the Milka-coated Oreo sandwich cookie. The most tender chocolate taste remains the underlying proposition for all these line extensions. It acts as the differentiator or *discriminator* against established brand offers in every single market subsegment where Milka is present.

Any established brand that considers stretching techniques to enter a new market segment with the objective of generating additional growth is well advised to take a fresh look at the definition of its brand positioning and core competence. The point here is not to categorically change everything, but to verify that the brand positioning is up to new challenges and that the way it is formulated provides a tangible and unambiguous direction.

Finally, even a seemingly well-defined brand may benefit from a redefinition of its brand essence with the goal of further sharpening its focus. In this case, the measure is not designed to make fundamental changes but to further clarify the overall understanding of what the brand stands for, providing more tangible meaning internally and externally to all stakeholders. A clarification of the brand positioning potentially offers concrete rewards, making the future brand management more tangible. As discussed in Chap. 8, many of today's brands consider themselves well-defined; however, many of them remain too abstract to provide clear and unanimous direction for marketing action.

Furthermore, substituting the brand essence with a *self-expressive human value* is a way to connect with consumers on a more emotional level. A reevaluation of the brand positioning may precisely serve that purpose. As we have seen in Chap. 5, consumers relate to brands through emotional connections and replacing the current brand essence by a *self-expressive human value* does exactly this. By no means does this suggest that you will change what your brand stands for. You simply say it with a different wording, leveraging the potential offered by self-expressive values.

It makes perfect sense to regularly take a fresh look at the *brand key* of any given brand and to seriously reevaluate its key components. The point here is not to induce perpetual change, which would clearly be counterproductive, but to double-check that all chosen terms, including the wording of the brand essence, continue to be right on target and coherent with all other fundamentals of the brand key model. A brand positioning only becomes workable if it provides the exact same single-minded meaning to all stakeholders, the people who actively shape and promote the brand, and the target audience for which it is intended. Brand positionings that remain abstract fail to do so, leading to inconsistent and weak brand messaging and resulting in less effective, costlier marketing programs.

# 13

# Brand Creation: Getting It Right from the Start

How to build a brand from scratch? How to turn a business idea into a viable brand proposition that stands up to competition with a differentiated and highly relevant offer? And how to translate that proposition into an identity, capable of engaging with the target audience emotionally? Even the most brilliant product or service idea will not succeed in leveraging its full potential, unless it has been transformed into a strong and recognizable brand proposition.

Building a brand from scratch does not only concern start-ups. It is also highly relevant to companies of all sizes that want to brand their product or service offers, and of course the corporate world with its constant business strategies relying on Mergers and Acquisitions (M&A). Apart from the motivation that drives the creation of a new brand, there is usually a lot of information to handle and to evaluate. Most of it will feel quite abstract since all those bits and pieces of information have never been connected to produce effective target messaging. Start-ups may have to content themselves with working from a product idea or if they are lucky, a first prototype. There might be an initial concept for a new service pitch or a management board's decision to harmonize corporate communications under one single roof, after a series of Mergers and Acquisitions. Under all these circumstances, what is lacking most is a clear vision to knit the available information into a coherent single-minded message, summed up in the logical concept of a brand and its *essence*.

There rarely is room inside the organization to look for guidance since the future brand has not yet left any traces. This is why succeeding to build a brand from scratch requires a substantial investment in resources and time. It also calls for the right set of tools and processes. Branding projects hold a lot of fascination for people and the decision to create and launch a new brand is often taken too lightheartedly, and without the necessary consideration and deliberation. Among other reasons, the costs and risks involved in building a brand are often underrated.

To avoid these risks, any product or service innovation should first be considered under the umbrella of any existing brand that may be part of the company portfolio. In most cases, this will be possible with a little bit of imagination and real determination to do so. Adding a new feature to a current branded offer might even strengthen the brand by creating news value and stature at the same time.

There are of course moments when creating a new brand is inevitable. This concerns all companies that either do not own an established brand yet or do but one that is not suited to carry a new product offer. When Toyota decided to enter the luxury sedan market, it decided to create the Lexus brand to do so. This was certainly a wise decision, seeing as the Toyota brand was unlikely to carry the image equity to succeed against established luxury car brands such as Mercedes-Benz, BMW, or Audi. Renault, which has tried several times to break into the premium car market segment, failed to do so with its Renault brand. Despite being well-engineered and designed, neither the Safran nor the Talisman became serious contenders in the high-end segment of the car market. The Renault car brand, mainly known for its subcompact value cars, simply did not have the brand equity to succeed in this very established and highly exclusive market segment.

Another reason to create or acquire an established brand may be for tactical reasons. The Volkswagen Group owns several brands that at times compete for the same customer, such as VW, Audi, Seat, and Skoda. Danone competes with Evian and Volvic in the international mineral water markets. In both cases, doubling up makes sense to gain a larger share of the consolidated market and to fight competition. Furthermore, all these brands were already strong at the time when they were acquired. Prior to being integrated into the respective holding groups, each brand already owned a business that justified maintaining the respective equities.

However, even owning a brand, success in business is not guaranteed, and according to the US Bureau of Labor Statistics, 20% of new businesses with staff fail in the first year, while seven out of ten are gone after just a decade. A well-defined brand will certainly not protect your business from failure, but it might give it a better chance to survive. This is a factor often undervalued in start-up ventures, where most of the resources and energy are spent on preparing the product or service for launch. This is not to say that start-ups or product and sales-centric companies ignore the importance of branding, but rather that they often lack the necessary skills, resources, and stamina to build one.

Turning a business idea into a brand has many merits. It makes the proposition more tangible for the target audience, as it spells out the benefits in a meaningful and relatable manner. Branding helps to build awareness and recognition, both essential elements of the purchase decision-making process. Most importantly, a brand will engage consumers on an emotional level, while products and services generally focus on functionalities. And branding obliges companies to develop a narrative that organizes the often-complex mass of information relevant to a business idea and its market environment into an easy-to-digest story format. The whole delivered by a well-ranked message hierarchy. In terms of methodology, there is virtually no difference between the creation of a product,[1] service, or corporate brand. Although the processes to achieve either one may differ.

A small- to midsize company or a start-up can follow this five-step process to create and define a brand prior to market launch. The launch typically starts with the retail presentations or, in the case of a service brand, with communication. Any brand in the process of being introduced must be fine-tuned and ready for this moment.

The first step of the brand creation exercise consists of getting to know your product or service. I mention this for a reason. One may suppose that anybody with direct responsibilities in brand development in a given organization has a solid understanding of the product or service in question. However, in many cases, a *solid understanding* might just not be enough. I therefore encourage you to dig deeper and to question every tiny aspect of your product or service, experiencing it yourself over time, personally examining the manufacturing or customer fulfilment process, asking the right questions to people who run these processes. Be curious and relentless. Your goal should be to become an expert on all of these subjects. Make time and find the means to testing the product or service with your target audience, prior to going live. Get feedback from the people who test it and try to personally relate the experience of your product or service by using it yourself over a longer period of time. Consider *mystery shopper* techniques where you pretend to be a customer for your own products and services.

Brands work like shortcuts for the product or service they represent and the *promises* they make to the target audience. The brand spells out that *promise* via its pre-learned identity codes that refer to a brand's image and stature. The

---

[1] Keeping in mind that the term *product* includes also people-, political-, and destination brands.

brand *promise* must be differentiating and *relevant*, meaning it must be perceived as satisfying a *perceived target need*. Consequently, understanding the exact nature of the *need* is paramount to formulating the *brand promise* in the most pertinent manner. Here, knowledge about your brand's production modalities and the consumer usage experience becomes essential. It will help you to identify and select the right words that will ultimately shape your brand positioning in all its key dimensions (*as defined by the brand key model*, discussed in Chap. 8).

The second step of the brand creation process should focus on the definition of the target audience. Not just from a sociodemographic point of view, but also leveraging insights from generational targeting and psychographics, all of which have been discussed in more detail in Chap. 9. The goal is to define who your brand's core target audience (bull's eye) and to fully understand the underlying motivational patterns and attitudes that drive your consumers' behavior. Knowing and understanding the target audience provides indispensable insights to shape the *essence* of your future brand. This understanding will also come in handy during the brand behavior phase (Chap. 11), when the brand positioning is leveraged for the brand identity and translated into tangible marketing action.

The third step is the analysis of the brands you will be competing against. The emphasis here is on *brands* and not on products, services, or corporations. The competitive brand map tool (Chap. 9) allows you to understand the four dimensions each market is competing on and how exactly your competitors and your own brand relate to them.

Fourth, it might be interesting to look at benchmarks in your own competitive set or in entirely unrelated markets. STYLEVAN, formerly a small French family-owned company in Burgundy, manufactures and promotes camping vans built on a Volkswagen T5 or Renault Traffic van platform. Camping vans are a hot item in the European leisure travel market, as they offer a large array of amenities in a compact format, travel easily through the narrow streets of historical cities, and are only charged according to the passenger car tariffs at highway toll stations. Camping vans are way more discrete than regular camping cars, which are generally conceived on small truck platforms. STYLEVAN had a brand name but no brand, or put differently, the brand was defined by the product itself and the customer reviews on the company's website. STYLEVAN did not really stand out from competing offers in the market, hence sales performance was constant but remained essentially flat.

Timing was sensitive when STYLEVAN decided to create its brand, as the market was just about to pick up. With little funding available for consumer research and target definition, we relied on online conversations to profile the target audience and to scout for consumer insights (sentimental analysis). Like many other product categories, such as gardening or pet ownership, camping vans have rather active communities who exchange on destinations and their personal experiences while travelling in the vans themselves. As it turned out, current owners were close to or had already entered retirement. They were very passionate about their vans, and all alluded to an adventurous state of mind that was well-dosed and far from the extreme.

These findings suggested two unrelated brands as benchmarks for inspiration: the North Face outdoor clothing and TAG Heuer sport watches. Both were from different categories, yet they somewhat related to the camping van universe. Road-trip afficionados, such as those travelling in a camping van, want sturdy outdoor clothing and technology features. The North Face and TAG Heuer, as already discussed, offered both and when combined hinted at a potential direction for the positioning of the future STYLEVAN brand. Both brand cases also somewhat suggested the value of freedom, procured by the performance of their respective product features in rough environments. And last but not least, freedom was clearly an identified need of the camping van core target community.

Most of us never go to the edge, but knowing that your equipment might allow you to do so makes us feel more comfortable. This form of *peace of mind*, potentially a powerful emotional brand benefit, quickly emerged as a hypothetical direction from the brand positioning funnel process. It clearly had the potential to give STYLEVAN an edge in the market and to significantly strengthen the brand's appeal to its target audience.

There was only one problem. The actual product reality did not live up to the concept of *freedom* or *peace of mind*. The new brand positioning required the product to change. This is not unusual and early in the process, product improvements might be highly beneficial for years to come. This is not easy to accept and generally translates into additional investments and time. Nevertheless, as with Cadum shower gels, brand positioning induced modifications in the product design generally increase coherence between the brand and its reality and produce a meaningful competitive edge.

STYLEVAN seized the opportunity to add important performance features to its camping vans, such as three-source energy sourcing to increase energetic independence, improved insulation against heat and cold, better ventilation through the new fabric of the push-up roof, and many others. Innovation transformed the STYLEVAN camping van into a *professional tool* for offroad leisure adventurers: a true ally for the target's leisure passions. Even though it was ready to take on even a serious *safari*, it was usually spotted near one of France's endless beaches or national parks.

Benchmarking can become a great ally in the brand creation process. It might not provide all the answers, but it always offers tangible inspiration and reassurance for the direction your brand's positioning might want to take. Be that as it may, benchmarking must not replace the brand development process as outlined in Chap. 8. The methodology prescribed by the brand positioning funnel and the related tools must all be employed to achieve a solid and lasting positioning platform for your new brand.

Many branding voices say that there is always time to correct things later. While this is true, a poorly defined brand positioning might not offer the opportunity for revision at a later stage. Like in human acquaintances, it is mostly the first impression that counts. Getting it right from the start does not only pay off, it also keeps the *brand ship* on course. Keep in mind that one-word brand positioning platforms work like a prism, which allows everybody in the team to produce and execute ideas in a manner that is strategic for the brand and its development over time. Brands require consistency to build awareness and traction with their target base. Only brands that stand for one thing really stand for something.

A few years ago, a special breed of brands emerged, which is referred to as *digital native vertical brand (DNVB)*. The particularity with these brands is that they are *online only*, from creation to operation. Among the first of these brands is Bonobo, a fashion brand created and launched in 2007. These brands own three distinctive characteristics: they are generally pure players who concentrate their activity in one single product category; their operation is entirely cost optimized, which means there are no intermediaries, neither wholesaler nor retailer; and they sell directly to the consumer (D2C) and are totally user-centric, providing the best product at the best price and with the best customer experience.

This is a high standard and consistently performing to match it requires an intimate understanding of the target audience at a level that few traditional brands might ever reach. *DNVB* brands are fully data-driven. Any small bit of information produced during the communication and selling process is processed and analyzed. Constant dialogue and reward programs help to build lasting relations. At the very center of these brands is the user experience. Through differentiated product offers, a more involving shopping experience, and a highly responsive customer service. These brands aim to build communities, which in turn add to the overall brand experience. Bonobo has recently opened a physical store, not for direct purchase but to provide a tangible experience of the brand world and to guide potential customers. In fashion, trying an item on prior to purchase remains important. Perhaps, despite all their innovation capital, these brands may also hit their limits with today's world of the *phygital*, which refers to the fusion of the physical and the *digital* in one fluid shopping experience.

Another example is Warby Parker, which started as a *DNVB* brand in 2010. Like IKEA, which made design furniture affordable, the founding partners, four students from the same business school in Pennsylvania, had the vision that well-designed eyeglasses should be accessible. Since the market at the time was dominated by an exclusive group of big manufacturers, this was far from being the case. Hence, the Warby Parker brand concept and product offer instantly disrupted the market with its stylish, premium quality prescription eyeglasses sold at a fraction of the standard market prices. Like Bonobo, the *DNVB* model allowed the brand to gain traction with consumers through data collection and analysis from interactions on the online shop and social media channels. Both allowed the brand to fine-tune its consumer profiling and to offer an exceptional, all-round user experience. Warby Parker has since evolved and now sells roughly 90% of its eyewear products through its 230 plus retail outlets in the United States and Canada.

Warby Parker also opted for a social entrepreneurship business model, right from the start. The program donates a free pair of glasses to anybody in need for each pair purchased. By the end of 2023, the program had provided 15 million pairs to people in need. And beyond offering great value prescription glasses, the brand offered *meaning* and with it an emotional bond through which the target audience could easily connect. According to the company statistics, average customers acquire 1.5 pairs every year. Doing good is indeed a great way to grow in the twenty-first century. By 2017, Warby Parker had also brought its manufacturing inhouse with a brand-new optical lab in Rockland County, New York, optimizing cost control even more.

Launched from scratch, the Warby Parker brand quickly gained traction because of its differentiated and highly relevant product and service offer. The brand also provided the emotional platform for consumers and its investors to deeply connect. Its involving brand narrative and an impactful brand mission, designed to be actionable and constantly measured by a set of board-approved key performance indicators, provided great push that continues to boost the brand's performance.

*Inspiring the world with vison, purpose, and style* continues to be the visionary mantra guiding the brand since its launch. Most prominently demonstrated by the *buy a pair—give a pair* program, Warby Parker's mission certainly rang a bell with Millennials and GenZ consumers, fostering brand engagement and building additional brand loyalty. Positioned as a value brand, Warby Parker's success story is also closely related to the brand's set of values that are fully and consistently lived by the company, even after it went public, and as it continues to perform under the conditions of a B-Corp company! Today, Warby Parker is no longer an isolated case and stands as proof that an alternative, more redistributive business model is possible: a model designed to share the generated value with a larger base of stakeholders, right from the start.

Other *DNVB* brands like Carbon 38 not only create or collaborate to shape their online collection, but they also enrich their offer through the curation of a wide range of established and emerging global brands. Also, Unilever has recently been experimenting with digital native brands in form of the Dollar Shave Club, a subscription online service related to shaving and grooming products.

Another vast domain of brand creation is corporate brands. In a world of alliances, joint ventures, Mergers and Acquisitions, a new brand entity might help consolidate an otherwise overwhelming number of fragmented brand propositions into one brand that stands out, providing meaning to customers, internal target audiences, the financial community, and any other stakeholder. Corporate branding is often reduced to a logo, a slogan, and a color palette and corporations sometimes forget that their customers are human beings who act and react in a B2B context, not very different from how they behave as consumers. I am referring again to the emotional side of branding and the purchase decision-making processes, which deep down only differ marginally from those found in mass consumption markets. Not in terms of the individual touch points or decision-making criteria, but the emotional way in which decisions are reached.

The repositioning of the corporate brand in general, or even the development of a new corporate brand to substitute a set of established B2B brands, makes sense way beyond the harmonization of the logo and the typeface. Defined in a crystal sharp manner and by just one word or *angle of attack*, corporate brands succeed in translating often abstract business concepts into involving messages that provide more tangible meaning to stakeholders. Corporate brands, too, just like FMCG brands, may generate positive brand experiences, effectively engaging customers and building loyalty over time. While self-expressive values may play a dominant role in B2C brands, B2B branding emphasizes functional, service, and ethical dimensions. The brand building methodologies, tools, and processes described in this book also apply to the corporate brand repositioning or brand creation.

Brand competence, differentiation, and relevance are as important brand building dimensions in corporate branding as they are for mass consumption brands. Corporate brands also gain from sharply defining what they stand for. Sometimes, doing so allows them to fully integrate corporate and product

## 13  Brand Creation: Getting It Right from the Start

brand dimensions into one brand concept, capable of carrying both. Coca Cola, Toyota, and Google, for example, operate corporate brands that fulfill this hybrid function. Admittedly, this is not always possible, and B2B corporate brands do not necessarily sell products that directly appeal to the general public. However, companies that may be able to leverage this dual role in branding will gain in efficiency and generally succeed in cutting costs.

The international PSA automobile group that had merged with FIAT Chrysler Automobiles (FCA) a couple of years ago rebranded the newly created entity using the *Stellantis* brand. The name suggests the strategic vision that constitutes the foundation for this new brand and the merged group alike. With its Latin roots—the verb *stello* meaning *brightening with stars*—Stellantis refers to the vision of the combined group to lead the automotive industry with sustainable mobility, diversity, and innovation.

Creating one brand with one vision and a set of common values is the right thing to do for a group that employs close to 260,000 people in 30 countries combining 160 different nationalities and owning 20 brands that sell in 130 markets. Here, the brand's role is to provide a common identity and to build a more homogeneous corporate culture, facilitating communications, mutual understanding, and acceptance. Corporate and product brands coexist and support each other image-wise. Visually and phonetically, the *Stellantis* brand suggests strength and trust with the brand logo's dark blue color and a modern, futuristic font, while the arrangement of white dots hints at the stars of the *Stellantis* galaxy. Stellantis has opted for a *house of brands* approach to organize its vast set of product and service brands (see Fig. 13.1).

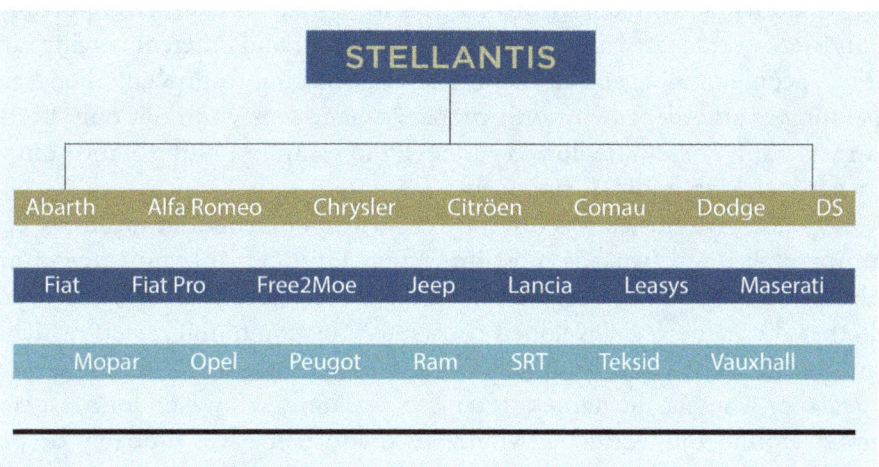

**Fig. 13.1** Stellantis *house of brands*. Author's own image

The *Stellantis* brand development is an example of the first level of branding in the corporate world. The new brand alludes to the ambitions of the merged entity and provides some general strategic directions for internal and external target audiences. It translates the corporate vision, and it has formulated a set of values that provide guidance and confidence to all the Group's stakeholders. However, there is more potential in corporate branding than naming, vision, and values. Corporate brands can aim for something bigger than just a business vision. Levering up to become a *purpose brand* would lend yet more traction to *Stellantis* and contribute to serving as a leadership vision for its employees and as an incentive to outside talent. Taking the *Stellantis* brand to the next level would require a thorough analysis of the groups combined equity, identifying the attribute that would allow for differentiation and the claim of a competence, which in turn could be leveraged to develop the purpose.

Purpose branding is less common in the corporate world; however, purpose is what today's consumer generations want. Any corporation, small or large, has the ingredients to define a brand competence and translating it into a unique and relevant *purpose*. Sure, it takes resources, time, and skills to do so. However, a stronger more relevant brand always pays back by providing stronger market differentiation and heightened motivation of internal teams, even in the corporate world.

The *Mondelez* corporate brand was established in 2012 after the spin-off of the snack foods division of the Kraft Food Inc. business, and it continues as a corporate brand in the grocery food market. Today, *Mondelez* is one of the world's biggest snacking companies with brands such as Riz, Oreo, Belvita, Tuc, Cadbury, and Milka, just to name a few. With its vast brand portfolio, Mondelez covers a large array of snacking occasions and different cravings and targets people of all ages and income levels. Splitting from Krafts Food and operating as an independent unit probably made sense, and not only from a business point of view. It allowed Mondelez to claim its unique brand competence in snacking, more distinctively.

As a name, Mondelez was carefully chosen to be neutral in meaning, easy to pronounce, and (what is most important for a global brand) free of any cultural or religious connotations. From the outside, it is difficult to say whether the name was developed consciously by combining *mond*, which is reminiscent of the Latin word *mundus* and *delez*, which might recall the word *delicious* or whether the name was chosen randomly. However, for most consumers around the world the Mondelez brand name will probably be perceived just as phonetically harmonious and without any specific connotations.

Unlike *Stellantis*, *Mondelez* has taken the next step to defining a vision for its brand. For many consumers, snacking is an ambiguous activity, as people increasingly strive to balance between indulgence and health. Building on its unique competence in different forms of snacking, Mondelez managed to define a brand purpose: *empowering people to snack right*. While this is credible given the many snacking options this corporate brand is offering, to what extent their snacking brands help to make more balanced choices is less obvious. On the other hand, from a branding perspective, making Mondelez a purpose brand was the right thing to do. It provides the brand with a societal role that provides meaning to employees and external stakeholders, both core target audiences for which corporate brands are primarily destined.

Reinventing established brands through renaming, creating brands from scratch, or developing a corporate brand to overcome the challenges of a fragmented brand portfolio and divergent corporate cultures, all require very similar intellectual branding processes.

The brand positioning funnel provides the methodological and structured framework for the development of any of these brands. It leads to the definition of the *one word* a new brand of any kind will ultimately stand for. Doing so in a time and cost-reducing way.

# 14

## B2C Versus B2B Branding

B2B brands (business-to-business), as the name suggests, target professionals. However, B2B target audiences are human beings who relate to brands, predominantly on an emotional level. B2B target audiences not only look for products or services that match a given set of specifications, but also a partner to do business with over the long haul. This marks a major difference with B2C branding, where consumers are less concerned with long-term relationships. Consequently, from the target audience's point of view engaging with B2B brands is often perceived as a high-risk/high-involvement proposition.

Not surprisingly, the decision-making journey in the B2B world is much longer and more complex. On average, procurement professionals take 7.5 months to work through a three-step process: researching potential supplier brands, short listing brands for quotes, and final decision-making. You can add another 3 months for Millennials and GenZ professionals, as they tend to look at more data, compared to professionals from previous generations.

B2B target audiences also reach their decision in a more complex and multilayered process in comparison to consumers. In B2B markets, decision-making is generally performed by a varying number of people with different levels of responsibility, evaluation standards, and potentially divergent preferences. In a recent survey conducted by B2B International, a business-to-business specialized market research company, 50% of enterprises with more than 250 staff members had decision-making units (DMU) of over four people. Compared to their B2C counterparts, B2B brands target a much smaller number of customers. From key accounts to small clients, the numerical size or the target audience also set these brands apart from those in consumer goods markets. Nevertheless, the decision-makers in these processes are human beings (at least for now) and as humans we build relationships with brands on an emotional level. In this respect, B2B brands are no different from B2C brands.

Procurement professionals, buyers, or executive managers all have defined sets of requirements, such as technical specifications or distinct competences in service-providing industries. Apart from the mere product performance, they may also look at factors such as productivity, capacity to innovate, sourcing, and ROI (return on investment) as defined by each customer's specification process. While rational logic and hard facts might be the dominant driver, these people also have a need for trust, confidence, reliability, and *pride*. In B2B branding, these emotional factors may tip the decision in favor of a given brand, when other performance measures are equal.

We have discussed the psychological process of *rational underpinning* during the emotional brand choices in B2C branding (Chap. 3). Consumers who relate to brands primarily via emotional dimensions may in certain *high-risk* or *high-involvement* purchase situations require *rational* product or service information to mentally prop up their decision-making. Premium or luxury brands make wide use of rational messaging alongside their image advertising for exactly this reason. In B2B branding, this principle is inverted, and a well-developed B2B brand is well-advised to provide the *emotional underpinning* in the predominantly rational purchase decision-making process. In branding, emotion and function always own distinctive roles. These roles may vary chiefly from case to case; though both have their own specific relevance in the decision-making process and neither performs well without the other in the course of concluding a deal.

Specifications in B2B purchases are designed to give purchase decision-making more objectivity. Distinctive performance criteria, availability, and pricing form the basis of each decision-making process. This is why on the surface, these processes might seem more functional and information or data-driven. Therefore, one might assume that decision-making is more objective. While this is certainly true in general terms, the rational reasoning also has its limits. *Impulse buying*, frequent in mass consumption purchases, is rare in B2B procurement and here the evaluation of competitive offers is a prevailing standard procedure. At least for as long as relationship-building and ultimately brand loyalty continue to be in the formative phase. Even so, emotional decision-making in B2B is more frequent than you might think. Keep in mind, B2B target audiences have a vested interest in not just identifying a product or service brand but also a reliable supplier to do business with in the long-term. In certain industries, procurement and specification processes may require up to several years to conclude and once the decision is reached, customers have a vested interest to maintain long-term relationships with B2B brands.

Trust, confidence, and reliability are indispensable for building these long-term relationships in B2B branding. All three are emotional triggers. In any given market, competitive offers might match or even surpass performance levels prescribed by a customer's specification process. This is precisely the moment when the B2B brand will play out its branding power, impacting the final decision-making on an emotional level.

When building relationships, product or service performance is key, but not nearly as much as the emotional dimensions of trust, reliability, confidence, honesty, transparency, and increasingly the sustainability dimensions as defined by the 17 SDGs (United Nations Sustainable Development Goals). In the real world, not everything works perfectly all the time and quality issues may occur in any industry. B2B brands that have built strong emotional connections with their customers are likely to weather these times more easily.

Several recent studies point out the importance of emotional factors in B2B branding, suggesting that these characteristics may play a more important role than previously assumed. A survey, by B2B International, a global market research firm, conducted in 2019 across roughly 2000 mid-sized and large companies in the United States, China, Spain, Germany, France, and the United Kingdom revealed that 56% of the decision-making in professional procurement situations is emotionally motivated. Emotional markers related to brands turned out to be most critical in the initial establishment of the *considered* supplier shortlist and at the final stage of the customer purchasing journey.

B2B target audiences rely on both rational and emotional factors when making their decisions. Objectivity and subjectivity prevail at different stages of the decision-making process, although both are equally decisive components that define failure or success. The B2B International research isolated four distinct dimensions that drive decision-making in B2B processes via emotional triggers: *trust, confidence, optimism,* and *pride*. All four are dimensions in which well-defined brands usually excel.

B2B brands are built on a distinct competence, an expertise, or know-how that supports the image of a reliable and consistent product or service performance for the customer. Both consistency and reliability make doing business more predictable and thus foster the perception of *trust*. Like with B2C brands, the brand competence must be translated into a brand essence, which defines what the brand stands for. A B2B brand that manages this task by reducing its meaning to just *one word* or angle of attack will mark its differentiation against its competitors more decisively, generating stature, hence infusing trust. As suggested by the above-mentioned research, brand trust appears critical at an early stage of the procurement selection process, with only two contenders retained in a customer's relevant set to enter the offer phase.

*Confidence* is another emotional dimension provided by brands. Purchase decisions in B2B markets are professional acts and unlike B2C decisions, buyers are judged by the results their decisions produce on their company. Nobody's job is on the line when buying a poorly performing mass consumption brand. This adds a substantial amount of psychological pressure to the process and buying from a well-known and important brand will reduce the perception of risk. Buyers rarely get blamed for choosing the market leader. This is an important factor in B2B branding and a key argument in favor of turning your business proposition into a strong and well-differentiated brand.

B2B brands also have the capacity to produce feelings of *optimism* through their values and brand personality. The above research revealed that decision-makers in B2B organizations develop preferences for brands that appear to positively contribute to their business in the mid- to long-run. A key role of B2B branding is to build and sustain long-term relationships with a company's customers. Strong B2B brands do just that. Their sharp brand positioning allows them to leverage brand stature, competence, and a unique expertise. This makes the prospect of making an active contribution to a customer's future business more likely. Inevitably, this also contributes to creating preferences, nourishing and fastening the relationship.

Pride is the fourth emotional value transported by B2B brands. Like in many areas of life, people want to be associated with winners not losers. By contrast, there are only a few true leaders in each market segment, and for most B2B brands getting there might be a long way to go. In any case, every brand started its journey at one point, and I do not think that being number three or four in the market really matters. In branding, what counts most is the impressions a brand leaves on its target audiences. When combined, these impressions allow target customers to form opinions about the brand over time. Brand performance, a differentiating and relevant positioning, visual identity codes, and messaging can provide these impressions even before a first personal contact is made.

The development of the brand awareness is often neglected in B2B marketing activities. Budgets allocated to build awareness of B2B brands are only a tiny fraction of those spent on B2B brands. Regardless, brand awareness in B2B branding is as important as it is for consumer goods. At the same time, building brand awareness is easier to achieve in B2B branding, since target audiences are more confined and easier to reach via direct or tailored marketing tools and social media channels such as YouTube, LinkedIn, and in certain instances Instagram. A brand that does not make itself known to its target audience will always struggle to make it onto the shortlist or into the specification process.

To build a B2B brand successfully, companies are well-advised to focus on the corporate brand first. Developing a brand positioning platform and establishing a new brand in the market is a costly and time-intensive exercise, which requires substantial human and financial resources and a specific branding competence to succeed. Under most circumstances, a corporate B2B brand will be able to support the entire product or service offer. That being so, additional brand development at an inferior level should rank secondary. As we have seen, B2B customers are motivated by trust and confidence and these two emotional values relate to the corporate brand and the company behind it.

It is important to remember that B2B brands are not reduced to just a logo, a slogan, and a color code. For B2B branding to work successfully requires a similar effort and analytic work as for B2C brands. These brands also need substance and strong messaging to succeed. The starting point for the development of the B2B brand positioning is the company's core competence, its expertise, or specific know-how that sets it apart from all competitors. In B2B branding, this competence might be defined by a unique product feature or a technology, a methodology, or a specific expertise acquired through experience and best practice. It is important to bring this expertise to the forefront, leveraging it to define what the future brand will stand for, ideally with a single word, the brand essence. The methodology to do so has been discussed in Chap. 8.

Like for B2C brands, the brand positioning of a B2B brand must be differentiating against competition and relevant to the target customers at the same time. You may use a simple scheme to help you in the process of defining your brand's USP (unique selling proposition; see Fig. 14.1).

Once the brand essence is defined, you may develop a set of values that your B2B brand will represent and act upon and will be instrumental in defining or adjusting your corporate culture. It might also be worthwhile to develop the benefits your branded offer proposes to a potential customer. Clarifying the benefits early on will later benefit your sales pitch and further help to highlight your brand's differentiation. All too often, B2B brands content themselves with stressing their product and service attributes without translating them into tangible or intangible benefits for their customers.

To execute the B2B brand building process professionally, you may refer to the brand positioning funnel and its associated tool, just like for any B2C brand. The B2B brand creation or redefinition methodology remains the

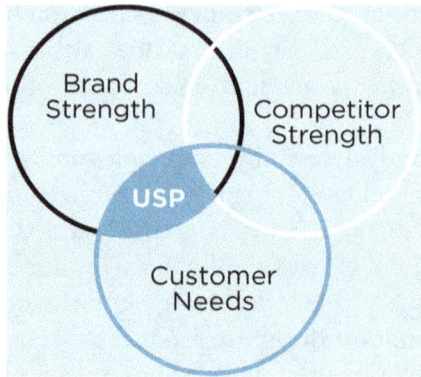

**Fig. 14.1** Standard USP model. Author's own image

same, what changes is just the information and data you put into it. Only once the brand positioning has been fully clarified and defined may the brand identity be developed. The briefing to do so is the brand positioning. Brand essence, values, and brand personality must now be translated into visual elements, potentially a brand slogan, ideally a vision and mission statement, and, in certain cases, also the brand name itself.

For several reasons, naming in B2B branding is important. The chosen name must be free of cultural and/or religious connotations, in order to potentially travel outside your home market. Phonetically balanced, pleasing, and possibly conceived with a logic in mind, the brand name will lend itself to the brand's storytelling efforts. This, in turn, creates involvement with the brand that favors brand retention. It also has a major impact on your internal target audiences and your employer brand. B2B brand names that tell a story and are easy to retain will significantly contribute to the brand awareness building effort (see Stellantis or Mondelez in Chap. 13).

B2B brands also benefit from a brand signature, which should spell out in a more colloquial and memorable manner what the brand stands for. Like for any brand, a signature will not easily end up in the collective memory of a given nation or target audience; nevertheless, it always represents great potential as a *jumping board* to introduce your brand's narrative or storytelling. And of course, it helps everybody internally and externally to remember what your brand stands for and in what sense it is relevant and different from competitors.

There are two distinct layers of branding in B2B. Company or corporate brands define the equity of the *supplier* brands, whereas *product* brands provide brand equity at the *object or service* level. Some companies also develop an intermediate *product or service category brand* level, although this might quickly become overwhelming and confusing. Sticking to just two branding levels and using a simple descriptor for the category level is a leaner and yet still efficient solution. As stressed above, it is the corporate level where B2B brands exercise the most impactful leverage. FEDEX is a perfect illustration of the unitary approach to branding (see Fig. 14.2). The FEDEX brand brings together all of the company's service brands by using a brief descriptor for differentiation at the sub-brand level. Here, the FEDEX umbrella brand provides the main push in the delivery services market, while its sub-brands correspond to specific target needs. As a result, FEDEX transformed itself from a *house of individual, disconnected brands* into a *branded house* where one brand covers all of the needs of a service provider with a very diversified offer.

Concentrating funds at the corporate level is also more cost-effective. Here, strong brands will provide a halo across all subordinate product or service brands. This branding principle is also frequent in B2C markets. Nike, for example, which sells hundreds of different product references, rarely develops any specific product brands (Air, Dunk, Free) and if it does, the Nike brand name is always part of it (Nike Air, etc.). This enables the Nike brand to provide strong caution to the entire product portfolio where each reference is branded primarily under the Nike name. This way, one strong and well-established brand is capable of selling hundreds of nameless products, just because all are supported by the Nike umbrella brand.

There is of course some merit to brands at the product or service level, but impact will be more limited. In general, B2B brands at the product or service level may gain a decent level of brand awareness with potential target audiences. Be that as it may, this generally happens only after they have been around for many years. No one single brand owns innovation. A product brand that is matched or outpaced by a competitive development loses its traction and part of the investment that went into creating it. This is why

**Fig. 14.2** Principle of a branded house. Author's own image

corporate umbrella brands that carry the product or service offer may turn out to be more resilient in regards to these market upheavals. Nonetheless, branding of individual products or services underneath the corporate B2B brand will challenge you to clarify the benefits that each product brand offers to potential customers, and this may become an asset for the sales pitch.

There is another valuable side benefit to B2B branding. Performed with scrutiny and diligence, the exercise might lead to a vision for the company's business and its market. This vision may translate into the definition of a purpose, which will further help to emotionalize the B2B brand, in particular for the Millennials and GenZ generations, who have started to climb up the corporate ladder, finding themselves in positions where decisions are being made.

Tarkett, one of the world's leading flooring companies with origins in Sweden, decided to take its company public in 2013. The Group had adopted the Tarkett brand name in 1997 and had since grown organically and through Mergers & Acquisitions (M&A). To protect its local or regional business, and afraid of disrupting the respective corporate cultures of the entities it acquired, the Group preserved most of the acquired brands in its quickly expanding brand portfolio. Tarkett gradually became a *house of brands*.

There was a clear strategy for those acquisitions, which allowed the Group to gain geographical scope and flooring expertise, eventually proposing a large range of flooring products and services from vinyl to linoleum, from stratified to hard wood, and from carpet flooring to artificial turf, athletic racing tracks, and tennis courts. Tarkett was primarily selling to B2B customers interested in large volumes, such as stores and shopping malls, office buildings, hospitals, hotels, airports, and sports venues. The brand also runs a B2C division, albeit, on a limited scale, selling mainly through distributors such as home depots and carpet specialists.

At the time, Tarkett's brand portfolio seemed as diverse as its product offer and even though the brand had developed a distinct identity, it lacked a strategic message. Preparing to go public via an IPO, an initial public offering at the EuroNext stock exchange in Paris, Tarkett recognized the need for a more differentiating corporate brand positioning that would equally play to its B2B target audiences. Furthermore, the value the newly defined Tarkett brand provided might become a significant booster for the valuation of the initial offering during the EuroNext introduction.

With its Swedish origins, Tarkett could look back on 130 years of experience in flooring, owning the most diversified product offer in flooring worldwide. As a world leader, it was also a very experienced supplier with strong expertise and the largest offer of different flooring types on the market. Last but not least, flooring also has a great capacity to transform a place. Even more so than walls, floors allow you to play with colors and patterns, giving interior architects almost unlimited options at the intersection of design and functionality to express their ideas and concepts.

From a branding perspective, Tarkett's ability to offer and to produce unique *experiences* was quickly emerging as one of the converging features on which the brand could be built. The brand was among the most experienced in the market, it offered unparallelled experience and know-how in products and services, and its large product range offered great latitude for producing experiences that had the potential to improve the *quality of life* in the spaces where Tarkett provided its flooring.

*Experiences* became the brand's essence, summarized in a new brand slogan: *the ultimate flooring experience*. The exercise allowed to revamp Tarkett's ageing brand identity and to softly integrate the other B2B brands owned by the Group via the application of new design codes and newly defined brand guidelines. After all, the brand positioning offered yet another potential, quickly sized by the Tarkett management. It provided a differentiating vision the brand could claim for the entire industry. This vision allowed Tarkett to transform its brand from a simple *flooring provider* to a provider of *life enhancing experiences*.

Through brand repositioning, Tarkett had transformed itself into a B2B brand that actively defends its *thought leadership vision*. A tangible demonstration of this was a first concept store and a large showroom in Paris, where its head offices are located, which Tarkett quickly opened. The new positioning helped to refocus the brand on its design competence and the commercial messaging played out Tarkett's new differentiation as a solution provider, capable of offering life-changing design on top of its products functionalities. Tarkett had found a new *emotional* way to engage with its target customers, leveraging a relevant point of difference to help build long-term relationships and to consolidate future growth.

The 2019 B2B International research project revealed that *thought leadership* is favored by 40% of B2B decision-makers in their brand choices. This makes perfect sense as thought leader brands are in the position to provide stimulus and new insights for their customers' business. This produces enriching experiences that translate into optimism, one of the four core values in emotional bonding, so important to B2B brands. And what customer would not rather work with a partner who demonstrates leadership in its market?

Brand value may translate directly into financial rewards. As shown by a Millward & Brown research study in 2014, this may be substantial. Analyzing the Standard & Poor's 500 (S&P 500) index, which includes the US most powerful companies, this international research firm concluded that the market valuation of the represented companies was boosted by an average of 30% exclusively by the value of their respective brands.

As we have seen, B2B brands have a double role to play. To succeed, B2B brands must address not only the target company needs but also those of the buyer. They must satisfy not only their customers' rational but also their emotional needs. Product and service performance on the one side and relationship building through emotional values on the other is what defines powerful B2B brands. Brand vision and a *purpose* are meaningful brand components in B2B as well. For all these reasons, B2B companies of any size should seriously consider transforming their business into a brand.

# 15

# Branding in the Corporate World (Crucial Implications for Corporate and Employer Brands)

As the name suggests, corporate branding refers to branding of a company or corporation versus products, services, people, or places. Corporate brands are generally more complex since they address multiple target audiences. They must also treat a more diversified set of topics, compared with product or service brands. As brands, they address and manage a rather complex ecosystem of diverse target audiences and subjects. The target audience of a corporate brand is generally referred to as the *stakeholder community* and its definition has grown increasingly multifaceted in the twenty-first century.

During the 1990s and 2000s, the stakeholder definition predominantly referred to the shareholder community with the intention of focusing management on the sole production of shareholder value, while today's definition of stakeholders has grown more complex and diversified. Now a corporation's typical shareholder community may include partners and suppliers, talent and candidates, local communities, government bodies, NGOs, the environment, or the planet in addition to the actual shareholders who are mostly motivated by financial interests in the company.

Successfully building and maintaining a corporate brand over time requires managing all these different stakeholder relationships, which may at given moments even overlap and interact. In that sense, employee motivation may impact product or service quality, which in turn may impact customer satisfaction and consequently shareholder value. Managing these relationships is not a static process either. Stakeholders may change as the company enters new market segments and stakeholder interests or needs may evolve over time, driven by trends or technological innovation. Managing these relations has become a matter of constant dialogue with the different stakeholder communities, mostly in direct exchanges (local communities, legislators, shareholders) and/or via social media community management. As a result, building and maintaining a corporate brand has become a multidirectional endeavor centered around a continuous, multiple communications effort based on true dialogue.

In theory, corporate branding and B2B branding (discussed in the previous chapter) are closely related or may even overlap. While corporate brands may directly represent a wide, multilayered product or service offer like a B2B brand (Tarkett), they may also exist as independent brand entities whose main role is to provide an image umbrella for an entire portfolio of independent sub-brands. Today, most of the world's large corporate brands in mass consumption or package goods sign the packaging of their product brands to provide cross-portfolio recognition and brand caution. Procter & Gamble (P&G) successively adopted this umbrella branding approach during the 2000s, introducing its corporate brand on the packaging of each newly acquired sub-brand. This way the reputation of each individual product brand somewhat pays into the image of the corporate brand, which in turn provides statuary caution to the product brands. The brand caution of a corporate brand may therefore contribute to prop-up less well-known brands in the brand portfolio by infusing trust and image value via the corporate umbrella brand.

Nevertheless, to apply this principle successfully, the corporate brand still requires a well-defined positioning platform of its own. Living just off the transferred image value of its sub-brands will not be enough to address the expectations and needs of today's multilayered stakeholder communities.

This brand positioning process again follows the principles laid out in Chap. 8, as prescribed by the *brand positioning funnel*. Corporate brands rarely have a single product attribute to differentiate from, but like B2B brands they usually have a unique competence to build their brand on. This competence may exist in the form of a unique technology, a specific know-how or expertise, a unique manufacturing process, a deeper, more intimate understanding of the target audience, a heritage from the founding years, or a set of standards in product or service quality that distinguish the brand offer.

Again, to define the one element that sets a corporate brand apart you need to do your homework, extensively mining for information inside and around the company. There will always be a meaningful point of difference from where to build the corporate brand positioning, too. However, the challenge is to identify it and to translate it into a relevant and differentiating *one-word* positioning or *brand essence*.

Quite possibly, the corporate branding exercise is where the *one-word* brand positioning methodology has its biggest and most diversified impact. Corporate brands have a more complex job to accomplish, and the one single angle of attack that the methodology helps to define serves as a powerful prism to unite all facets of the complex corporate brand ecosystem. Only the corporate brands that stand for *one thing* to all stakeholders succeed in providing the ultimate in message clarity and consistency.

Achieving this kind of corporate brand positioning is not a question of identifying the smallest common denominator. On the contrary, this is potentially the biggest trap to avoid. All too often, branding agencies proceed to interview senior management to listen, learn, summarize, and then define the brand essence. Rarely is this exercise paired with a deep dive into the company's product or service reality, its history, its unique competence, and knowhow that may be derived from this data. Instead, the distillation process becomes focused on a positioning line that pretty much everybody can agree on: somewhat like a statement at the end of a controversial political meeting. In the context of a corporate branding process, this inevitably rhymes with compromise, and often results in defining the positioning platform on the smallest common denominator. Compromising on the exact definition of a brand positioning almost always results in a lack of focus that challenges employees' ability to transform it into tangible action.

One-word corporate brand positionings, such as those for product or service brands, must be anchored in the corporate reality (tangible and true), provide a high level of relevance to all stakeholders, and be differentiating at the same time. *Truth*, *relevance*, and *differentiation* render the corporate positioning operational and usable to all and for all communication purposes.

How many of the world's CEOs can say what their brand stands for? And how many can say it with just *one single word*? Those who struggle to do so still have an unexplored potential to redefine the positioning of their corporate brand. Without a doubt, corporate brands are particularly complex and abstract. Yet, they too can be defined with a single word that prescribes tangible and precise action for everybody inside and outside the company. This is where the power of such positionings resides. *One word* that points to the direction in which all stakeholders will take.

In the corporate world, the merits of the *one-word* brand positioning may reach way beyond the obvious. Like for product and service brands, they provide tangible direction for employees, thus helping to improve motivation and productivity. All the company's inherent energy and creativity is channeled in a single-minded unique direction. This alone may render the entire organization more cohesive. Teams grow tighter together; employees feel more in control, generating a significant motivational uplift, potentially translating into enhanced productivity. Danone's corporate *active health* positioning, first introduced in the early 2000s, and discussed in detail in Chap. 10, provides strong testimony for this approach. The corporate brand positioning mantra of the time, *active health*, prescribed tangible action at every hierarchical level, obliging everyone in the organization to provide and emphasize the health benefits offered by every Danone product brand. This was not always easy to accomplish, but the task was clear, and this made everybody's job more tangible and meaningful.

*Active health* provided the corporate Danone brand with a strong and relevant brand vision and mission statement, still relevant today. Danone's corporate brand positioning was sourced in its past. Little known to most of us, Danone's origins are in Spain. In the aftermath of WWI in 1919, many people were suffering from intestinal disease, often related to poor drinking water quality. At the time, Issac Carasso, Danone's founder and company owner had met the Russian scientist, Elie Metchnikoff, who had spent years at the Pasteur Institute in Paris researching live yogurt cultures, establishing their benefits for human health.

That being so, the active health positioning of the Danone brand was no coincidence. It was the obvious choice for a company that had believed, throughout most of its existence, in the vision that our *nutrition represents our first line of health defense.* This belief nourished Danone's corporate vision for many years, only to evolve recently to include the planetary dimension, particularly important to younger generations. At the same time, *One planet. One health.* is just the logical evolution of the original corporate *active health* positioning. It reflects the belief that people's health and that of the planet are intimately correlated.

Simultaneously, the corporate vision, which Danone was able to formulate based on its corporate brand positioning, also defined its corporate mission and its brand purpose: *Bringing health through food to as many people as possible.* On the other hand, one could rightly argue that some Danone products (such as desserts, dairy drinks, or products targeted to children) contain substantial amounts of sugar, rendering their health benefits somewhat questionable. While this is certainly true, these products still provide calcium and vitamins, which, compared with other product choices in snacking or desserts, makes them somewhat healthier.

Taking the time to properly define the positioning of a corporate brand always pays off in another sense. Determining what a corporate brand really stands for may also contribute to sharpening the strategic direction the company might want to take for its future development and growth. The driver behind this strategic insight is the brand competence. Reflecting on what a company is best at as part of the brand development process and turning this competence into the brand essence may help senior management to clarify and refocus its strategic direction. This, in return, may impact internal and external innovation processes, eventually leading to a stronger competitive edge.

The corporate brand development exercise almost always generates positive impact for the employer brand as well. While Millennials and GenZ generations are still attracted to money, they also seek meaning. A well-defined corporate brand is clearly in a better position to provide this meaning, most often through the definition of a visionary corporate *purpose*.

In corporate branding, purpose refers to the contribution a company can potentially make to positively impact society and/or the planet by directly leveraging its unique expertise, know-how, and related competencies. This suggests that *purpose* must be real. Like the brand essence, it must be rooted in the company's tangible or intangible equity. The brand positioning exercise will almost always directly suggest a brand purpose concept as one of the process outcomes. However, like with brand values, the brand *purpose* never succeeds as an empty shell, and it must be talked about and acted upon by everyone.

Most of the world's powerful corporations have fully adopted this approach, regrettably not always in a truly sincere manner. After the *green washing* of the 1990s and 2000s, *purpose washing* continues to be quite commonplace. While companies like Unilever, Patagonia, Danone, Johnson & Johnson have all adopted competence-specific *purpose*-inspired programs with the goal of addressing and remedying urgent societal or environmental problems, others like Nestlé remain stuck in old day practices and repeatedly produce content for scandals. More recently, these have included food safety issues (Buttoni Pizza) as well as cruel and hazardous animal welfare issues (Herta). Revealed by the L214 NGO in France in 2023, this latest scandal even pushed several retailers like Whiterose in the United Kingdom to delist all Nestlé-owned Herta products from their stores. With transparency becoming an ever more important factor in brand behavior, these practices are likely to enter into direct confrontation with today's ethics of increasingly sensitive and well-informed consumers.

As a global corporate brand, Unilever strives to make *sustainable living commonplace*. The Unilever purpose program was initiated by Paul Polman in 2015 during a remarkable speech at the United Nations in New York. The program, founded on and supportive of the 17 UN Sustainable Development

Goals (SDGs), was visionary right from the start and advocated a more responsible form of capitalism that would address climate change, poverty, and inequality in addition to financial performance and shareholder value in the traditional sense. Unilever has since enacted the program through corporate initiatives and product innovation in the areas of hygiene, health, and the environment.

As one of the first FMCG product brands and part of the global Unilever brand portfolio, Dove pioneered its brand purpose back in 2004. Initiated in Germany, it may be seen as a precursor to the larger Unilever corporate effort. At the time, global research had revealed that only 4% of women considered themselves beautiful. While shocking in absolute terms, these findings were not really a surprise after decades of massive advertising by the beauty industry. The industry's communication efforts had managed to establish impossible (and, most importantly, fake) beauty standards that became universally recognized and used as a benchmark for women (and men) to compare themselves against.

Born as a simple photo exhibition in Düsseldorf, Germany, the campaign has since grown into a global purpose effort for Dove and Unilever, alike. Dove's *campaign for real beauty* now relies on a vast communication campaign, leveraging social media and local workshops where women come together to exchange. Helping women of all ages to gain self-esteem is a noble task that pays directly into one of Unilever's purpose domains, inequality. By 2030, the Dove purpose program projects to have helped some 250 million women around the world to feel better about their own natural beauty. As an important side-benefit, the program will no doubt also foster the emotional bonding with the Dove brand. More than ever, doing good has become a great way to grow.

Google defines its global brand purpose as *organizing the world's information, making it universally accessible and useful*. If it is true what some scientists believe that humanity's combined knowledge currently doubles every 2–3 years, Google's purpose is clearly no easy task. Tesla is set to *accelerate the world's transition to sustainable energy*. A corporate brand purpose that has already produced some very tangible results, Tesla being the first car manufacturer to succeed in creating any universally significant demand for electrical vehicles. While the Tesla example is remarkable, the brand is also at risk due to some of the overreaching purpose declarations of its founder and chief shareholder Elon Musk, who is disrupting conventional ethics in other, unrelated markets perhaps best illustrated by the Twitter/X fiasco and a charity foundation with questionable practices.

However, still numerous corporate brands would gain from taking a fresh look at their brand purpose definition. Toyota claims to *lead the way to the future of mobility, enriching lives around the world with the safest and most responsible ways of moving people*. While this is fundamentally correct, the statement neither feels differentiated nor inspired. It contains too many messages to make it truly focused and actionable.

Brand purpose statements are most efficient in providing direction and traction to staff and potential candidates when they project a single-minded message claim. Like defining the brand essence, not all messages can stand out at the same level of priority. In which case, corporate brands are well advised to make a tough choice. This does not mean that important messages are lost. They are just placed at a different level in the message hierarchy. Chapter 16 will elaborate on the principles of message hierarchies in more detail.

Fully aligned with the corporate brand positioning, the brand purpose is a powerful tool to translate the corporate brand essence into a meaningful and actionable marching order, everyone can easily identify with and act upon, at any level of responsibility and professional experience. A mutually shared corporate brand purpose may unleash substantial motivational forces, not just with Millennials and GenZ generation but also with long-serving employees, thus lifting everyone out of the daily routine with the inspiration of a higher goal.

Another important domain of corporate branding is the definition of the employer brand. Unlike for other generations at least in the Western world, the available workforce is shrinking, making it harder for companies to identify, recruit, and retain talent. Often referred to as the *war for talent* (McKinsey in 1997), the situation is not new, but it is not improving either. Korn Ferry, a global recruitment and consulting agency, estimates that the global talent shortage may reach 85 million people by 2030. This trend is likely to become accentuated by the technological transition of the current Third Industrial Revolution that will transform our global society in many key areas such as energy (from fossil energy to sustainable electricity), industry (from production to knowledge), and the claims for true *purpose* or *meaning*. Younger generations increasingly base their employer choices on a company's ability to propose a true and relevant purpose. Within this context, demographics are changing and not only skills but *branded purpose* will become determining factors in firing up the *war for talent*. At the heart of this struggle is the *knowledge worker* (Peter Ducker), who will move the needle of success of entire corporations and industries. Everything plays out in a global world, where geographic barriers have become marginalized.

In addition, many companies strive to adapt to this change by researching talent needs, offering more job flexibility, thus creating previously unheard-of working conditions. Free five-star breakfast or lunch buffets, flexible working hours and locations, a work–life balance baby boomers were unable to even imagine, more paid vacation days, free coaching and gym memberships, personal out-time, just to name a few. Today's *knowledge workers* sure value an all-inclusive package.

All of these conditions and perks aim to attract and retain talent. A special 2012 issue on corporate governance by *Business Horizon* suggested that the cost of training a new employee may add up to 1.5 and 2.5 of that position's annual salary. Job evaluation platforms like Glassdoor add another layer of complexity, where millions of employer brands are reviewed and evaluated by its workforce communities, thus serving as a powerful decision-making tool for job seekers from Europe to India and from the Americas to Australia. The reach of these platforms is further expanding and likely to soon stretch far beyond the tech-related industries.

Within this global context of ever-tighter labor markets, the employer brand becomes another important pillar of the corporate brand ecosystem. The corporate and the employer brands corelate with each other and while the first one may ambition to primarily shape the perceptions of external target audiences, the employer brand is both inner and outer directed. However, both must coexist in a perfect symbiosis, thus projecting an attractive, authentic, and cohesive image of the company. Sourced from the same brand essence, the employer brand must also be fully aligned with a corporation's vision, mission, purpose, and values. The foundation for the employer brand is the corporate brand positioning and as a corporate *sub-brand* the employer brand also gains from defining itself by a single word or angle of attack.

Besides attractive working conditions, benefits, and other amenities, the focus of the employer brand must be to provide meaning and purpose. Google has fully embraced this concept by signing its employer brand with its *do cool things that matter* slogan. The line suggests precisely what knowledge workers look for: fun, visibility, and meaning. Tomorrow's leading managers want to make an impact while living their own personal values. Employer brands fully aligned with the corporate brand and labeled accordingly, signal more authenticity, and hence offer better traction in the market. Like so often in branding, what ultimately swings the pendulum is not the product or service attribute itself, frequently matched by competition, but the emotional experiences that these attributes produce (or claim to produce). It is those experiences that build strong and lasting brand preferences.

Employer brands, as siblings of the corporate brand, are no exception and the time and effort that might go into building them is clearly worth the investment. Well planned out, they become a strong driving force behind the development of an attractive, inclusive, and cohesive corporate culture. There are of course many other dimensions indispensable for successful employer branding and the purpose of this short section is simply to stress the importance of the flawless interconnection between the corporate and the employer brand, both built from the same brand foundation. Perfectly aligned, both brands may make a significant contribution to the business success.

CSR (Corporate Social Responsibility) and, to a lesser extent, ESG (Environmental Social Governance) represent yet another layer the corporate brand must address within its complex messaging and target audience ecosystem.

While CSR programs are usually less formal and more flexible in terms of the areas they address and cover, ESG is mostly used as a financial evaluation tool that measures the risk potential a company carries regarding environmental, societal, and governance issues. Accordingly, ESG is more closely linked to a company's overall business strategy than its corporate brand. In recent years, ESG programs have become increasingly regulated and now have to correspond to certain regulatory frameworks such as the Global Reporting Initiative (GRI) or the Sustainability Accounting Standards Board (SASB). ESG programs generally come with a strict annual reporting.

On the contrary, CSR programs impact the corporate brand more directly. They are designed more freely to best reflect the company's abilities and to address the expectations and needs of a respective stakeholder community. CSR messaging is data based, whereas KPIs (Key Performance Indicators) are mostly defined by the company itself and not by independent regulatory organization such as GRI or SASB. Often, they are defined to fit the overall narrative of the corporate brand.

Necessarily, it is crucial to align any CSR program directly with the corporate brand positioning. Again, the *brand essence* directs the development of all dimensions of the corporate brand, defining what it stands for, developing its identity codes (potentially even the brand name), its vision, mission, and purpose statements, as well as distinctive messaging for the employer brand and the CSR effort.

A company's CSR program has an important role to play in today's environmental context and, in particular, resource scarcity, biodiversity, and climate change. Most consumers now express some degree of concern or even anxiety regarding these issues that increasingly impact their behavior, including their brand choices. In this overall context, B2B customers are no exceptions. Similarly, assigning certain brand messages to a designated CSR program offers the advantage of relieving the message load of the corporate brand. Corporate brands must also define a stringent message hierarchy, where all relevant messages are organized at specific levels underneath the differentiating and single-minded corporate brand message, the *brand essence*. Like for the positioning of consumer brands, defining this message hierarchy does not mean that any message is lost. At any rate, a well-designed CSR program allows any corporate brand to package all sustainability-related messages into a designated and meaningful communication effort, which will feed directly into the equity of the corporate brand.

To make a significant contribution to the equity of the corporate brand, any CSR program must be genuine and authentic. All program parts and the intention behind them must be honest and sincere. Numbers quoted must be verifiable; achievements must be tangible as measured by a set of predefined KPIs. CSR program objectives should be realistic and attainable in the short- to mid-term. Boasting program goals that your company stands to miss might backfire, projecting a negative image on the corporate brand. In my experience, too many companies still consider CSR programs as a great way to simply boost the image of the corporate brand, providing too little tangible substance for it to be perceived as real. This quickly raises suspicions of *green washing*, for which public tolerance is quickly vanishing, in particular, for Millennials and GenZ generations.

The space a CSR program takes within the corporate brand platform may vary. While one could argue that Patagonia has merged its CSR, corporate, and product brand platforms into one and the same brand entity, IBM has developed a freestanding approach to CSR, which stands almost as an independent brand pillar next to its corporate brand. Over decades, IBM's CSR program has grown organically, often ahead of the general societal consciousness. Its origin dates all the way back to the early twentieth century when IBM first included dimensions of equality.

A great source of inspiration for smaller or mid-sized companies, IBM' CSR program is worth taking a closer look at. It provides deep insights into the evolutionary principles CSR may encounter in any corporate organization, no matter the size. IBM first pioneered a more institutionalized CSR program during the 1970s. It included initiatives toward community engagement, diversity, and education. A significant environmental dimension was added in the 1990s, and with the rapid rise of IT technology, IBM introduced its *Smarter Planet* CSR Program in 2008. The program, while still including the traditional CSR components, recognized the impact technology could make to transform public infrastructure and entire industries through data analytics and first AI solutions.

The *Smarter Planet* program was directly aligned with the IBM corporate brand and helped stress the company's tech leadership across multiple industries such as health care, transportation, public services, water management, and so on. Simultaneously, it designated IBM's corporate brand *purpose*, illustrating how well corporate brand and CSR program had become aligned. Responding to emerging societal challenges during the 2010s, IBM yet again remodeled its CSR program introducing *IBM Impact*, which takes a stronger focus on societal issues such as sustainability, education, diversity, and community engagement. The program includes a proprietary workforce development initiative SkillsBuild (free online courses for high-school students, academics, and adult learners) and P-Tech (Pathway to Technology—a program designed for students to bridge the gap between academic learning and workplace skills). The program targets students from lower income classes, promoting employability among other topics. The *Impact* program simultaneously amplifies IBM's role as a purpose brand and true solution provider. It plays a decisive role in IBM's efforts to win over the best future knowledge workers.

The corporate brand is undeniably the most challenging of all brand types to define. It must manage a complex ecosystem of diverse target audiences and stakeholder communities, requiring more message diversity to address multiple and often dynamic expectations and needs. In addition, most corporate brands operate in a global marketplace, with accentuated competitive pressure and important challenges through continuous technological innovation. Combined, these represent an environment of permanent, multidimensional threats where a strong and well-defined corporate brand might come in handy to compensate for a temporarily lagging product or service performance. This explains why the effort that goes into the positioning of a corporate brand, no matter the size, always offers great returns.

# 16

# Organizing the Brand Message Mix

Never in the history of mankind has branding been more popular. Today, there is barely any product or service, destination or cause, which has not turned itself into a brand—not to mention personal branding, powered by social media networks. This massive proliferation of branding concepts does not come without a cost. Markets have become more competitive; brand choices have grown more complex and brands must fight harder to grab their target's attention. Within this context, the brands that know what they stand for and are able to communicate their single-minded difference and relevance in a clear and distinctive way are the most likely to stand out. The indispensable first level for brands to be remembered and desired.

The one-word brand positioning methodology, discussed in this book, always comes with a challenging side effect. At its center stands the single-minded brand value proposition: the *brand essence*, the one and only central message that sets the brand apart and produces relevance for its target audiences. This pure and single-minded positioning angle constitutes a sort of prism through which all brand activities will be seen, evaluated, and executed. Developed and introduced seamlessly through the *one-word* brand positioning exercise (as defined by the *brand positioning funnel* in Chap. 8), it will succeed in pointing everybody in the same direction, internally and externally alike. All the company's inherent energy and creativity will be channeled toward a single-minded strategic objective, thus building a coherent and consistent brand equity in the shortest possible period of time and under the most cost-efficient conditions. One-word brand positionings make staff more autonomous, making strategically relevant decisions and producing and evaluating fresh ideas. In sum, this will directly support growth objectives, and in the mid- to long-run contribute to enhancing the overall company value, as demonstrated by the 30% brand valuation factor identified in the Millward & Brown research project related to the market value of S&P 500 companies in 2014.

However, rarely is a brand holistically described with just *one* word or one angle of attack. What happens to all those other brand messages that are generally considered equally important? How can these messages be best leveraged in a supportive and proactive manner to build and foster the brand? And how can the multitude of messages be organized to maximize the communication impact?

This is the role of the brand *message mix*, a sort of framework that organizes and prioritizes all relevant brand messages, designating distinct roles for each of them within the brand's message hierarchy. Its underlying objective is twofold: first, to develop and select the strategic content most relevant to your brand and second, to organize this content in a message hierarchy with clearly defined priorities, assigning designated roles to each strategic message in the mix. Not all potential brand messages, no matter how important you may think they are, can be communicated at the same level of priority or urgency. This would simply make your branded communication too complex to be absorbed, inevitably leaving consumers or customers with blurred image perceptions of your brand.

Besides the pure organization and hierarchization of the strategic brand messages, the objective is to provide maximum message consistency. Consistent messaging of what your brand stands for will help you establish your brand's identity faster and more cost-effectively. All messages embedded in your communication strategy will thus converge to create clear and lasting brand impressions that your target audience may easily relate to and process cognitively in the form of the brand equity.

Delivering a consistent and well-prioritized pool of brand messages applies to all communication channels. The concept must be performed transdepartmental. Brands that fail to provide this consistency, either in content or across channels, will find it harder to build their equity. As a result, consumers might only gain a faint idea of what these brands stand for. Brands with a somewhat diffuse equity will struggle to make it onto a customer's relevant set. They will also underperform in building trust and loyalty with its target audiences.

In theory, the definition of the brand message mix will follow the same basic methodology and pattern, no matter whether you work on a FMCG, service, or corporate brand or whether your business model is B2C, B2B, or

B2B2C. There are of course some differences, but the underlying theory applies to all.

Defining the message mix is a strategic exercise for every brand. It must be translated into your business objectives and establish the brand as defined during the brand positioning process. It ought to be taken seriously and definitely deserves the right resources. As the brand message mix lays down the master plan for all brand communications, it will ultimately inform crucial parts of the marketing and the media strategy. Both of which directly impact budgets and costs.

To develop a sound and efficient brand message mix, the brand essence is the departure point. It defines what the brand stands for, rationally and emotionally. It is both the brand's DNA and soul. All strategic brand messages must support the claim embedded in the brand essence. They are conceived to substantiate the brand essence using content that intellectually supports and elaborates on its single-minded claim. One way to think about organizing these messages is to consider them as part of a dynamic *message galaxy* (as shown in Fig. 16.1), where all message interactions are reciprocal. Where message formats evolve over time to keep the brand up-to-date and relevant to its target audiences.

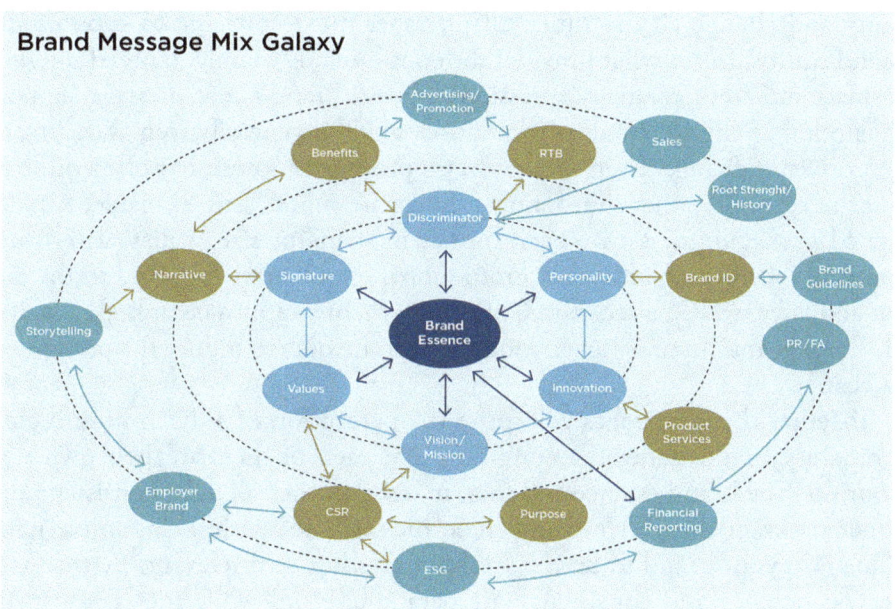

**Fig. 16.1** Brand message mix galaxy model. Author's own image

Within the mix, different messages have different roles. The galaxy offers inner and outer spheres where distinctive messages can be placed and organized to relate with each other in logical coherence and supportive of the differentiating brand claim, defined by the brand essence. The challenge here is to identify the logical thread that ties all messages together and allows for each of them to contribute to the brand equity.

A well-designed brand message mix tells the story about what your brand stands for in varying degrees of detail and coming from different angles to cover every aspect of your brand's equity. Vision, mission, and purpose, values, brand promise, and benefits translate the brand essence into meaning that consumers can easily relate to. All individual messages do so in their own manner. In short, the brand essence is captured by the brand signature that translates it into a catchy, relatable, and memorable tagline. Sales and innovation-inspired messages present the brand essence from a business point of view. Advertising and promotional messages, narratives and storytelling, CSR messaging, and PR help to keep your brand up-to-date with your target audience. And employer brand messages entice outside talent and invigorate staff. They must all converge in the same meaning, as defined by the brand essence, even though their wording will differ and evolve over time.

Within the messaging process, brands must simultaneously manage continuity and change all the time. All messages must converge to support the brand equity. This is what provides the continuity. Dynamic, tailored message formats and fresh creative expressions of your brand's core message support the notion of change. So does innovation which is generally seen as the strongest driver of change. Even so, significant product innovation is often difficult to achieve, while other innovation formats are more easily available. A redesigned packaging or a new pack format in shape or size, a new advertising campaign (online or offline), a promotional effort, news funneled to the target audience via PR, a sensitive CSR program, or simply a paraphrased strategic message may in one way or another, all contribute to induce the perception of change.

Together these messages will foster the perception of a dynamic and contemporary brand under the condition that each of them in their own way nourishes the brand essence and that, in essence, they all tell a consistent and coherent brand story. Updating these messages regularly helps inject news value into your brand to keep it fresh, interesting, and relevant. Be that as it may, coherence and consistency are paramount and while message formats may evolve, the strategic core message content must stay the same. Correctly performed, the entire brand message mix works like a little musical tune, without any false notes.

The brand essence is the centerpiece of the galaxy model. It has been defined using the *brand key* tool (see Chap. 8) and is directly derived from the discriminator that relates to the brand's core competence. The brand essence now informs the meaning for each core brand message at the central strategic orbit of the brand. Vision and mission statements, brand values, brand personality, and brand signature, which translates the brand essence into a memorable catchphrase, combined make up this set of priority messages. All core messages communicate the brand essence in a slightly different light. The vision coins the brand essence using a larger, philosophical view, a sort of brand *belief* that it claims and defends in its market and toward its target audiences. The brand mission translates this vision into a concept for tangible action.

Nike (my apologies if this reference starts to bore you, but it is just the perfect example) believes that *everyone who has a body is an athlete*. This is a very powerful brand vision directly mirroring its "empowerment" brand essence. Nike's brand mission directly bounces back on this vision, making it actionable: *to enable athletes* (professional or leisure alike) *to find their personal greatness*. Nike's brand signature captures the brand essence from yet another angle. Developed by the San Francisco ad agency Wieden & Kennedy in the late 1980s, the "Just do it" slogan has served the brand ever since. Today, it is probably one of the very few slogans that most of us know and actively remember.

Consistency in branding always pays off. Stepping back for a second to look at Nike's essence, vision, mission, and brand signature, you will realize how well the brand has translated its core brand messages without losing the fundamental truth of the brand essence: *empowerment*. This logic applies to varying degrees equally to the subordinated message of the second orbit and the tailored messages in the outer one. The innovation effort must also, in one way or another, deliver the tangible proof of what the brand claims to stands for. Every new Nike product or service will empower athletes to find their *personal greatness*. The same holds true for the sales pitch, which captures the Nike essence all the way down to the store level, where sales staff would often encourage hesitant customers with the *Just do it* line. In this sense, Nike has excelled in writing its *brand tune* without false notes.

Most of these messages will have been defined already in the Brand Key tool and you may simply revert to this tool to use them for your brand's message mix. At this first level of hierarchy, promise, benefits, and RTB interact directly with consumer needs. Brand identity codes developed against the brand essence will portray the visual stimuli for brand recognition, awareness build-up, and the brand personality.

Words are powerful image builders, but visual clues are even more powerful and easier to grasp in today's stimuli-overloaded world. Purpose messages will provide a platform for emotional bonding through personal identification. This again serves brand awareness building efforts. Finally, CSR messages address more delicate secondary consumer needs, while advertising and promotion push consumers to act.

All of the brand's core strategic messages must be ownable, differentiating, and relevant. They are central to defining and building the brand's equity over time. Each of them is defined by expanding from the brand essence. This ensures that all messages pay into the brand's differentiating value proposition (brand positioning), actively shaping the impressions consumers perceive and memorize about a given brand over time. A process no brand owner should leave up to chance.

In the galaxy model, all messages are formulated factually, they spell out the precise meaning, even if they might not yet be in their most communicative form. This way, messages stay pure and to the point. The right moment to translate these messages into a more communicative format is when you are getting ready to run a campaign at the operational level: one at a time, to preserve its single-minded focus. This way, core messages preserve their strategic meaning, while leveraging the flexibility you might need to tailor them to different target audiences or when communicating in a specific context or market environment.

Prioritizing your various brand messages allows you to define them with utmost precision. Each message that has its designated role will remain pure and uncompromised. Once these core messages are defined, they are used across all communication channels and across all departments of your company. This is best achieved by conceiving fully integrated marketing campaigns (Integrated Marketing Communication or IMC, see Chap. 10), locally, nationally, and internationally.

While message consistency primes over anything else, this does not imply repeating the exact same message formulations everywhere and all the time. It is the meaning that must remain aligned, not the message's executional form and shape. A literal language translation rarely works when brands cross national borders or when they enter markets with radically different cultural backgrounds. The point here is that the meaning must remain the same, while the actual wording may be paraphrased to account for specific target groups, local customs, or needs and understanding.

Nothing is written in stone, and you may amend your brand messaging at any level and any time. There is some merit in testing an initial message mix to gain feedback and input for improvements. Rarely, a brand message mix is a perfect match right from the start, and adjustments are frequent and legitimate. They will not put your brand at risk. There are several ways to monitor and test your message mix effectiveness. Qualitative or quantitative consumer research, customer service feedback, awareness levels, and social listening may provide regular indications for your brand's message impact and receptiveness.

The message galaxy model can be adjusted depending on your brand, target audiences, or target-subsegments, the industry or the market context you are operating in, or any specific communication needs you consider important to address. It may be simplified or expanded. Given the complexity in different brand settings, no one model fits all and the one presented here is just meant for illustration purposes. What counts most is the underlying logic behind your model, referring to both the messages and the architectural structure. This logic is what you need to work out. As a cohesive framework of dynamic (regularly refreshed) brand messages, your model must cover all communication needs.

An auxiliary tool to help you get started on the logic of the message mix is the positioning statement for your brand. It helps establish a first blueprint for core brand dimensions, next to the brand essence. The format itself obliges you to focus on the essential. This is important, because expanding your messaging from the brand essence early on in the brand messaging process bears the risk of losing focus. This in turn might reintroduce some degree of complexity. Complexity is the biggest threat in branding and almost always results in the loss of focus.

The brand positioning statement is a short phrase that summarizes the core elements of the brand positioning with the intention of defining core brand dimensions for the operational phase to follow. It is written in a lightly formatted manner as shown below:

**To the (target audience), (brand name) offers (promise/discriminator) because (reason to believe/RTB).**

Applied to Milka (discussed at various points in this book) the brand positioning statement would read like this:

**To the whole family, Milka is the chocolate with the most tender taste, because it is made with Alpine milk.**

Written this way, the brand positioning statement defines several single-minded strategic messages. In addition, its role is to provide clear direction for action. Targeting families requires the brand to be omnipresent in mass distribution (including impulse buying channels such as kiosks, gas stations, vending, etc.). The brand claim (promise) of the most *tender chocolate taste* becomes a staple for any future product development. It provides the consistency in product performance across the entire product range. Among many factors, Milka's global success is also due to its capacity to reach out across market segments and stretch its brand and product offer into multiple categories. By doing so, Milka leverages its core competence of *tender chocolate taste*, which differentiates the brand beyond its core market across all snacking segments where line extensions have allowed it to be present. However, *tender taste* is also what Milka must communicate. And finally, the RTB mandates that each Milka product must contain Alpine milk. Alpine milk is a core strategic message for the Milka brand. It has gained relevance beyond the brand's RTB to also determine the brand's *territory*, consistently set in the Swiss Alps.

The Milka brand positioning statement is a good example for precision, clarity, and focus. It defines the brand's strategic brand claims that interact in the message mix to build the brand equity. Simultaneously, the statement produces a first indication for the message hierarchy, demonstrating how "tenderness" is surrounded by supporting claims that all support Milka's brand essence. Aside from FMCG brands, the brand positioning statement serves all brand types, corporate or B2B brands, service or destination brands alike.

Another aspect of the brand message mix is the distinction of strategic versus tactical messages. While strategic messages are primarily used to build the brand equity, tactical messages allow you to communicate with more flexibility, addressing specific target audiences and their respective needs. However, they also contribute to building the brand equity.

In due course, with testing and with sensitive adjustments having been made, your brand's message mix will identify the perfect spot for every message you want to convey. Your strategic and tactical messages will work in synergy to provide consistency, target appeal, and repetition.

The brand message mix also has some financial implications. Its overall ability to streamline the brand development process makes it more linear and consistent. It ensures that messages converge throughout all target touch points. This way, all messages, although distinctive, converge to build a clear and single-minded brand equity through homogeneous holistic image perceptions. Branding today has achieved unseen dimensions, hence brand clutter has dramatically increased. This makes it harder for target audiences to develop brand awareness and to collect and process lasting brand impressions. Proctor & Gamble believes that *advertising works through repetition*. This principle is obviously true for brand messaging, as well. Strong brands are built via the repetition of single-minded, tangible meaning, which produces urgency through relevance. Inconsistent or unfocused messaging will simply produce the adverse effect. To build a brand that constantly flags non-convergent messages will at best take longer or might never succeed. Here, time and resources are wasted, and the full potential for creativity and motivational energy is never released.

Like for your brand's visual identity, the brand message mix deserves its own formalized guidelines. Guidelines not only allow you to mentor and share, putting them in writing forces you to really put your mind to it. It helps to better reveal the logic behind the brand message mix. As a brand manager, you may seldom work on your brand alone. Other people in the team across departments or even across borders will also have a say. The brand positioning process is performed in small, experienced teams, while the roll-out and brand building effort is a task shared with many others. Your role is to bring them on board. Turning these colleagues into true *brand ambassadors* is the right thing to do. Without them experiencing ownership and in the absence of clear and mutually agreed directions, consistency might again be at risk. Messaging guidelines always provide a deeper understanding of your brand, which in turn will encourage and foster ownership.

There are two prerequisites for brand ownership: deep brand understanding and personal contribution to the branding process. There is no better antidote to the *not invented here syndrome* (NIHS) than the ideas your internal brand ambassadors contribute during the branding exercise. That being so, training people who have potential impact on your brand should be considered a must-do exercise. It will serve your objective of message consistency and open your brand development up to fresh ideas, while preserving the focus. For international or global brands, messaging guidelines are indispensable. Often, local markets experience some degree of autonomy, especially in companies that *think global and act local* (referred to as *glocal* management). Here, brand ID and brand messaging guidelines are crucial to guide local teams in their endeavor for cultural adaptation. Any message adaptation is a delicate task and understanding the essence and detailed meanings of your brand is indispensable for local colleagues who want to join the process. This is best done in writing, well-thought out and clearly formulated.

The brand message mix plays a strategic role in branding, and message consistency is what ensures its success. It is always strategically aligned with the business objectives. The message mix will oblige you to define, select, and prioritize your brand messages. The brand essence provides the focal point and the road map to formulate all claims that constitute your message mix. Consequently, each branded message on its own will contribute to building the single-minded meaning that you have decided your brand will stand for, either through words or suggested by images. This way, each touch point between the brand and its target audiences will be leveraged to achieve maximum consistency and operational efficiencies.

# 17

# The Current and Future Role of AI in Branding

There is probably not a single industry that is not staring at artificial intelligence (AI) and asking itself how this new generative tool will transform the way we currently run our businesses. AI is at the very heart of the Third Industrial Revolution, which is under way. It is transforming our global community from a production to knowledge society, with electrical energy entirely and permanently replacing fossil fuels. There is no doubt that AI will have a major effect on branding, too, and as a matter of fact this is already the case. Maybe AI's greatest contribution to branding is and continues to be its ability to produce highly personalized and pertinent communications that stand in stark contrast with the one-size-fits-all approach of mass marketing techniques, which have already been partly replaced by the introduction of social media networks in the 2000s.

Historically, major technological breakthroughs have always created apprehension and excitement at the same time. In the sixteenth century, the Swiss scientist Conrad Gessner opposed the printing press. He believed that the sheer number of books would produce a knowledge overload and chaos for human civilization. Gottlieb Daimler, the father of the automobile, estimated that the number of cars in circulation would remain limited to 2000, as there were just about that many qualified drivers available at the time. AI is no different. Generative artificial intelligence models have made deep inroads into our civilizations and the technological applications that serve it. Most of these AI applications are running in the background, invisible to the average eye. Simultaneously, AI-powered services such as ChatGPT, Google Bard, Midjourney, Deepl, or Jasper have already gained wide visibility and popularity. In little time, they have succeeded in making the benefits of AI tangible for the average person everywhere around the world. ChatGPT boasts close to 200 million regular users who generate an average of 1.6 billion visits per month. In early 2024, Open AI, ChatGPT's parent company, claimed to produce 100 billion words per day, representing the equivalent text volume of 1 million novels (NYT, 8/24).

Despite the enthusiasm on one side, AI is also raising many questions. As this new technology remains virtually unregulated, the unethical use of AI is felt as a major threat. AI relies heavily on large data pools to become efficient. Consequently, concerns are mostly, but not exclusively, related to data privacy. AI search results are not always reliable, which turns unverified AI produced content into a potential issue, once published without the necessary scrutiny. Fake news is certainly as old as mankind, but AI-generated *deepfakes* make misinformation way more difficult to detect.

AI has also been accused of being biased, a point we shall address more deeply later in this chapter. All this may have serious implications for our societies as a whole, for example when applied to election processes (as was supposedly the case in the 2016 US presidential race). Also, entire professions are believed under threat, with AI already outperforming humans in multiple areas from medical diagnosis to law, from financial services to manufacturing. The world of branding, again, is no exception.

Today's AI language learning models (LLM) still have their limitations. Incapable of reproducing humanized emotions and sensibilities, they are unlikely to entirely replace creative talent and the need for emotional psychology in branding anytime soon. That being said, AI already assists humans in the creative process, providing stimuli for example, thus allowing graphic designers to explore greater numbers of design options more quickly. While this is improving productivity, AI-generated designs are still a long shot from simulating the emotional values and sensitive subtleness humans are capable of. Current AI models also lack the *psychological* dimensions required for effective branding. Therefore, even as AI gets better at providing basic design options and message content, humans will for the foreseeable future stay in charge of humanizing it.

This might change with the arrival of the next generation of *general artificial intelligence* (GAI) models, which are believed to emerge in the coming decades. There is a lot of money being poured into the development of these technologies and mankind might indeed succeed in turning the imagined performance of GAI into reality. As far as branding is concerned, this would give AI vast creative, emotional, and even psychological capabilities.

Nonetheless, today's generative AI models might become increasingly threatened by their own workings. As the use of artificial intelligence increases at an exponential rate, AI feeds increasingly on content it has produced itself. This may become a downside with significant impact, as the equation between original human and AI-produced content continues to shift. Without a technical solution to prevent this phenomenon from happening, AI will increasingly analyze self-produced content, making it somewhat *degenerative*. First, experiments in controlled laboratory settings to reproduce this down-spiral evolution indicate that generative AI might become degenerative after as little as 20 content recycling rounds. The trend is further accelerated by AI's ongoing technological improvements, making generated content ever harder to detect. Chances that content slips into the next level of data analysis slowly but continuously increases, thus watering down the pertinence and accuracy of search results over time. Obviously, the industry is aware of this problem, but has yet to come up with the solution.

A recent article by the *New York Times* refers to experiments conducted to demonstrate this degenerative side effect that threatens the viability of AI as it feeds increasingly on its own content. Here, a number of random handwritten numbers was run repeatedly through AI algorithms. The result after just 20 runs is shown in the illustrations from one of the tests shown in Fig. 17.1. The industry is well aware of this problem and works frantically to find a solution. However, with AI output becoming increasingly sophisticated and harder to detect, it is difficult to imagine how future LLM models will solve this issue.

There are many areas in branding where AI is already playing a significant role. AI's biggest asset is its capacity and ability to analyze massive amounts of data, providing meaning and intelligence for branding and marketing professionals at many levels. This data analysis is by no means limited to the internet and includes other data sources provided by credit cards, loyalty cards, search engines, social media, for example. AI crossed with *big data* offers near limitless possibilities for cross-analysis. This may generate a multitude of tangible

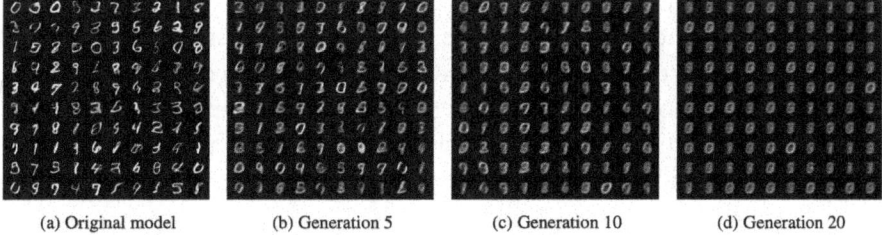

(a) Original model     (b) Generation 5     (c) Generation 10     (d) Generation 20

**Fig. 17.1** The curse of recursion: training on generated data makes models forget—arXiv:2305.17493v3 (cs.LG) April 14, 2024. Permission: Ilia Shumailov, University of Oxford

benefits for branding professionals such as improved target understanding through behavioral and sentimental analysis, preference scouting and predictive analysis, messaging and design generation, just to mention the main areas of application. All of them are already available and increasingly used in branding and marketing alike. Conversational AI and virtual assistance tools like AI-powered chatbots and augmented or virtual reality tools try to engage customers in personalized dialogues, hence providing more meaning to conversations. All this may help to engage entire target audiences who long for memorable brand experiences.

On the other hand, this raises ethical questions. For many years, AI has served to improve the performance of internet search engines and in areas such as SEO marketing or yield management. Dynamic pricing, for example, is extensively used by the service industry for demand forecasting or to promote certain offers with dynamic discounting. While the use of AI in data analysis may in theory be legitimate, not much different from what basic computing did a couple of decades ago, having AI produce creative content in forms of visuals and words might be a bigger matter of concern.

The key question here is how transparent brands should be about the use of AI in generating brand content. Consumers clearly do not welcome the use of AI in branding and marketing. More than half of Americans express concern according to a recent study published in the *Journal of Hospitality Marketing & Management*.[1] For brands to use AI in this way may indeed pose a certain dilemma. In the absence of more specific regulations, these brands must weigh the benefits against the downsides of being transparent regarding the use of AI. Knowing that a brand uses AI in its targeting and messaging processes might in fact lower consumers' purchase intensions. The study essentially looked at categories such as household appliances, as well as consumer and health services. Products with a higher associated risk in purchase fared worse than those considered low risk, yet, in all categories, purchase declination was the dominant reaction to the declared presence of AI.

The study concludes that in absence of a deeper understanding of AI and a general lack of trust in this new technology, consumers revert to emotional decision-making models. Privacy, too, may play a role in peoples' rejection of AI technologies. While this study clearly applied to purchases of products and services, one could assume that similar trust patterns also apply to brand

---

[1] Mesut Cicek, Dogan Gursoy & Lu Lu (19 Jun 2024): Adverse impacts of revealing the presence of "Artificial Intelligence (AI)" technology in product and service descriptions on purchase intentions: the mediating role of emotional trust and the moderating role of perceived risk, Journal of Hospitality Marketing & Management, https://doi.org/10.1080/19368623.2024.2368040.

imaging and messaging by FMCG brands, when generated by AI technologies.

As will be discussed in the following chapter, *transparency* is the next big thing in branding and consumers are likely to hold companies increasingly accountable. The reach of social media channels makes this more than real. Transparency favors the development of trust. For consumers and customers alike, the trust factor will gain in importance over time and in an ever faster changing world, where the perception prevails that increasingly fewer things can be trusted.

On the other hand, brands might benefit from being transparent about their use of AI in marketing and communication programs. The challenge is to translate the use of AI into a perceivable benefit for the target consumer. AI is already being leveraged to improve target distinctiveness in messaging and visual brand identity. When applied to promotion and sales tasks, AI might help better cater branded offers to consumers' real needs. AI is also a powerful tool to identify trends in color, design, fashion, or other lifestyle-related areas early on, allowing brands to offer their target audiences a head start in up-and-coming product and service cycles. In 2017, the Italian Ferrero Company, owner of the Nutella brand, used a precursor version to AI in a major product promotion, referred to as *Nutella Unica* (see Fig. 17.2). The algorithm was developed by HP Mosaic and was programed to produce 7 million unique labels, sourced through analytics of latest color and design trends. Nutella was outspoken about the use of the algorithm in this promotion, which generated not only massive sales but also a lot of social media buzz for the brand. The limited-edition jar sold out in less than a month and became a collector's item, while the promotion helped Nutella to project an image of a brand that is ahead of its time.

**Fig. 17.2** *Nutella Unica* range of HP Mosaic generated labels. Permission: Ferrero Group

In Nutella's case, the use of the AI-like algorithm was leveraged as an asset. Being transparent about its use in the promotion paid off. Other examples include Sephora, a cosmetics retailer belonging to the LVMH French Group, which uses AI in its virtual beauty advisor or Starbucks that makes extensive use of AI for its Deep Brew initiative, responsible for its customization program. The company employs machine learning algorithms to track and analyze customer behavior based on locations, dayparts, seasons, and even weather patterns. This allows Starbucks to manage staffing needs on an hourly basis. It enables the brand to customize its offer to seasonal or regional preferences, pushing hot beverages in cold weather and refreshing ones when it gets hot outside. It has also led to adapting menus to local or culturally driven needs, such as proposing a larger array of teas in Asia, for instance. Nevertheless, while Starbucks has managed to micro-tailor its offer to different target audiences around the world, it might have overstretched its in-store servicing capacities, leading to longer waiting times that have recently turned off an increasing numbers of loyal customers and contributed to a decline in sales.

Nike has been using AI algorithms to power its Nike Running Club (NRC) and its Nike Training Club (NTC) apps. The apps measure sport activity in real time, capturing live user data. People who subscribed to the Nike, *Choose GO* program, for instance, get inspired by work-out plans, running tips and training schedules. AI technology then kicks in to coach users, motivating them to stay active and continuously progress toward their fitness goals. This might seem like old news, but AI has the ability to perform these tasks in real time, making Nike's declared brand mission tangible and real for consumers. At the same time, the campaign allows Nike to collect data from users worldwide, providing valuable insights into its targets and its athletic habits. In return, this allows the brand to promote certain products with more precision and higher relevance.

Two distinct areas of AI applications are frequently used to address offer distinctiveness: preference analysis and predictive analytics. With the help of machine learning tools in branding, consumer preferences may be identified and analyzed using vast amounts of data from various sources including chatbots, forums, social media, reviews, purchase histories from loyalty and payment cards, and many more. AI may sift through huge volumes of data, analyzing and providing market intelligence. This way business decisions become more reliable as they are backed by hard data and facts. This not only allows brands to adapt their product and service offers, but also to optimize brand imaging, messaging tonality and SEO key word strategies, for example.

Predictive analytics covers several branding and marketing functions. It empowers brands to design proactive marketing programs and more need-distinctive offers. Be that as it may, it provides brand owners with data to back up decision-making by predicting future consumer behavior and trends. The principle of these machine learning algorithm is to analyze past consumer behavior in purchasing or through past information searches to forecast future behavioral patterns. Predictive analytics may provide insights into purchase motivations, enabling brands to improve target distinctiveness and engagement in brand messaging, for example by message personalization that addresses needs more directly while considering previously identified pain points. Streaming platforms like Netflix, Deezer, or Spotify use predictive analytics models to propose future content or playlists to their customers that are better targeted to match their preferences and needs. Needless to say, this improves the service quality ratings, which in turn has a positive impact on customer satisfaction and retention.

Identifying the *lifetime value* of certain target profiles is another way to employ predictive analytics in branding. AI algorithms may help brands identify and select those consumers or customers who are most likely to become loyal users over time, designing brand offers and communication strategies that eventually turn them into brand ambassadors. Predictive analytics is increasingly used for trend forecasting, generation of product and service innovation, all the way to ROI forecasting and modeling of future pricing strategies or even *anticipative shipping* in the retail business. Here, predictive analytics uses online search results, wish lists, and order history to analyze target preferences and to identify a potential future product purchase.

Initial formats of predictive analytics were explored by Amazon as early as the 2010s in California. The objectives were to increase warehouse productivity and customer satisfaction by pre-shipping identified goods prior to customers making a final purchase decision. Amazon went as far as to literally ship goods to consumers, prior to them clicking buy. Apparently, the patented *anticipative shipping program* was predictive enough to have Amazon accept the associated financial risks. The program offered returns free of charge and leveraged discount incentives or even gifting if consumers refused the unsolicited shipment. Even without going that far, the potential benefits for e-retailers like Amazon include more pertinent and personalized product recommendations, shorter shipping times and improved warehouse productivity.

AI-powered predictive analytics is also increasingly used in the fashion industry to identify trends and forecast sales.

Heuritec, a Paris-based service company analyzes millions of real-world pictures from social media and other digital sources to scout and define tangible insights for the fashion industry. This form of sentiment analysis helps predict trends and demands more accurately, thus offering fashion companies a tangible competitive edge. Developing new products with the help of AI-powered technology also contributes to making the fashion industry more sustainable, reducing or at least helping avoid fashion waste. During the development of a luxury sneaker model, Heuritec analyzed 3 million images from three distinct panel clusters: edgy, trendy, and mainstream. Technology was used to scan product types as well as design details such as patterns, colors, shapes, and so on across 2000 products. Lastly, the agency used proprietary technology to forecast how trends in the luxury segment of the sneaker market would travel from edgy influencers to mainstream consumers. Complementary to experience and intuition, AI made the development process more data-driven, which produced some sort of decision-making safety net and contributed to turning the launch of this new shoe into a success.

Sentiment analysis is yet another activity that relies on artificial intelligence and its machine learning algorithms for branding and, in particular, brand management purposes. Sentiment analysis has played an important role in branding for quite some time; regardless, AI has allowed to scale it significantly by tapping into larger data sources. This type of analysis helps companies understand how their target audience feels about a particular brand, product, or service offer. Sentiment analysis leverages data such as social media, forums, surveys, reviews, or any other publicly-generated conversations to provide insights into public opinion. In these instances, AI applies natural language processing algorithms (NLP). NLP analyzes large volumes of texts, for example, from social media posts to determine feelings and attitudes people have toward a brand or a certain subject. More advanced AI models can now recognize brand names, locations, or products mentioned in these texts, a process referred to as *Name Entity Recognition* (NER) or even identify basic levels of emotions, such as joy, anger, or sarcasm. *Recurrent Neural Network* (RNN) models such as *BERT* have the capacity to analyze words in the larger context of a text, hence identifying irony or sarcasm. A sentence such as *Great, my car broke down again* is correctly analyzed as delivering a negative emotion, despite the use of wordings that express positive sentiments (*great*).

Certain AI applications offer image and voice analysis. In video-enabled conversations, these versions not only analyze words but also criteria such as language speed, voice tonality, and degree of tension, as well as body language and gestures. The obtained data is capable of evaluating the level of customer satisfaction or frustration, even when the words used during the conversation come across as neutral. All this in multiple language models, including slang and local dialects. While the word *sick* used in an American context refers to something regarded as *great, fantastic or cool*, the word has kept its original meaning in most of the world's other regions. By now, language learning models know how to make this distinction. The level of subtleness that AI has acquired in sentiment analysis is quite amazing and allows marketers to tailor their brand messaging with more emotional relevance, hence engaging their target audiences more effectively.

As AI technology progresses, other imaging tools become increasingly integrated to provide a continuously enhanced user experience. Augmented reality (AR) or virtual reality (VR) are likely to take just a few more years before they go mainstream, offering new possibilities for more holistic and immersive brand experiences. Nevertheless, this also means that brand managers will have to imagine totally new communication formats designed to run smoothly and seamlessly on these new technological devices, without causing stimuli saturation within the designated target audiences.

Generative artificial intelligence is seen by many as the next big thing after computing and the internet, globally introduced just 30 years ago. A new generation of AI technology that will transform not only the world we live in, but also the way we live in this world. Yet, as AI technology advances and ever bigger sums are poured into its development, critical voices rise in greater numbers.

Job losses or the disappearance of entire professions has always been feared (and also materialized) during both previous industrial revolutions. This will certainly also be the case in the age of AI; however, while certain jobs may vanish, entirely new ones will be created. If the previous periods of industrial disruption are a measure, the problem as such might not be the decimation of entire professions but the time lag that develops during the transition. Training and education are crucial for preparing people for the new responsibilities that await them. I do not think that branding will see this happen within its industry any time soon. Current AI machine learning models are trained to recognize recurrent patterns in the data that we feed them. AI has so far failed to handle abstract concepts, which define crucial thought processes in branding. Nevertheless, for the foreseeable future, AI will no doubt increasingly assist humans in their branding endeavors. Just the same, it is hard to imagine how current AI models will replace human creativity and subtlety, indispensable for emotional bonding. Coca Cola learned this the hard way with its 2024 AI-generated Christmas ads, which were met with significant criticism on social media platforms for being creepy, strange, and far from *the real thing*, which had been Coke's advertising slogan for years.

The environmental and climate impact of ever bigger data centers with an unsatiable appetite for energy used for data processing and cooling is another side effect of the AI revolution. With renewable energies still lagging behind, the next generation of AI technology is likely to produce an even bigger carbon footprint.

Today, AI provides stimuli for creative processes in visual arts and messaging. It is also instrumental in helping brand managers preserve message consistency across all media channels. All of this in an increasingly personalized manner that allows brands to provide deeper meaning and higher relevance. With its capacity to process massive amounts of data, AI applications are highly effective in providing market and consumer intelligence to be leveraged in branding tasks such as targeting and messaging, both heightened by insights gained from sentiment analysis.

With all the benefits AI offers marketers today, caution also applies. All AI models, to some extent, have proven biased, sometimes underrepresenting consumer groups based on color, gender, or disabilities, for example. The reason for this bias is linked to the fact that human-produced content itself is often biased and machines are trained to feed on it. Bias can quickly get companies or brands into trouble, producing lasting negative effects for a brand's reputation. This does not only relate to branding tools, but to the use of AI-powered applications in general. Take software applications, for instance, already widely used by HR departments to help pre-scan the hundreds of CVs that large and attractive companies receive every day. Here, an AI algorithm, oblivious to bias, may produce highly damaging effects, excluding potential candidates unfairly and potentially depriving the company of much needed talent.

Current image generation platforms, like Stable Diffusion, produce images based on written prompts. While these images may feel surprisingly realistic, they have also been shown to represent a dangerous distortion of reality. Analyzing 5000 of these AI-generated images in 2023, Bloomberg identified a strong bias that was summarized as: *The world according to Stable Diffusion is run by White male CEOs. Women are rarely doctors, lawyers or judges. Men with dark skin commit crimes, while women with dark skin flip burgers.*[2]

The introduction of language learning algorithms and, in particular, Open AI's ChatGPT in 2022 sounded to many governments and regulatory organs like a wake-up call. These publicly available and easy-to-use algorithms showcased for the first time the power AI could unfold on our societies. Concern about the potential outreach of AI is now also shared by its major industry players, which clearly adds to the sense of urgency. Numerous governments around the world have rushed to establish regulations and the administrative

---

[2] Humans are biased. Generative AI is even worse. Bloomberg Technology + Equality, by Leonardo Nicoletti and Dina Bass, June 9, 2023.

bodies to enact them. The EU was the first to introduce a comprehensive regulatory act in August 2024. This new law will come into force gradually, over a period of 3 years in all 27 member states of the European Union. China, Canada, the United States, Britain, Brazil, and many others are currently also defining their own regulations.

The debate about how to best regulate AI is still underway and many industry players believe in regulating AI's applications rather than its models. In theory, this would lighten regulations for language applications like ChatGPT and tighten them for AI use in medical fields, for example. Whatever the final regulations will end up looking like defining them quickly is the right thing to do. Still, new AI-powered versions go public almost every day and the breathtaking pace of this evolution is only likely to increase. Estimates of funding being allocated to next-generation AI range from hundreds of billions to several trillions of dollars over the coming years. These massive sums of money are not only going toward funding new versions of AI, but also new quantum computing technologies, likely to increase data processing capacities manifold. This will make it challenging for legislators and fulfilment bodies to keep up. In this context, local regulations are probably the appropriate strategy to crank out legislation quickly. However, in the long run, only a worldwide consolidated approach might provide effective protection since the technology itself is global by nature.

# 18

# The Transformative Responsibility of Brands in the Advanced Twenty-First Century

Brands are powerful instruments that can be used not only in business but also in politics, as well as in charitable initiatives and NGOs. Micro branding has become commonplace through social media and has helped many achieve fame and riches. There is little debate about brands being capable of yielding significant influence on their target audiences. This is indeed the key objective of branding. From their very beginnings, brands have been designed to change consumer behavior. This was initially achieved by creating preferences using competitive offers (price, quality, innovation) and with time by establishing strong emotional bonds with consumers. There is nothing wrong with that. As a matter of fact, branding over the course of the twentieth century has contributed in a big way to pushing progress forward and raising the standard of living for large portions of the global population. However, the power of brands has not always been leveraged in an ethical way and this last section of the book intends to discuss brand ethics in more detail.

The intimate processes on how brands develop these capabilities has been central to this book. Be that as it may, successful branding relies on multiple techniques. Brands might create preferences through tangible product attributes, or through the experiences that these attributes produce. In service sectors, these experiences may be enhanced more by how well staff incorporates and lives the brand, than by a given service feature itself. Others see brands as convenient shortcuts to complex decision-making processes. Loyalty might be seen as the ultimate measure for leadership brands, yet the most loyal Coca Cola buyers only buy one or two bottles in a given year and hardcore Harley Davidson fans generate just 3.5% of the company's revenue (The Economist, Aug 30, 2024). While this debate is probably useful, in the end it might not really matter. What matters is that brands do perform as influencers of opinions and acts. This makes them highly sensitive agents of positive but potentially also negative or perilous societal change.

Media proliferation has transformed the way people access and consume information. Never have media choices been as fragmented as today. *Mass marketing* still dominated branding just 30 years ago and has now given way to the *market of one* (P&G). Consumers now play an active part in the branding process, and their opinions weigh on how brands are perceived. Brands used to be what we wanted them to stand for, while today they have increasingly become what consumers say about them. Buying a brand is now intimately linked to *buying into a brand*. Decades of intensive advertising and promotion have left entire target audiences more commercially educated and marketing savvy. This also impacts their attitudes and expectations toward brands.

All brands have self-expressive dimensions that constantly expose them to the cultural shifts that take place in our national but increasingly globalized communities. Our societies are in constant movement and to stay relevant, brands must move with the times. Brands are never built in cultural isolation; they are always the result of their times. Branding always scouts for new trends. While this is important, many trends are talked about long before they turn into truly popular behavior with the masses. Unless you operate in niche markets or against highly selective target audiences, trends may be hard to instrumentalize for your brand. Nonetheless, what helps your brand gain maximum traction is understanding and incorporating the currents of their times.

Those times are defined by major cultural shifts that are strong enough to move mainstream, successively transforming themselves into the new conventions of society. To penetrate an entire population, these cultural shifts may take a full decade and generally the following decade becomes the answer to the previous one. The past 70 years provide some testimony on how entire societies have swayed from one *behavior* to the next. These shifts often have global repercussions, and they definitely affect brands.

With its global reach, many of the important societal swings that marked the twentieth and twenty-first centuries originate in American society. The postwar economic growth of the 1950s favored an economic boom with significant urban development and the proliferation of the American suburban way of life. These were times marked by family values, rigid gender roles, and patriotic conformism. These were the years of the original *American Dream* that prescribed a tangible and popular model for success.

Success in the 1950s also came with conventions and conformism. This prepared a fertile ground for the counterculture of the 1960s, marked by a quest for freedom. Civil rights, the birth of the hippie movement, sexual liberation kick-started by the anti-baby pill, and growing protests against the Vietnam war marked the proliferating enthusiasm of this decade. While social movements spread, loudly calling for change, a strong sense of enthusiasm and optimism continued to progress far into the 1970s. The Vietnam war, followed by economic pressures from the oil crisis in 1973 started to give way to a general state of disillusion. This provoked the arrival of pop culture in all sorts of performing arts, which aimed to fight the disillusion with a new form of hedonism.

The 1980s brought back a new type of conservatism and the beginnings of ultra-capitalism. Trickle-down economics, materialism, and consumerism became the dominant drivers of the 1980s societal model, best incorporated by the stereotype of the yuppie (young urban professional) who strived for status through wealth and for whom professional success was considered the highest goal in life. Technology and globalization transformed the 1990s society. Deregulation of financial institutions, the democratization of IT technology, and the dissolution of the Soviet Union in 1991 marked the end of the Cold War, which in turn boosted the concept of the global economy. There was a strong belief that economic progress would be the best way to preserve peace. And for those who remember these times, it really felt like a wonderful peaceful world, where opportunity was waiting around any corner and at any turn that your life might take.

The speed of progress accelerates the speed of change. Most of us will remember the 1920s as the decade of social media, smartphones, and the internet. However, it is also the decade of cultural fragmentation and isolation, in which many of us innocently leaped into the social media *bubbles*, where algorithms define what you will read and see, and social recognition was reduced to the simple number of *likes*. This also contributed to increasing polarization in many of our societies. Terrorism, regional wars, and the fallout from the 2007 subprime crisis, the pandemic, the increasingly visible prospects of climate change as well as the pace of change have again reintroduced the notion of an unpredictable, unsafe world. This underlying current is somehow reflected by a strong emergence of retro-style design in many areas, reminding consumers of times when life was less complex and more predictable and might also explain to some extent the rise of ultra-conservatists or populists in many of our well-established democracies.

Brands must maneuver through these societal swings, adapting to evolving consumer needs, attitudes, and preferences. More than ever in our amorphic world, brands are perceived as offering some form of stability and hold through *meaning*. They offer continuity in a world of change, and they provide meaning, where overwhelming complexity produces confusion and fear. They may promote values that many of us perceive to be fading in our post-globalized societies. Within this evolving societal context, brands face great opportunities to also incorporate the ethical cravings of their target audiences.

Honesty, transparency, and authenticity are no longer what many of the world's powerful elites incorporate and live by. This book has widely discussed and illustrated not just what brands are, how they operate, and how they are built and managed over time. It also aims to highlight the transformative power brands hold on consumers and on society as a whole. This gifted power brand must act ethically.

As commercial or ideological entities, brands may wield impressive influence over people. When developed and managed professionally, brands are and will continue to be a great source for value creation. Even so, this value creation must not come at the cost of those who are not at the receiving end. For those who have *not won the lottery ticket of life*, as Paul Polman, Unilever's former CEO would say. Neither must branding be abused for ruthless and unethical purposes, in whatever sphere of modern life anywhere around the world.

It would be naïve to think that these words will prevent these missteps from happening. They have and continue to do so as you read these lines. Yet, for those who mean well, this chapter about the transformative responsibility of brands in the twenty-first century is intended as a manifest for a responsible and ethical use of branding techniques and methodologies. Far from moralizing, these lines are meant as a call for brands to refuse being abused as sole instruments of capitalistic greed, but to be embraced by marketeers as allies for participative value creation and positive societal change. Leveraging the power of branding to create value through sincere meaning and not through delusion, I do not suggest a complete overhaul of today's prevailing business models. However, I do suggest accepting the fact that giving some of the brand-induced gains back is not a cost but an investment in the future of society.

Ethical branding consists of three fundamentals: truth, transparency, and authenticity. They are also essential values for the cohesion of our society. They must not be seen as a self-fulfilling prophecy. Living and acting upon these values genuinely pays back. Recognized ethical standards foster stronger and longer relationships between brands and their target audiences. And doing good has become more than ever a great way to grow, as recently showcased by brands such as Warby Parker, TOMs, and Patagonia, just to name a few.

There is nothing new about dishonesty in branding and without today's laws and regulations, it would no doubt be more widely spread as was the case before these regulations did exist. That being said, honesty in branding is well advised. Exaggerated or even false promises are short-lived and product performance gives consumers an effective tool for finding the truth themselves. The lightest form of bending the truth are somewhat carelessly overstated brand claims. Unfortunately, the proliferation of branding has not grown at the same speed as the professional understanding of brands. During my work I have seen many examples of textbook marketing techniques combined with best-case benchmarking. This mostly produces poorly defined brands with wordy claims that do not match their product or service reality. These claims are often pompous and overstated and today's consumers are increasingly oblivious to them.

While consumers may show some forgiveness for *overrated* claims, they show much less tolerance for deliberate lies. The *Diesel Gate* scandal in 2015 demonstrated the risk brand's take when they consciously labor to manipulate public opinion. Volkswagen was the first to get caught, while other manufacturers also tempered their emission rates. In the end, *Diesel Gate* became closely associated with the Volkswagen Group and tainted its reputation for many years, while continued lawsuits keep the scandal topical in the global news until today. Technically, the brand had manipulated engine software to recognize procedures linked to emission testing. The software switched the engine to a programmed *testing mode* that allowed it to live up to regulatory standards. In everyday usage, however, Volkswagen's diesel cars emitted up to 40 times higher nitrogen-oxide emissions than limited by law. Most of its customers felt cheated at the time and many turned away from the brand to never come back. Even if this was not the only reason, Diesel Gate significantly contributed to the serious threats the VW Group faces today.

The environment and sustainability are other domains where bending the truth has been and continues to be common practice. Oftentimes, elaborate storytelling and clever wordings are used to distract from the truth. The oil industry has a long history of using branding and communications to master these skills. For example, take Humble that merged with Exxon to become one of the world's leading fossil fuel companies. Humble's national print campaign in 1962 provides an early example of these techniques. In today's context, one of these ads would come across as ludicrous. The double page full-spread print ad in *Life Magazine* shows a frontal shot of the Taku Glacier in Alaska and features the following headline: *Each day Humble supplies enough energy to melt 7 million tons of glacier!* In the following body copy, the company continues to brag on about the fact that *this massive glacier has remained unmelted for centuries and that the energy Humble provides daily, produces enough heat to melt 80 tons a second.*

As it happens, the relationship between fossil fuels and climate change was already a well-known fact in the industry. By the time the campaign appeared in *Life Magazine* on February 2, the scientific community had already officially established the direct link between burning fossil fuels and climate change. It must be assumed that as a market leader then and now, Humble/Exxon was very much aware of this and leveraged its brand to divert the general public's attention, via clever messaging. Nevertheless, what this ad illustrates is just the peak of the (melting) iceberg. Massive investments in PR and lobbying by the entire oil industry made sure that the sensitive topic of climate change stayed out of the larger public domain.

And it still does today. Regrettably, over 60 years later, things look all too familiar. Total Energies, an international French company and global leader in fossil fuels, changed its name from *Total* to *TotalEnergies* in 2021. This move was intended to stress the fact that Total had diversified its energy offer to include those from renewable sources. Total's brand equity was meant to evolve from a fossil energy provider to one that offered more sustainable energy options, in line with its development strategy.

The statement in the following press release describes the brand's strategic and environmental vision at the time:

> "Energy is life. We all need it, and it is a source of progress. So today, to contribute to the sustainable development of the planet in the face of the climate challenge, we are moving forward, together, towards new energies. Energy is reinventing itself and this energy path is ours. Our ambition is to be a major player in the energy transition. This is why Total is transforming itself and becoming TotalEnergies," declared Patrick Pouyanné, Chairman and CEO of TotalEnergies.

As the leading fossil company, Total supposedly felt pressured to give itself a new and more sustainable brand image. From a branding point of view, this is what you do. However, this does not happen overnight, and nice words must lead to tangible deeds. This is where Total fails. Despite its declared goal of carbon neutrality by 2050, many environmental groups denounce the company's continued heavy investments in the exploitation of fossil fuels. According to Total's 2023 annual report, only 25% of its capital expenditure goes toward renewable energies. In 2023, the French Advertising Ethics Body formally ruled against some of the brand's sustainability messaging as misleading its target audiences. While brand transformations of this kind certainly require time and big investments, a brand like Total would fare better in the public opinion by keeping its claims down. Staying with the truth and demonstrating strength by more transparency and why not by some humility.

Telling great stories to overemphasize efforts related to positive change just to divert attention from the *dirty facts* has long lost its attraction with today's younger target audiences. Too much self-confidence may also lead to self-delusion, lowering the moral barrier for making false or overstated claims. *Fake it until you make it*, the mantra for some brands in the tech industry is a widely reported attitude example for this. For the average person, *green washing* and *purpose washing* are not always easy to detect. At the same time, scrutiny from environmental and consumer protection groups are here to stay and the internet has a long memory. Never has finding facts been easier and quicker than today, particularly facilitated by generative AI. Whatever the reasons why brands bend the truth, doing so might provide some short-term relief. In the long run, overstated claims or even outright lies are short-lived and always come back to haunt your brand.

Transparency is another core value every brand should embrace. It is fundamental in building trust with your target audiences. This in return favors brand loyalty and brand advocacy. Transparency is also somewhat a generational phenomenon that has gained significant importance with the Millennial and GenZ generations. These well-connected and well-informed consumer groups are the ones experiencing the impact of change the most harshly. They have little or no recollection of times where perpetual change still offered some understanding and meaning. I recently discussed AI technology in the context of teaching with one of my very bright and talented international students. She was 21 years at the time and *already felt left behind*. Consumers who feel lost may intuitively revert to strong brands that provide them with powerful reference points and tangible meaning.

Transparency is an important principle in brand communications. As a fundamental attitude toward doing business, it should guide everything your brand does and claims to do. Product formulations, ingredient sourcing, offer clarity and pricing models, data management and data usage, corporate finances, environmental impact, and CSR programs are just a few examples where transparency defines executional messaging formats. This does not suggest that a company or brand must open all its books. Proprietary and confidential information must of course be treated as such. However, transparency in branding should be understood as a way of communication in which things are clear and where messages are comprehensive and complete. Where important facts are not left out or instrumentalized to cover up for the less glorious ones.

Patagonia recently acknowledged publicly that the company would miss its 2025 sustainability targets in carbon emissions. The brand could have simply remained quiet about it and continue to focus on what it does well. Speaking about this failure was a great act of transparency, which directly feeds into consumer trust. The Patagonia brand courageously transformed an apparent weakness into a strength. By announcing its missed targets, Patagonia also demonstrated humility, which further strengthens its emotional bonding with its target audiences.

At times where AI is extending its reach into branding, transparency will acquire a totally new dimension. Research has shown that consumers are wary of this new technology and that brand choices are impacted by admitting that AI played a role in the branding process. What is the right dose of transparency in those cases? What does your brand risk, by leaving the AI fact out? Both questions have already been addressed in Chap. 17 and I do not want to answer them again. For the sake of transparency, being outspoken about the use of AI is a matter of transparency. If its use produces value for your target audience, consumers will understand and go along with it.

Authenticity is the third core value to guide ethical responsibilities. It refers to the differentiation that sets a brand apart. For this very reason alone, it should be the nature of any brand. Even so, authenticity refers to more than this one dimension. Integrity, respect, uniqueness, and realism are other traits that designate authentic brands. Brand differentiation is defined in the positioning process. No brand really owns its unique position unless it claims and starts to own its differentiation through consistency in messaging. Authentic brands stay true to what they stand for. They walk the talk.

Like truth and transparency, authenticity is a guiding principle that instructs brands on how to act and live up to their transformative responsibilities. They are fundamental brand dimensions and contribute to defining the brand personality, which ultimately guides the brand's behavior and the tone and attitude it employs. The traditional sources that power brand strength have started to shift. Recognition and image value are still important, but alone they are no longer enough to secure the long-term traction of any given brand. Brands more than ever must show that while they are good at what they do, they also do good by what they do. A higher purpose is what will set brands increasingly apart and those that do not walk the talk will become more exposed.

Throughout contemporary history, brands have leveraged their transformative power in many ways. While most have done so with great ethical standards, some have been abusive. Considering the challenges humanity faces in the twenty-first century with its hyper-performance societies, brands play a pivotal role in the quest for societal transformation. They have the power to engage millions of people to consume and act in different and more sensible ways. They own the opportunity to serve as role models for positive change. Demonstrating that purpose is sincere and that a purposeful life provides meaning to all.

This comes with responsibilities and requires a strong vision to direct change. This vision might not always be fully aligned with short-term business objectives. However, with a slightly more long-term view, brands create value way beyond sales and reliable returns way beyond the iconic corporate reporting culture.

GPSR Compliance

The European Union's (EU) General Product Safety Regulation (GPSR) is a set of rules that requires consumer products to be safe and our obligations to ensure this.

If you have any concerns about our products, you can contact us on

ProductSafety@springernature.com

In case Publisher is established outside the EU, the EU authorized representative is:

Springer Nature Customer Service Center GmbH
Europaplatz 3
69115 Heidelberg, Germany

www.ingramcontent.com/pod-product-compliance
Lightning Source LLC
LaVergne TN
LVHW010339260326
834688LV00036B/783